LONGMAN SOCIAL RESEARCH SERIES

The Limitations of Social Research

Marten Shipman

4th Edition

LONGMAN
London and New York

Addison Wesley Longman Limited
Edinburgh Gate
Harlow
Essex CM20 2JE
United Kingdom
and Associated Companies throughout the world

*Published in the United States of America
by Addison Wesley Longman, New York*

© Longman Group UK Ltd 1973, 1981, 1988
This edition © Addison Wesley Longman Limited 1997

First published 1973
Second edition 1981
Third edition 1988
Second impression 1995
Fourth edition 1997

ISBN 0 582 31103 9

British Library Cataloguing-in-Publication Data

A catalogue record for this book is available from the British Library

Library of Congress Cataloging-in-Publication Data

Shipman, M.D.
    The limitations of social research / Marten Shipman. — 4th ed.
      p. cm. — (Longman social research series)
    Includes bibliographical references (p.) and index.
    ISBN 0–582–31103–9
    1. Social sciences—Research. I. Title. II. Series.
H62.S4641997
300'.72—dc21   97–30721
                                             CIP

Set by 35 in 10/11pt Times
Produced through Longman Malaysia , TCP

UNIVERSITY OF
WOLVERHAMPTON

THE LIMITATIONS OF
SOCIAL RESEARCH

LONGMAN SOCIAL RESEARCH SERIES

Series Editor: Professor Maurice Craft, Goldsmiths' College, University of London.

Reading Ethnographic Research, 2nd edition
Martyn Hammersley

The Philosophy of Social Research, 3rd edition
John A. Hughes and Wesley W. Sharrock

The Limitations of Social Research, 4th edition
Marten Shipman

CONTENTS

INTRODUCTION

This fourth edition has been revised as radically as social research itself over the quarter century since it was first published in 1973. Accepting the depth of those changes in social science and research is not easy. It means acknowledging your own prejudices. But any contemporary establishment in the production of knowledge about the human condition will have short-lived authority. Social research is motivated by an urge to clarify and to change. Its credibility is determined by informed criticism. That maintains its momentum and undermines its authorities.

Everybody produces evidence on the human condition. The brave make it public and await criticism. That is also the procedure for establishing the credibility of research evidence. Here, too, the review is expected to be 'friendly-hostile' (Popper 1945). The invitation in this book is to join in that informed but critical review. The major influence now, as in previous editions of this book, has been Sir Karl Popper. The sceptical assessment of evidence is a condition not only of accumulating credible knowledge, but of democracy itself. Social researchers should invite criticism and never close their work to outside scrutiny. The users of research evidence should be active participants in that review.

The need to spell out the limitations of social research arises from the power of research to convince. Unlike other authorities it does not depend on reference to external sources in religion, mystery or folklore, but on agreement among peers. Yet research evidence is often stretched too wide. Peer review is often too narrow. Readers cannot assume that quality has been controlled. They too have to be involved, informed and review without deference.

The book is divided into three parts. Part One examines the underlying assumptions of different traditions of research that justify different research methods.

Part Two examines the techniques for collecting evidence and preparing it for publication.

Part Three examines the processes and restrictions in publication: crucial, because credibility can only be assessed if the work has been made fully public for review.

Each chapter is preceded by a Controversy, usually chosen from education, illustrating the problems discussed in the chapter that follows.

These show why critical review is necessary – not just from within academia, but by those who use the evidence. Too much damage has been done, particularly to children, for social research to be above criticism.

In the revisions since first publication, the picture of the social researcher has changed. Then it was of a surveyor accumulating evidence from a detached position. After 15 years, in the third edition, the image was of a researcher crouched in the Wendy House of an infant classroom trying to be inconspicuous. A third image, the social critic, a shadow in earlier editions, is now more prominent. In each case the motives were different, ranging from a detached search for truth, through a search for the way those observed understood their situation, to the exposure of injustice.

These three researchers are making different claims. The detached surveyor may only be testing a theory, without claiming that this has any necessary validity in the confusion of everyday life. Participant observers will not claim that their work can be checked for reliability by repetition. The critical researchers reject the idea of universal validity, seeing knowledge as relative, imposed by groups with power. However, all three publish and hope to convince, usually under the title of social 'science'. Hence they owe the reader sufficient information to answer the questions that follow. Many researchers will not make such claims, but it is their responsibility to spell out why not. In turn, the reader should use that information to assess the work.

Is there a claim for VALIDITY?

This is a claim about the evidence made public. Does it reflect reality, reach the truth? Is the case made convincing, given our existing knowledge? Is it supported by other evidence? Does it explain current problems? Does it help in understanding how and why humans behave as they do? There are no established bodies of knowledge in the social sciences against which validity can be assessed. The responsibility of the researcher is to lay out the claim for review. The reader should take up the offer.

Is there a claim for RELIABILITY?

This is a claim about the methods used. Would the same results be obtained if the research was repeated? By someone with different political views? At a different time, in a different place? A claim to high reliability is usually based on 'scientistic' research described in Chapter 2. But each human situation tends to have unique features and, in the 'interpretive' research in natural settings described in Chapter 3, such a claim is unlikely. There should be sufficient information for the reader to assess how much is evidence and how much is opinion.

Is there a claim to a basis for GENERALIZATION?

This is a claim about the particular as a basis for wider conclusions. Is the work based on a sample or a case? If it was a sample, how representative was it? Was non-response a limiting factor? If it was a case, how and why was it picked? In all research, from a single case study to a large-scale social survey there is likely to be generalization of results. But cases may be unique, samples may be unrepresentative. The reader needs sufficient detail to gauge whether claims have been stretched too far.

Are the bases of the claims made PUBLIC?

There should be enough detail to enable the reader to answer the three questions above. That should include the rationale underlying the work and accounting for the choice of subject, methods and the treatment of results. It should also include the reasons why any of the three questions above were not relevant.

PART ONE

Approaches to Social Research

CHAPTER 1

Social research

Our ancestors, faced with a problem, were likely to consult a priest, an oracle, some hopefully wise old neighbour, custom, holy writ. That reference to authority persists. But we are as likely to engage in or look to research. Here the concern is with research that is published. That still leaves an overlap with filling in a tax form and peeking over the garden fence. Further, that overlap is a clue to the limitations that are the subject of this book. Social research is about humans investigating humans. That raises philosophical as well as technical problems. It also means that the motivations to research are often mixed up, particularly the urge to discover new knowledge, to benefit humanity and to raise awareness of injustice.

There are then many routes to understanding the human condition. The mystic and the priest have their own maps. These are often private, based on some external source and jealously guarded. Authority is not negotiable. The authority of research as a claim to knowledge is distinctive because it rests on publicity not privacy. It is disclosure that enables others to examine and assess the work and hence establish its authority. This is a social activity dependent on scientific communities that are organized to assess, approve or reject without deference (Popper 1945). But this cannot be exclusive. Social research is reviewed by government, professions and the lay public who bring their own informed if distinctive criteria to bear to assess the evidence for use. They need sufficient information to be able to do this. But researchers can leave out essential details from published accounts. Peer review can be inadequate. Claims for research as a source of knowledge can be as private as those from any cabala.

The claims for research as a path to knowledge

Research is a public exercise

Secrecy belongs to the era of arcana, when knowledge was produced in communities of priests or scholars jealously guarding their sources from the public. The alchemist, the quack, the mystic, the priest, claimed privileged access to the truth but denied it to outsiders. The distinguishing feature of research is that it is published so that it can be reviewed by peers. Only then is a claim to truth accepted or rejected. The claim to knowledge is based on surviving criticism, not by reference to mysteries beyond human reason.

This is the most important claim. Publication should enable readers to assess credibility from initial conjecture to final conclusion. Only when sufficient detail is made available can strengths and weaknesses be assessed. That is not only essential for the peer review that decides reliability and validity, but for the professional and lay-users of the evidence. It is the major focus of this book because publication can often conceal rather than reveal. Conventions of reporting today can be as secretive as the mumbo jumbo of alchemists. The researcher is often concealed behind third-person language. The published reasons for doing the work this way, selecting that data, analysing the results like this, drawing those conclusions are rarely sufficient for those outside the often small research community involved to make an informed judgement. Those inside often have to use knowledge that is not in the public domain.

Research makes explicit claims to knowledge

The second characteristic of research is that from start to finish its procedures are claimed to be explicit. To count as research, enquiry has to be more than the collection of prominent features of an interesting topic as they strike the inquisitive. It has to have defined and restricted aims if it is to be a claim to knowledge. That is often achieved by using models that simplify the confusion of the world by concentrating on a few features related by a theory. The research design and its rationale will be spelled out and justified. The analysis of evidence and the conclusions drawn will be referenced to the aims and methods.

This does not rule out changes in direction as research progresses. Indeed, in fieldwork described in Chapter 3, this is common as new leads look promising. But it does mean that this should be planned for and made clear in reporting. It is legitimate to raise awareness or promote change, but not published tangled up with a search for knowledge under the common title of research. The implicit cannot be assessed. There should not be any need for the reader to puzzle over what was really being investigated, how this was done and why.

The explicit nature of research is most marked in its systematic procedures. There is a design and progress recorded in fieldnotes. It is thought through, carried out, recorded and reported in ways that can be justified and are made public. The design will have been chosen because it is suited to the issue being researched. But it will also be chosen on the basis of assumptions in the discipline of the researcher. It is a discipline because its members share views on the nature of the world, how we can get to know about these, what limits there are to the knowledge produced. There is both method and methodology because the various approaches are rooted in different views of the world that is being investigated.

The responsibility for ensuring that research is public, explicit and systematic lies with the researcher. This may be difficult. Time and resources may be limited. There are constraints on space in publication. But there are too many examples in this book of influential but flawed evidence for this responsibility to be ignored. There is also a responsibility on the readers of research. If evidence is to be used it has to be assessed. There is never complete agreement among peers. Further, if reality is indeed what is defined as real, each reader is likely to review research differently. The claims are based on exposure to review. The more perspectives that are brought to bear, the less likely it will be that faulty theories will be developed and misleading practices promoted. Further, the greater the number engaging in review, the more likely is the flawed or fraudulent to be exposed.

Thus there is particular emphasis in this book on public disclosure as central to all enquiry titled as research. There is also the assumption that the reader will adopt the sceptical stance that ensures that any published work, including this book, will be critically assessed as it is read. The guiding principle comes again from Popper. There must be no deference in the scrutiny. That is the condition of the open society and the accumulation of knowledge (Popper 1945). Unfortunately the conventions of publishing tend to exclude the crucial first stages of research that are in the biographies of the researchers and the models used in their specialism. This often missing information accounts for the style of research. It can be scientific, trying to reduce the effects of extraneous factors. It can be freeranging, designed to follow leads that look promising. The evidence collected can also be used to try to remedy injustice. But the bottom line is that if it is under the title research it should be public not private, open to review not a mystery known only to a closed group.

Behind these two basic features of research lies the communal organization of science. The lone alchemist jealously protecting results from spies was doomed once scientists organized for communication and review. The Royal Society and its French and Italian counterparts, established in the seventeenth century, gave a seal of approval to science as a profession and provided a forum for public debate and review. Today academic libraries are bankrupted by the proliferation of journals to facilitate the publication that informs colleagues, attracts money, advances careers, brings prestige to institutions and adds new knowledge. It is now so specialized that there are barriers to the necessary communication. But there is a vast array of users of social research capable of reviewing critically. Too often they are denied the chance.

There is one more necessary comment before looking at research within social science. Scientists are a varied lot, not just in their range of subject specialisms, but in the way they go about their work. Medawar (1986) distinguishes two conceptions of science. The romantic conception is of a speculative excursion into the unknown. It is poetic, imaginative and should not be constrained. In social science this is often found in the interpretive research described in Chapter 3. The alternative conception is that truth lies in nature and must be extracted, examined and judged on the evidence. That scientistic social research is discussed in Chapter 2. But it remains a creative, human, often funny and hence fallible activity. Here then is the unhappy case of the discovery of N-rays.

The discovery of X-rays by Röntgen in 1895 led to a search for other rays with other wonderful properties. In 1903, Blondlot announced the discovery of N-rays. By 1904, 77 scientific publications described their detection, properties and applications. But there was a mystery. Outside France nobody could find them. One explanation from inside France was that Anglo-Saxon senses had been dulled by exposure to fog and beer. Then a sneaky American visiting Blondlot's laboratory removed a crucial lens from the apparatus during a demonstration, yet the N-rays continued to be observed. The N-ray disappeared from science and poor Mr or Professor or Prosper, or René Blondlot, Blondot or Blandot, recipient of either the Lalande or Leconte Prize, went mad. Even in death he has not been respected for all these versions of his name and his prize appeared in the references used here (Good, 1962; Eysenck, 1965; Firth, 1969; Broad and Wade, 1982).

The human subject in social research

The step from natural to social or human sciences such as economics, psychology and sociology, means that the subject is now thinking humans and their transactions. They will be learning from and acting on the research situation. Social researchers are also part of the world they research. Their activities provide clues for those they study. Across the years humans in the social sciences have been modelled as driven by instincts, drives, the id, needs. They have been modelled as actors playing roles written for them, or as making roles, as manifesting rational expectations, as information-processors, through to enquiring scientists. Human behaviour is still modelled by experimenting with apes, pigeons and rats at one extreme and by comparisons with gods at the other. Each metaphor or model leads to different ways of defining the human condition and hence of designing and reporting research. The questions asked will be varied and many answers will not even be comparable.

In this book it is assumed that humans are active, enquiring, interpreting, trying to make sense of their world. Thus researched and researchers are both modelled as trying to find out and understand what is happening. Both bring to bear their personal, political as well as professional beliefs to give meaning to events and take action. All are members of groups that share beliefs, ways of finding out and criteria for judging validity. Through those groups they gain prestige and influence others. Beware, for questions from such a popular model lead to optimistic answers. Those who assume that life is nasty, brutish and short reach different conclusions.

The distinguishing marks of professional researchers are that their work is focused and made public for review. But they too belong to groups, disciplines and specialisms where they learn to use, develop and validate models. They 'see' the world through these models. They depend on colleagues to judge their work and hence to determine their careers. These research communities can be tight-knit, with membership, reputation, qualification and promotion, as well as the assessment of research, controlled by a few authoritative figures. They can hold in common views that are openly political. They can also be loose associations of buccaneers. But the individual professional is still influenced by the group through which their work is assessed and their career determined.

The importance of assumptions about the human condition lies in determining the questions asked and in conjectures about answers. Experimental methods, or approximations to them, are appropriate if humans are modelled as the product of stimulus-response bonds. Other 'scientistic' methods may be legitimate if humans are modelled on the computer or as information-processors. But if the model is of humans who are always working out and sharing new meanings of the world around them, a social science has to be 'interpretive', in order to study those shared meanings. That subjective world seems self-evident to those involved. That means getting into the field without disturbing it and looking and listening, until the lay meanings are understood in lay terms. There can be no imposition of meanings through hypotheses formulated in advance.

It has not been easy for social scientists to give up the idea that there were laws of human behaviour to be found equivalent to those in the natural world. It must have been gratifying to claim you knew why and hence could predict future developments. But humans are slippery subject matter. It is reasonable to assume that beyond simple knee-jerk reactions, little is predictable in human behaviour, especially over time or across cultures. Humans think, particularly about what the researcher is doing. There have been two major responses to the arguments against a science of human behaviour. Some social scientists, particularly in sociology, rejected science as an appropriate method. Others redefined it to accommodate the study of the human condition.

Once the change of model of the human switches attention from the experiment, the test and tick-the-box questionnaires, to observation in the field, classroom or bedroom, the opportunity for fun increases. The models now overlap with those in the arts. The divine comedy, the naked ape, the noble savage, the concrete jungle, all the world's a stage, paradise lost, all produced new insights. The social sciences have as much variety. From here on this will be reduced to the conventional distinction between the scientistic and the interpretive. Both of these approaches to research can be used to go beyond informing to reforming, emancipating. But this is a gross simplification. Each of the many metaphors leads to specialization within social sciences and hence to different research questions, designs and results. That is realistic. Human life is varied and unpredictable. The grand theories, the metanarratives and the systems of much early social science, telling how human society developed, are now recognized as fallible. Contemporary social research tends to aim at revealing the variety and the diversity of human life. But that revelation, if it is through research, still means explicit definition, systematic enquiry and full disclosure of procedures and results for peer review.

Social researchers at work

There is a continuing demand for research. The Economic and Social Research Council spent more than £40 million of research and nearly £20 million on research training in 1995–96. The explanation lies in the human concern to give meaning to events. We need to know. We also need to believe that we can know. That questing marks out researchers. They are imaginative and adventurous. It is tempting to describe social research just as techniques for collecting information. Even accounts that show how methods are related to their underlying assumptions tend to concentrate on two models: one, scientistic, sharing the assumptions of natural science, the other interpretive, aimed at understanding and building on the way humans make sense of their world. Yet that is an impoverished version of a varied and exciting occupation. From fact-gatherers to consciousness-rousers researchers exercise a variety of skills in pursuit of a variety of objectives.

Much of this book is about the contrasts between these two research traditions. Yet both can be used not just to study but to expose injustice and hence suggest how to improve the human lot. There is a long and honourable tradition of such critical research. The limitations of social research can only be appreciated if the intentions as well as the procedures of the researcher can be assessed. The justification for a claim to research lies in it being restricted in its ambitions and a public exercise open to scrutiny. Validity rests on review by peers. But this review cannot be just the preserve of a few in academia. Evidence from social research is widely used by professionals, administrators, policy-makers and the general public. Before use it is assessed. Peer review cannot be confined to a few academic colleagues where the subject is human transactions. Those researched and others sharing the evidence produced need to be able to act as peers and review from an informed position.

Social science is now big business. It contains the large numbers in higher education. It feeds the media. It is an important influence on policy and practice. We all use its ideas and evidence. We should also be active participants in assessing its quality. Peer review should not be left to a few experts, often colleagues of the researcher. For such a lay review to be possible there has to be sufficient information published. Research has to be genuinely public if those who use it are to be in a position to assess its credibility.

The crucial information is on the assumptions about the human condition built into the models that are used to produce hypotheses about social life and guide the choice of research methods. If humans are modelled as computers there will be a very different logic to enquiry than if they are seen as scientists. One will treat them as information-processors, the other as producers of that information. The former will proceed through setting them problems to solve, the latter will observe how they think through and test hunches for themselves. There are hundreds of metaphors and models of the human condition and hence hundreds of research methods. They change rapidly and vary country by country. Assessing limitations is not easy.

To illustrate the relation between methods, the models that justify their use and the way they have changed, here are three sketches of social research at the start, middle and end of the twentieth century.

First, come into the London School of Economics (LSE) shortly after Hobhouse had been appointed as the first Professor of Sociology in 1907. With two collaborators, one of whom, Ginsberg, succeeded him as Martin White Professor, he was throwing anthropological accounts and traveller's tales into wastepaper baskets according to the stage of development each society was judged to have reached. Hobhouse pulled in evidence from any source into this evolutionary bucket model. The product of this particular effort was a statistical study, extracted from the baskets, comparing the cultures of 'simpler people' at different stages of their evolution (Hobhouse, Ginsberg and Wheeler 1915).

Now return to the LSE in the early 1950s. Floud, Halsey and Martin are researching into the chances of boys from different social classes entering grammar schools. The design is quasi-experimental. The boys are categorized according to their father's occupation and measured for intelligence. The chances of middle, lower middle and working-class boys being selected at 11-plus are then compared (Floud, Halsey and Martin 1957). Note that the study was of boys only, although in the text the references are to 'children'.

Now leave LSE and move on to the late 1980s. Browne and Ross are investigating the way gender affects the way children view science. Over four years the researchers observe, record, question in 29 schools. They capture the ways boys and girls in nursery and infant schools have constructed their world in relation to science in contrasting ways. The key to this research is allowing these views of children, and of their teachers, to emerge and be recorded with minimum interference from the researchers. Gender differences are at the centre of the work (Browne and Ross 1995).

These three groups of researchers share the focusing of their work through conjectures about what they will find. There is no collection of facts preceding theorizing, even when data is being sorted into buckets. Hobhouse and his colleagues had already labelled each according to an evolutionary model. At mid-century, Floud and her colleagues had very strong views about the injustice of selection along social-class lines following the 1944 Education Act. Underlying the statistics is a model of social differentiation and mobility with social-class differences at the centre, developed first at the LSE in the department of social biology directed by Hogben which links these first two studies. The observation of infants in the late 1980s and early 1990s is modelled on the social construction of reality. All three studies have been guided by prior theorizing arising out of very different contexts.

At the start of the century, Hobhouse and his colleagues were using a comparative method, albeit with some very doubtful data, that was developed as part of science influenced by evolution. Tracing stages of development required the use of historical and anthropological documents. Marx in the British Museum, Spencer, Tylor, Maine were all engaged in such comparative study, used so productively by Darwin after his voyage on the Beagle.

By mid-century Floud and her colleagues were using a quasi-experimental design to produce quantitative results that would convince policy-makers worried about the way the new selective secondary schooling was developing. They were taking a problem that needed solution following the development of selective grammar schools and secondary moderns, and the testing at age 11 that followed. The quasi-experimental design produced influential results criticized mainly for not asking more searching questions about the morality and reliability of selection.

Browne and Ross towards the end of the century were trying to find out how the children were constructing their own identities, particularly in relation to science. The research was open-ended and its subject 'made', by the researchers, in the field, not taken from policy-makers. Behind this approach lay the assumption of interpretive social science that researchers cannot adopt a detached stance but must understand through involvement in the everyday construction of the identities being researched.

Behind these three examples are very different models of the human condition and of ways of finding out about it. The logic and hence the methods are different. The methodology changed as models changed across the century. This link between assumptions in the models of the human condition and the methods used to investigate can be examined through questions starting with techniques of enquiry and ending with questions about what actually exists and how knowledge of it can be obtained. Thus research design can be seen as a series of increasingly profound questions to be answered, each dependent on answers to the one below.

1   Questions about methods

Here the focus is on techniques for collecting evidence. These are the subject of Part Two of this book. Surveys, observation, questionnaires, interviews, experiments, documents are all possible sources of evidence and there are variations of each, with rules for securing reliability. The choice is determined partly by the topic itself, partly by the discipline of the researcher and partly by the time and resources available.

The important decision is over methodology, for this links the methods chosen to the underlying assumptions.

2   Questions about methodology

Here the focus is on the 'logy', the logic of using the methods selected. This is determined by reference to the assumptions in the theoretical models guiding the work. A feminist sociologist and an experimental psychologist researching sexual relations may use very different methods because they refer back to very different models in their different disciplines, even though they are interested in the same issue.

3   Questions about how we can come to know

Underlying the models used in social science are assumptions about how we can come to 'know' and the limits of that knowledge. This is epistemology. It is an integral part of each model. Scientific method is based on the assumption that science is primarily concerned with testing conjectures against observed facts and that values and beliefs have to be excluded by research design. Interpretive methods are primarily concerned with those values and beliefs and the way they are constructed in social life.

4   Questions about reality itself

The basic questions are about what is actually out there in the world. Was it created by God? Has it evolved since a big bang? Whatever it is, is it out there waiting to be found, or only to be known through our perceptions, our concepts, our models, including those constructed within the social sciences? The study of these assumptions about reality is ontology. These fundamental assumptions load the answers to previous questions. If the world is out there open to the senses it can be discovered by imposing scientific method. If it is constructed through human interpretation, it can only be understood by leaving the natural situation undisturbed, getting involved in it and hence getting to the way those involved have made sense of it.

Thus the questions that in theory finally justify the methods used are the basic 'What is the nature, the essence of things in the world?', through 'How can we know about this nature?' to questions about methodology, the logic, the rationale for selecting one research design among the many possibilities. Only then can questions such as 'Given this topic, my resources and the models established in the specialist community in which I am working, which methods shall I use?' These questions range from philosophical to practical. But few researchers have the time to work through such questions. They just get on with the job. They are pragmatic realists. Yet many do confuse methodology with methods by leaving out consideration of the 'logy' and many a failed doctorate has resulted from this omission. Many research reports have also been rejected because the stages outlined above don't hang together, are incoherent.

It is conventional to distinguish two major social research traditions aimed respectively at explaining and at understanding the social world. One tradition shares the assumptions of natural science. It aims at explanation by discovering the causes of events and at producing laws for prediction. This research tradition uses scientific method to investigate a world of facts, open to the senses, waiting to be discovered. It will be labelled scientistic and is the subject of Chapter 2. It is however necessary to be sensible about the pioneers of social science who adopted this view. Major thinkers such as Durkheim and influential reformers such as Booth are often displayed as idiots believing that humans automatically responded to social pressures like zombies. Dividing social research arbitrarily into two traditions not only ignores many variations in between, but can demean the pioneers.

The other research tradition assumes that the human, social world can only be understood through getting to know the way those involved have given meaning to events. This tradition rejects the idea of a social world out there waiting to be observed and hence of the suitability of scientific method. Here it is labelled 'interpretive'. Once again, it is misleading to assume that those who developed these approaches were unaware of the existence of customs, beliefs and norms that constrain humans and which are open to observation and natural experiment. But they saw that the human world can only be understood as the product of human thought. Hence research had to be aimed at understanding how humans themselves constructed a meaningful life. There could be no laws of human behaviour and hence no prediction because humans were always reinterpreting, reconstructing, often with the help of social researchers. The methods of natural science could not be applied. This is the subject of Chapter 3.

Range and change in social science

The rest of this book follows the conventional division of social research into scientistic and interpretive. But this can be misleading. There have always been contrasting research designs. Change has been rapid, particularly around 1960. Those changes were not just technical arguments over the use of the methods of the natural sciences in studying human behaviour. They were disputes about what we can know, how we can know, about our own human condition. The claims have become more modest over the years. But we want to know, to understand, even where this is impossible. Social research is usually the best buy available. Its public and explicit character also means that its credentials can be checked.

The range of social research

The most striking aspect of social research to outsiders is that it is organized within specialisms that don't cooperate and hardly communicate. Within psychology and sociology there are numerous specialisms, each based on different models of the human. In psychology, Skinner's reacting human has nothing in common with Kelly's scientist. In sociology the role-takers contrast with the role-makers. All contrast with the rational human in economics.

A look at researchers at work again shows a broad spectrum. Here are focus groups in a hotel room discussing a product with a market-researcher. There are students in a laboratory responding to the stimulus of pornographic photographs. In libraries they are deconstructing texts, accessing databases and searching piles of old theses. Much of this research is individual. Public library shelves now contain books titled *Do your own research* specially written for A-level students engaged on projects. At the other end of the spectrum, the City University Social Statistics Research Unit is managing the 1 per cent sample study of successive censuses involving data from about 500 000 people, the National Child Development Study following up another 17 000 born in March 1958, the British Cohort Study of another 17 000 born in April 1970 and the massive 16-to-19 follow-up study combining survey and ethnographic studies in Britain and abroad (Bynner 1992).

There are three broad overlapping categories of social researcher. First, there are the theory-builders and testers, mainly concerned with the development of academic social science. Second, there are those most involved in guiding policies and practices. Third, and probably most numerous, are those employed to collect and analyse descriptive information. Most engage in all three activities.

Fact-gatherers appear in the Bible. The *Doomsday Book* was for Norman tax-inspectors. The first Census was in 1801. Today fact-gathering is a major industry, concentrated in the Office of National Statistics, market research, pressure groups, government, business, commerce and research units within academia. The data collected is essential for administration but is also mined to elaborate theory, guide policy and practice and raise awareness.

But it is ideas rather than facts that guide most research. Induction, starting by collecting facts, has been described as a 'bucket' theory (Popper 1959). You collect observations, examine them and theorize. The shortcomings can be gauged from the 'Mass Observation' movement after 1937 (Calder 1985). Volunteer observers were given a topic such as the coronation of George V1 and asked to take notes of what they saw. The results are often interesting, but add up to very little. To select 'May 12' as a research topic and depend on enthusiasts to note what struck them is interesting. But bucketfuls of facts need have no theoretical significance. It requires an hypothesis to collect the relevant facts, test them and give them meaning. Research starts with imagination.

Thus the most productive model of scientific method is hypothetico-deductive. The start is a hunch, a happy guess. This is tested by experiment if you work at CERN or in the field if you are observing gorillas. Popper describes this as the 'searchlight' theory of science (1959). The hypothesis guides the collection of evidence, and in turn is either confirmed or falsified. This however still depends on assuming that there are facts out there, independent of the theory, that can be observed, that are open to empirical investigation. In the social world that is a problem, for the thinking human and the deducing researcher clearly are interacting. The scientistic social researcher has to be a pragmatic, a naïve realist who ignores this conundrum.

The two strands of social research, one to develop theory, the other to inform practice are often combined despite their contrasting goals. There is inevitable loss. The few interested in theory are liable to be starved of funds. Those who aim to influence practice will often relate factors to practical issues without further consideration of their place in models which give them meaning. In scientistic social research that means that research is often designed to establish causal relationships, laws, explanations, often out of context, but used to guide education, business, management, social work. Similarly a case study based on assumptions of a world constructed by humans is often used to generalize and predict. The assumptions, the logic of social science, are ignored. Theory is divorced from practice. Further, research-funding is concentrated on topics deemed to be of economic or social importance, again ignoring the dependence of such work on underlying theory.

Theory and research are developed together. The logic of the former determines the methods in the latter. In academia it is still argued that the main purpose of research is to build theory. There is vigorous defence of basic research not only because it improves theory, but because it is more effective in improving practice, albeit indirectly through enlightenment, than attempting direct influence through applied work (Kerlinger 1977). This view has to be respected, although the idea that there is nothing as practical as a good theory doesn't stand up to investigation (Sandelands 1990). Research is not the mechanical application of techniques. That is what is implied in the term methodology. To Mouzelis a widening gap has opened between theory and research in the twentieth century (Mouzelis 1991). Both are consequently impoverished.

Finally, there are a wide range of political motives for researching. Many will use their work to enlighten, emancipate, raise awareness. Further, the motives for researching the human condition have always included the hope of improving it. That 'do-gooding' is not only a motive of students, but of the founders of social science. With Comte it had the fervour of religion. Max Weber was passionately engaged in politics and the cause of peace in Europe. Booth and the Webbs saw the collection of facts as pointing the way to reform. The London School of Economics was founded to provide evidence from enquiry to help produce a fairer and juster society (Dahrendorf 1995).

The changes in social research

The founders of both psychology and sociology at the start of the twentieth century tended to be eugenicists, worried about the quality of the human stock. This concern persisted to mid-century even at the London School of Economics where research of lasting value was done in the Department of Social Biology under Hogben. By the end of the century even researching the issue was labelled biological racism. Yesterday's priorities are often today's embarrassment.

A typical transition occurs in the routine attacks on positivism in most books on research methods. This is treated as a design issue only. Yet to Comte, sociology, the 'science of society', the 'final science of Humanity', was the culmination of human intellectual thought. It would lead not just to knowledge but regeneration. Positivism would bring 'Feeling, Reason and Activity into permanent harmony' (Comte 1848: 355). French philosophers are difficult to translate, but positivism did mean more than experimentation and quantitative methods.

The changes in social research range from technical to philosophical. They have been dramatic. The researcher squashed into the Wendy House trying to observe how infants understand their schooling assumes that they are constructing their own reality. It's sure to be different from that of the teachers. An interesting outcome of the research is ensured as a result of this discrepancy. This psychologist measuring the reaction times of students to different colours displayed on a screen has them wearing ear-plugs in a darkened room to control 'extraneous' influences. Here the assumption is that the world impinges directly on the senses.

The drama of these changes underlying social research can be detected in discussions over the promise of scientific method. Here is Sully, friend of Charles Darwin, designer of the first psychology laboratory at University College, London:

The relation of Education to Psychology is, however, a closer and more pervading relation. Being a theoretic as distinguished from a practical science, it does not, it is true, give rules for regulating mind. But it gives us an account of mind as a whole, the way in which it operates, the laws of succession and dependence which govern mental phenomena, and lastly a theory of mental growth or development. And since Education in all its branches is engaged in producing some mental result (e.g. accurate knowledge, good feeling), it needs to continually revert to Psychology.

(Sully 1884: 17)

This claim for psychology as a basis for educating seems exaggerated today. Yet until government intervened in determining the curriculum of teacher-training it was argued that psychology and sociology, and other components of an education course should replace courses on the teaching of school subjects (Price 1966; Webster 1976). The dates here are significant. The confidence in social 'science' peaked among users after its demolition by academics (Mills 1959).

The attacks on a science of society also gained support from the tough criterion of falsification advanced by Popper (1959). If the criterion for accepting evidence was confirmation, social science was possible. But if a single case that refuted was decisive, Marx, Freud, economics, sociology and most of psychology were not sciences. This was not just an academic debate. One consequence was that Sir Keith Joseph had the word 'science' removed from the title of the Social Science Research Council (SSRC) and had it renamed the Economic and Social Research Council (ESRC). He first lectured committee members on Popper's criterion of falsifiability as essential to science, but missing from the work funded by the Council.

The internal and external attacks on the relevance of scientific method produced a swing to an interpretive stance in social research around the 1960s. Simultaneously feminists, gays, Blacks, were attacking the assumed objectivity of social science as a White, male front for sexism and racism (see Controversy 1). Many researchers, including myself, took aboard interpretive, ethnographic research as just another set of useful designs. Simultaneously, science was redefined as the public, explicit, systematic definition used in this book. This may not have satisfied Keith Joseph, but it enabled even the most virulent critics of science to continue to call themselves scientists.

This has not been an easy transition. It has meant accepting that you were not a detached expert who could stand outside and study other humans with detachment. You had to be inside the everyday framework of ideas and not disturb it. You learned by observing rather than imposing a questionnaire or test. Experimental methods were no longer appropriate. This resulted in a wave of exciting studies of the way different groups, oppressed and poor, powerful and rich made sense of their world. But this involved the abandonment of the conventional image of social science as explanatory and predictive. However, there is now less chance of doing harm. Marxism has a lot to answer for. There may be only modest conclusions from unobtrusive methods derived from models of the social construction of reality, but they are unlikely to lead to increasing misery and are great fun to do.

The benefits from abandoning natural science as a model for examining the social accrued mainly from attacks on determinism. The confidence that human events had detectable causes and that these would be found and built into laws enabling predictions to be made has now evaporated. Yet the ambition to predict persists. In 1992 and again in 1993, the American Sociological Association (ASA) set up programmes to find out why the collapse of the Soviet Union in 1989 had not been predicted by social scientists (American Sociological Association 1995). A few economists, psychologists and sociologists had been unwise enough to make predictions for the year 1992 at the start of the 1980s (Wallechinsky, Wallace and Wallace 1981). These ranged from 'correct' predictions to those seeing the whole world except the USA and Australia as communist-controlled. However, 'correct' predictions also included the collapse of capitalism as the whole world disintegrated.

Some consolation can be obtained from the predictions of the strategic and Soviet foreign policy analyst at the Central Intelligence Agency who predicted that by 1993, not only would the USSR be approaching hegemony over the rest of the world, but that the USA would no longer be a Great Power. The outcome of the programmes of the ASA were, predictably, that more research was needed.

The quantity of research evidence is however more of a warning than a promise. It usually means that the issue is too complicated for any conclusions to be reached. In Chapters 2 and 3 research evidence on the teaching of reading in schools will be discussed. This looks like a straightforward topic. Take two classes, teach one this way, the other that way and compare how well they read at the end. Hundreds of research projects later the design will have improved and become much more expensive. There will be a lot of evidence on the complications in the teaching and learning not just of reading, but of language. Meanwhile teachers, inspectors, language experts will be confidently emphasizing that they have the secret to success.

There is no need to be depressed about failure to be conclusive, to explain, to predict. It is also a reason for hope, for humans are demonstrating their ingenuity. Further, the conceptual and technical advances from researching will continue. Eminent natural scientists often guessed wrong. Lord Kelvin, President of the Royal Society from 1890 to 1894, buried next to Newton in Westminster Abbey, predicted that 'Radio had no future,' that 'Heavier than air flying machines are impossible,' and that 'X-rays will prove to be a hoax' (Pile 1988). Kelvin was in good company alive as well as dead. Simon Newcomb, first President of the American Astronomical Society, published an article on 22 October 1903 proving that aerial flight was impossible. On 17 December in the same year Orville Wright flew 850 feet in a minute at Kitty Hawk, North Carolina. Even in 1905 the *Scientific American* was claiming that the flight was a hoax. In that year the Wrights flew 24 miles in a half-hour flight.

Can there be objectivity in social research?

It isn't easy for old, White Anglo-Saxon males to accept that their youthful research, treasured as objective, was actually sexist, racist and homophobic. These uncomfortable accusations from feminists, from Blacks and from gays have been accompanied by condemnation of the work as positivist. There is little consolation in the feminist view that men have used the term objectivity to display and impose their own subjectivity as the truth.

It is easy to detect subjectivity in social research. It is impossible to confirm objectivity. Each Controversy that follows is concerned with conflicting evidence, redundant theories, bias in design, in action and in the interpretation of results. I see this is a detached look at social research. You will rightly detect my prejudices. Those who threatened litigation have seen previous editions as libellous. Objectivity is a central concern to all researchers. But when the research is about humans there is always controversy. If truth is socially constructed, there will be different versions, for there are many involved in that construction inside and outside social science.

Bias can enter at any of the three stages of research that form the three Parts of this book. Conflicting beliefs about the nature of the human condition and how we can come to know about it enter at the conceptual stages discussed in Part One. Bias as well as errors can accumulate at the technical stages discussed in Part Two. Publication, the subject of Part Three, is often loaded with views that are not derived from the evidence presented. Yet objectivity remains the public image of research. The title 'researcher' bestows status as detached. So does social 'scientist'. The third-person dead-pan reporting, the jargon, the formal layout of the research report all reinforce an image of objectivity. Yet that is controversial as both aim and stance.

There are a range of views among social researchers over the possibility of detachment in researching humans. Some maintain that their intellectual detachment places them in a position from which objectivity is possible. Others believe that the world was revealed to us and that knowledge is accessible through prayer or sacred books. Most researchers probably accept that humans, including social scientists, construct their own knowledge of the world around them and that there is no detached position for neutral observation. But they are in social science because they are passionate about current issues. Thus detachment is difficult, among just those who claim it. Hence the passion in this dispute between those defending their past record and those criticizing it as biased.

An example of the conflicting ways in which the objectivity of research can be assessed can be found in a debate over the classic 1968 study, *The Affluent Worker* (Goldthorpe *et al.* 1968). This was a study of the thesis that rising prosperity was eroding the foundations of class structure. It was criticized at the time in parallel studies of similar workers (Blackburn 1969; Beynon 1973). Across the years its male views have also come under fire. It ignored gender and failed to ask women about their political affiliations. Goldthorpe (1983) had defended the then conventional position adopted. But Hart (1994) returned to this 'relic' of a study which she saw as telling readers more about mid-century Sociology than about Vauxhall Motors workers in Luton in the 1960s. Goldthorpe (1994), responding to Hart in the same issue of the *British Journal of Sociology*, defended the design, particularly the way the control of age and social class removed bias resulting from not directly asking questions of women. The two authors never seem to get on the same wavelength. Goldthorpe's objectivity was sexism to Hart.

This is a conflict over the possibility of objective social 'science'. The conflict can also be seen in the exchanges over feminist methodology in the journal *Sociology* in 1992 and 1994 (Hammersley 1992, 1994; Ramazanoglu 1992). Hammersley maintains that the aim of research is to produce knowledge, not to raise consciousness, educate or change the world. Ramazanoglu sees the aim as the transformation of gender relations. With these contrasting ambitions, the importance of getting beyond technical issues to the assumptions behind research design and the presentation of results is obvious. If such conflicting assumptions drive social researchers, they cannot be disinterested, detached, objective.

Critical, emancipatory social research aimed at raising awareness of injustice has a long history on the political left. Research here is aimed at correcting the way knowledge has been used to ensure the passivity of the weak. Marxists and others looking at the way the world has been organized by those with power have simultaneously attacked assumptions built into the base of the social sciences and social research. This is an attack on claims to objectivity in both scientistic and interpretive research (Gitlin, Siegel and Boru 1989).

The feminist's case, alongside that of Black and gay social scientists, has brought home the depth of this controversy. The extreme case is based on the view that women and men have a different view of the human condition (Gilligan 1982). Women define the self in terms of relations, men in terms of distinctiveness. Women, with the experience of being exploited, are best able to research exploitation. A feminist social research would be based on women's experience. The idea of objectivity is a masculine concept resulting in the researcher controlling the researched. Feminist research has to be qualitative because of the way women see the world. The researched must not be exploited. Feminists consequently press for qualitative, interpretative research as non-exploitative. But this has been criticized as excluding quantitative research which remains influential and engages women who do not take a strong feminist line. Thus there are a range of feminist views, from a rejection of the whole ideal of objectivity as masculine exploitation, to its acceptance by women researchers, with many positions in between accepting both quantitative and qualitative research but sensitive to the possibility that both may still be designed in a way that demeans women (Jayaratne and Stewart 1995).

This controversy arises from acceptance that reality is not out there, created or waiting to be discovered, but constructed through our models in the mind. Consequently there can be no pure and unadulterated knowledge of the world as it really is. The researcher has a particular position in society and will see the world from there. This is not a detached position and cannot be the basis for a claim to be objective. The resolution of this problem comes from the organization of procedures for reviewing claims to have produced new knowledge. This is peer review. The researcher may not be detached, but the procedures through which research and the evidence produced is made public, scrutinized and assessed for validity can produce agreement among experts. That view, derived from Popper (1945), recurs in this book, but with the rider that lay as well as peer review is important when the subject is human behaviour.

The organized review of research bypasses questions of objectivity. It depends on research being open to the 'friendly–hostile' assessment of peers. If research from start to finish is open to scrutiny, reported fully and if there is agreement that it is sound, questions of researcher objectivity will have been taken into account. Doubts of course remain. Different research communities will come to different conclusions. There will still be questions. Who are the peers? What if they are the established, or a clique who know the author? What if women, Blacks and gays are excluded? How can there be agreement beyond a narrow group of specialists sharing a research tradition? How can the users of research, often knowledgeable and sophisticated, have their say?

The dependence on peer review means that research has to be fully public. That is a repetitive theme in this book. But it is not easily achieved. Publishers and editors are not keen on much space being given to a methods section. In books of readings this section is usually cut completely. In later references, the results are given without any detail of how they were obtained. Readers rarely know the many professional, financial and political features that can account for the choice of model and method and the conclusions drawn. Peers within a research community can read between the lines, relate the work assessed to the life history, the current political views, the personal friendships and animosities, the gossip in senior common rooms, as well as the models favoured by the author. But that is no longer peer review in an open society.

The examination of doctoral students has included defence of the thesis in the face of seniors for more than 800 years. Examiners probe below the printed words, concerned that model, method, evidence and conclusions have produced consistent and new knowledge solid enough for others to use with confidence. Peer review may no longer be a search for heresy, but the sceptical, critical attitude remains the key to deciding quality. If that is the way academic examination is conducted, it should apply to the publication of evidence in article and book. The researcher has the responsibility to provide sufficient information for such a review. The reader has the responsibility to carry it out without deference. When human behaviour is the subject, the wider the review the less chance there will be of a small unrepresentative group making a biased judgement and of this being widely accepted.

CHAPTER 2

Scientistic social research

Comte writing in 1848 claimed that the application of the methods that had triumphed in mathematics and natural science would prevail in politics and produce a science of society (Comte 1848). It was a widespread belief. In Britain Bentham pressed for the collection of facts to ensure that legislation would produce 'the greatest happiness of the greatest number'. In Belgium, Quetelet was examining social issues statistically. Le Play in France was testing theories of the family against their domestic budgets. Engels was social surveying in Manchester. Marx wrote the Communist Manifesto in 1848, the same year that Comte published *A General View of Positivism*. There was an American Statistical Society from 1839 and these existed in many of the large towns in Britain. Theorizing and description have always guided policy and practice, and been used to try to change things for the better. The promise of social science and social research was international and irresistible.

The grip of the scientistic view remains strong. For more than 100 years social scientists claimed they were in the business of explaining and hence predicting human behaviour. That claim has left the public with the belief that social science and research are 'scientific'. So do the key questions in the Introduction of this book. In practice, between the laboratory experiment at one end and the observation that is intentionally freeranging at the other there are a range of methods described in Part Two that can each be structured or unstructured, and overlap with physics at one extreme and popular journalism at the other.

The conviction that a science of society was possible was shared among those who established departments of psychology and sociology at the start of the twentieth century. Research, however modest, could produce exciting results. For half a century at least it remained in the scientistic tradition. Here is Thomas in 1935 writing about the work of Spearman on intelligence. 'But the purpose of this book is that of positive science, not speculation; and, when phrases like the laws of the growth of knowledge occur in the following pages, it must be understood that such laws only summarise certain observed facts about the acquisition of knowledge' (Thomas 1935).

These claims for science in the study of humans remain strong. Here is Fontana in the introduction to a *Psychology for Teachers* published for the British Psychological Society. 'The application of psychology to eduction has a long and honoured history, and stretches back to the first occasion when adults tried to influence the behaviour of the young. But it is only in comparatively recent years that the association between the two subjects has been given a firmly scientific basis' (Fontana 1995). The use of scientistic research to test theory gave the social sciences an authoritative basis. They have held on to the title 'science'. Being able to back hypotheses about the relation of class and attainment, personality and political views and so on was convincing. But you cannot write QED at the end of a social research paper. Laws explaining behaviour are porous and prediction is perilous. Indeed, if there were such laws, human ingenuity would soon be exercised in making sure they broke down.

Scientistic approaches, looking for explanations, for laws, are deterministic. Effects have causes. It is a short step from there to a view of the social world where humans are driven by forces beyond their control. The causes of behaviour can be seen to lie in preceding events rather than in human effort. Intelligence is seen as inherited and fixed at birth. Low achievement is caused by poor social background, criminality by a broken home, lack of affection by maternal deprivation, lack of achievement by low self-concept. Humans are denied understanding of their condition and the potential to improve it. They are swept along by historical forces beyond their influence.

Determinism accounts for many of the failures of social research. Assumptions that there are laws has often meant that relations between variables are assumed to be causal rather than just occurring together. The frustration–aggression hypothesis is plausible, but the aggressive are also more likely to be frustrated. It may seem obvious that parents bring up children. But children turn adults into parents (Shipman 1972).

Laws, such as one relating frustration to aggression, also break down because of confounding factors. Is the tendency for frustrated people to get aggressive anything more than spurious? Are there other factors that cause both frustration and aggression? Is the relationship accidental? We never know. Further, it is often the processes, treated as extraneous in much scientistic research, that link factors. It may seem obvious that the most useful research into schooling would focus on organization, teaching, learning. But the attempt to relate inputs and outputs had priority and it was only in the 1970s that attention was switched to the curriculum, the teaching styles, to school effectiveness. It is easy to interpret coincidence as explanation, especially when laws ignore contexts. There is a relationship between the number of storks and the number of births, but a look at urban–rural birth rates is a safeguard against blaming the stork for our own behaviour.

The key to breaking through the armour that the title 'science' gives to social research is to adopt the 'friendly–hostile' attitude recommended by Popper (1945). That scepticism is essential for the peer review that secures or denies credibility to research. But it cannot be the monopoly of academics. Once it is accepted that the evidence from social research has provided concepts, ideas and evidence, not just for a few peers, but for making sense of everyday life, we all become peers and we all have a responsibility to review sceptically.

The human subject in scientistic research

It is unusual to consider the human in scientistic social research. The individual is usually hidden among the statistics. The claim to a science of society was based on the idea that social phenomena were collective, objective and factual. These qualities hold the clue to the claim that the social could be studied in the same way as the natural, scientifically, excluding values and prescriptions, collecting facts and explaining them.

The twin nineteenth-century developments in the collection of statistics and theorizing about laws of human development and transactions came together in attempts to organize distinctive social sciences. One group of models were sociologistic, seeing the individual as dependent on the social. These models were influenced by the theory of evolution. Spencer (1820 to 1903) wrote massive, multivolume texts on sociology and psychology using the model of human society as organic. This was an important model through to the decline of the functionalism in the 1960s. The human was modelled as an actor swept along by the evolution of societies from primitive to advanced, simple to complex, status to contract, community to association, theological to positive. Some were two, some three-stage models. Marxism, substituting revolution for evolution, similarly predicted an advance from feudal to classless via capitalism. These typical nineteenth-century models shared a certainty that buried the human under models of development.

Another group of models were psychologistic, seeing the social as dependent on the relationship between individuals. This was Adam Smith's basis for economics. The common good was the product of the individual self-interested. Two hundred years later economics is still based on theories of individual rational expectations. Individual motivation clears markets without any necessary intervention. Psychology is concerned with individual differences. Social psychologists study the relationship between individuals, overlapping with sociologists such as Goffman, viewing humans as negotiating, constructing their relationships and hence institutions and organizations. But critics of the individualistic focus within psychology are still a small minority (Harré 1993).

The most influential attempt at reconciling the psychologistic and the sociologistic came from Durkheim (1858–1917). Here the collective effects of individual actions was seen to be more than the sum of the parts. There is a collective consciousness resulting from individual thought and action, producing a transcendent pressure that influences individuals. The most convincing research using this model is *Suicide* (Durkheim 1952). Here statistics are used to show that rates of suicide vary with different social conditions and cannot be explained by reference to individual psychology. Durkheim's *The Rules of Sociological*

Method (1966) spelled out how social facts could be treated as things. Hence social research could use the methods of natural science. This concentration on the social as fact remained as a polar if isolated position. Not many statistics have significance beyond being a collection of possibly useful data. It is difficult to detect evidence of a collective consciousness from much of the Census. But Durkheim gave social research its rules, usually described as positivist. The individual was modelled as acting within institutions that imposed roles. The focus of research was on education, the family, law, social class and so on as patterned, rule-governed behaviour, learned by those involved. The individual was socialized into the roles necessary for these institutions to persist and ensure continuity in society.

Positivism therefore assumed a passive human subject to laws. The social world was determined. There were causes of events. Research would discover these laws by producing indicators of those events and relating them through statistical analysis. In Psychology behaviourism could reject the relevance of the thinking human and concentrate on measuring responses to stimuli. In Sociology positivism could ignore the meaning of events for those involved and concentrate on the relationship between behaviour and social positions defined by categories such as age, class and sex.

The assumption of a law-obeying human in social research meant that there had to be control over the human subjects being researched, whether in the laboratory or through allocation into statistical categories. As the laboratory experiment was impossible in Sociology, naturally occurring experiments had to suffice, particularly comparisons or tracing changes across time. Data was collected, used to establish relationships such as social class and attainment or criminality and urban conditions. Control was imposed through statistical analyses.

Laboratory experiments could reduce the human subjects to responders to simple stimuli. Sitting in my office in County Hall, London, in the 1970s, I received a desperate phone call from a primary school headteacher to rush over to stop a psychologist forcing children to pedal an exercise bike until they were exhausted. This followed the completion of a personality inventory, probably equally stressful. The most famous example of such exploitation is Milgram's study of the extent to which humans would go to punish others (Milgram 1963). Put in charge of a machine discharging electric current, they administered shocks of increasing intensity to others who gave wrong answers and had learned to give cries of pain appropriate to the rising voltages. A few went on increasing the charge, thinking that they were actually torturing the 'learners'.

Thus scientistic research designs control or distort normal human interaction. The instructions on a standardized attainment or intelligence test constrain researcher and researched. There are instructions for environment, procedures, start, finish, scoring and reporting. What matters is the answer, not how it was obtained. The way problems were solved, the states of mind of those involved, the way they adjust to the test situation, their understanding of the subject outside the questions are seen as a cause of possible unreliability. They are extraneous and unwelcome. Standard procedures, the detachment of the researcher, securing the attention of the researched to a defined task are ways of restricting human activity in order to detect the relationship between variables and hence to explain behaviour. Humans in scientistic research are subjects. Their thoughts, interpretations and asides are controlled because they are potentially confusing and confounding. Yet they will always intrude and indeed are often the keys to understanding what has really happened.

Scientistic researchers at work

The influence of scientistic research should not be underestimated. This is not just due to public perception of what constitutes science. It is certainly not due to agreement over the role of quantitative methods in the social sciences. But it is very difficult to research without falling back on the traditions of science. Positivism, objective methods, hard data sound solid. Readers will have already detected this persisting influence, even in the Introduction to this book. This can also be seen in the frequency with which facts and figures appear in what is described as qualitative research. A lot of information can be collected at low cost through the use of a questionnaire. Unstructured interviews are often the source of structured data. Most frequently 'soft' interpretive evidence is reinforced by some 'hard' stuff to impress the reader. Above all, social research is part of social science. That title is retained even when 'science' itself is rejected.

My own lapse came in an interpretive study of a Schools Council curriculum project (Shipman, Bolam and Jenkins 1974). After chapters describing how the participants in the Council, the university, the schools and local authorities viewed the project there is an embarrassing attempt to quantify inputs and outputs. A quarter of a century later I can only attribute this garbage to cowardice and the lure of the 'hard' data. Even today theses for a research degree often include quantitative measures that seem to have no justification in the methodology chapter. Examiners do tend to be aged and may still see research as scientistic. But they are also likely to detect that methods have been confused with methodology and that the student lacks conviction in their own research design. Nevertheless such insertions recur.

Other researchers have been retrospectively surprised. Having taken 'voluminous fieldwork notes' in his study of Suffolk farmworkers, Newby looks back with surprise at his book because it contains little on the participant observation and a lot of survey data (Newby 1977a). Stierer, reviewing Southgate *et al.*'s *Extending Beginning Reading*, notes that reading test scores are used as the true measure of the children's reading rather than the teacher's assessments against which they are compared (Stierer 1982). Stierer justifiably asks why heavily criticized tests should be taken as the objective baseline against which the subjectivity of teachers could be assessed.

A mixture of quantitative and qualitative evidence can ensure that numbers are related to the complex social situations from which indicators have been extracted. The two perspectives can add insight, although the mixing does require justification in the form of reference back to the underlying assumptions of each. Often questionnaire results or other measurements appear without explanation amid observational research reports. Visualize, for example, research for the article 'Striptease: the anatomy and career contingencies of a deviant occupation' (McCaghy and Skipper 1970). Our two sociology professors observe the ladies in ten cities from New York to Honolulu. Having watched the show they went backstage, introducing themselves as preparing an anthology on burlesque. They managed 35 interviews. But they also managed to measure the height, weight, bust and hips of the sample for comparison with those of Playboy Playmates and the average American woman. A promising but hardly essential empirical elaboration. Significantly, the example in Chapter 3, 20 years later, is herself a stripper doing the research for her research degree.

The convincing appearance of scientistic social research is a warning that readers should be cautious. When the issue of the effectiveness of schools is raised in Chapter 11, it should be remembered that a century of research has uncovered the complexity of the factors involved, but little else that can be used by teachers or government. This may enlighten, but it cannot guide. But that is comforting. Scientific research starts with models of the social world that are often controversial and always simplified. It depends on concepts and on indicators of them that can be quantified. Measurements can be flawed and response low. Over the century the models have been progressively elaborated as new factors have been recognized as important. Statistical techniques have had to become increasingly complex. But the evidence still reflects the model rather than the reality. The former should not be reified into the latter. Ronai, the table-dancing social scientist in Chapter 3, is likely to get nearer to the human condition than any attempt to measure and question.

The procedures of scientistic research

Dian Fossey living among gorillas in the wild had little in common with a high-energy physicist working at CERN and living in Geneva. That variety is why natural scientists protest at efforts by social scientists to describe how they go about their work. It's too varied to characterize. Similar objections are raised to the efforts of philosophers to analyse the strengths and weaknesses of science by reference to the nature of the world they study and of ways of getting to know it. Most scientists are pragmatic or naïve realists. They just assume that there is a concrete world out there and set about the task of examining it. So do most social scientists, even though the issue of the human as subject is far more complex because of our capacity to think.

The dangers in this tendency to take research designs off the shelf without considering their underlying rationale is not just to leave the 'logy' out of the methodology. It also means that results are often presented without considering possible flaws in validity. The major cause of misleading interpretations identified in Chapter 1 was extraneous or confounding factors that can provide alternative and plausible explanations. In the human world these spurious factors are numerous. We are rarely certain what caused the value of the pound to fall, stress at work to rise, or our manias or depressions.

The multiple factors behind any development are a problem for researchers. They may be testing out the relationship between the amount of homework set and attainment in school. Other relationships can be controlled by collecting information on the age, sex, social background of the children and factors in school such as the marking of work set. But the hours worked by teachers, their quality, the help given by parents could all be influential and confound results. Many other influences can only be guessed at.

The true experiment avoids this problem of extraneous factors by allocating subjects to experimental and control groups at random. With sufficient numbers, that ensures that any extraneous factors are distributed randomly between the two groups and will not have any systematic effect on the results. But that is impossible in most practical situations. Teachers, for example, will not engage in such social engineering. Either all children receive the innovation or none. The alternative, to match by age, sex and so on always leaves unmatched and possibly important confounding factors. We either cannot control them all or we don't know what they are.

These procedures to remove the effects of possible extraneous factors are only possible in genuine experimental designs. In social research these are usually too artificial or unethical to be practicable. The greater the control, the less the chance of confounding factors surviving the planning, but the more artificial is the research. The popular natural experiments using comparisons or follow-up of actual developments depend on reconstructing what happened. There is then no control over or even knowledge of extraneous factors. In social surveys, control is exercised through statistical procedures. The variables under investigation, such as social class, attainment at age 11 at age 16, can be related while controlling others mathematically. But many of the measures of these factors are ambiguous and unreliable. Receiving free school meals may be a measure of social class, but itself contains several spurious assumptions and exceptions. The spectre of unforeseen, extraneous factors confounding results haunts all scientistic social research. This point is elaborated in Chapter 7.

There are then limitations in the attempt to apply social scientific methods to practical issues. Weaknesses in design are often not appreciated. Research to test and improve theory does not tell practitioners and policy-makers what is right or wrong, or the most promising way forward. All research can enlighten. But that is rarely why research is funded. Further, policy-makers often have plenty of ideas and professional colleagues suggest many more. They fund research to provide description, evaluation and the most cost-effective action. They rarely get it and hence go back to inspectors, advisers and others who can give instant opinions based on experience. The claims of scientistic researchers often exceed their capacity to deliver the goods, as ordered and on time.

However, the demand for research continues. That is partly because it can deliver descriptions that are essential for administration. But that description is also the basis for theory-building and for guiding practice. Most social researchers are engaged in this routine descriptive work. But it is not divorced from theory. This guides the conception, design and reporting of research. There is always implicit or explicit reference to theory. The notion of an inductive science in which facts are collected in the bucket and then sorted through until relations between them are revealed is no longer influential in theory or practice. The world is always modelled before research. There is always a searchlight lighting up possibilities before fieldwork starts. There can be no naïve observation of facts, no pure empiricism. There are always preconceptions.

The confounding factors, even when experimentation looks possible, partly explain why it has been so difficult to come to any conclusion over the best way of teaching reading. Hundreds of methods have been promoted, used and evaluated in thousands of research studies (Smith 1978). Smith's conclusion was that all the methods worked with some children. That is a clue to the apparent failure to set up a conclusive experiment to assess the value of such opposed techniques as phonics, the learning of letter sounds, and learning to read by reading 'real books'. That looks like a straightforward experimental task. Arrange for two parallel school classes to be taught by one of the two methods. Control for their ability and test at start and finish. But the confounding factors can void any conclusions. Thousands of studies have only fed the conflict.

First, the methods of teaching reading contrast, but are not precisely defined. Nor could they be, for the second factor is the flexibility employed by teachers. They use a variety of approaches and will not stick to any one method even when cooperating in experiments. Further, they see themselves as facilitators. Children learn to read. Teachers provide the materials, the encouragement, the help. They won't stick to any of the two methods being compared. That also follows from a third point. School classes are large and make individual attention by the teacher difficult. The ambitions don't match the reality. Once the researcher leaves the room, teachers adjust. The experiments are ambiguous. But outside the classroom the ambiguity increases. At home children can be taught by a variety of methods by parents, or ignored. They can be in homes with or without books. Their parents may be literate, enthusiastic or not interested. The possible confounding factors mount up. No randomization or matching can take them all into account.

However, the problems don't end there. The acquisition of language itself is itself the centre of conflict between those who see it as mechanistic, the acquisition of a skill by trial and error, and those who point to the wonder of the human capacity to utter sentences that we have never heard before. The conflict between Skinner, with his emphasis on stimulus and reinforcement, and Chomsky emphasizing the deep structure of language is a classic in social science (Mennell 1974). One points to experimental control as the way forward, the other rejects this as just the way to conceal what is actually happening. On Skinner's view research should control as extraneous, all but a stimulus and its effect. On Chomsky's view, most of the factors carefully organized into the thousands of experiments and surveys on reading become extraneous because of the human capacity to acquire language naturally.

The contribution of scientistic research

Most books on research methods devote much space to an attack on positivism, scientism, the attempt to apply the methods of natural science to the study of human transactions. But the authors usually focus on physics in the laboratory rather than the study of gorillas in the wild and ignore the extraordinary variety among scientific occupations. In practice, natural and social science have both contributed to the process of demystifying the world. Both use combinations of theorizing and observation to accumulate knowledge. Both are explicit, systematic and public activities. Beyond that, however, social research runs up against the construction of reality by humans. To get to know that constructed reality means close observation, getting involved with the humans concerned. It cannot be known through experiment or survey. That sets the limits to scientistic social research.

Social research usually takes place in departments labelled science. Even researchers who reject the reduction of human behaviour to numbers, who see scientistic research as invalid, still retain their title as scientists. They publish in journals with scientific titles. When they criticize the methods of school inspectors or journalists they use the criteria of scientific method. Even when scientistic research is seen as another manifestation of oppression or even rape, the language and format of the article or book follows the conventional third-person, dead-pan style that seems designed to intimidate all but a few colleagues who will perform the peer review. Above all, these publishing conventions help to sustain the public view of social research that it is 'scientific'.

It is easy to see why scientistic language and procedures survive. This research tradition, for all its faults, has made an immense contribution to improving the human condition. This contribution has come from theorizing and guiding policy and practice, both fed by description. We understand our lives by using ideas such as the self, social class or markets. We make decisions on the basis of evidence on child development, the incidence of poverty or unemployment. All depend on description that has to be quantitative because numbers condense a lot of information that can then be manipulated statistically.

Thus many social researchers get on with their work without concern for philosophical problems, just like their peers in the natural sciences. An example of the value of this pragmatic realism came when the Office of National Statistics announced that the General Household Survey, which had been the major source of data for the annual publication *Social Trends*, was to be suspended from 1997. The General Household Survey had tracked and related basic statistics such as income, jobs and housing since 1972. It was an important part of the Essex University data archive. Yet the categories, the definitions, the analyses in the Survey were open to criticism for not reflecting changes in social conditions or social science across the quarter century. Nevertheless, academics, whether concerned with developing theory or guiding practice, felt threatened. Description provides the raw material for all social science.

Scientistic research, with standard designs and tight controls, can also be repeated, replicated. That repeatability enables knowledge to be accumulated with confidence. That is why there is a question on reliability in the Introduction to this book. Valid research need not be reliable. Peer review often promotes work that could never be repeated. But when methods are systematic, designed to control extraneous factors, including the researcher, and follow conventions that are shared among researchers, the chances of accumulating knowledge are increased. Further, data can be stored, checked, reanalysed and replicated. The *cause célèbre* of social research has usually been scientistic. But that is a strength. It survived repeated review.

When researchers have cooperated in the reanalysis of data it has not only settled disputes over validity but led to improvements in techniques. The *Teaching Styles and Pupil Practice* study caused a furore (Bennett 1976). It seemed to suggest that class teaching was related to high attainment. Ten thousand copies were sold in its first day of publication. There was massive media coverage. Critics both damned and praised. To their credit, Bennett and his colleagues opened their data up to reanalysis (Aitken, Bennett and Hesketh 1981). This appeared in an academic journal with little publicity. All the significant differences caused by teaching styles disappeared with the new ways of classifying them and allowing for variations within each style. The most important findings, however, were the recognition of the difficulties in defining teaching styles and establishing how they were linked to pupil progress. The causes of pupil progress are manifold and interrelated. It was a warning to inspectors and other evaluators.

The accumulation of knowledge comes through a concentration of researchers interested in the same subject, using similar research designs, replicating and building on previous work. In the natural sciences that has produced a 'third world' of knowledge (Popper 1989). This is the outcome of such sustained agreement among peers that evidence can be taken as objective. You pump up your tyres and then feel the heat as the air is compressed. You put too weak a battery into your torch and the bulb dims. If the definitions and limits of pressure, volume and temperature, volts, amps and resistance are respected, Boyles and Ohms law holds. Don't jump from a high window chancing the fallibility of gravity. Even where methods are closest to those used to study humans, there is predictability. You don't win betting on the foal of two cart-horses.

Popper does not identify any social science as attaining the status of 'third world'. There are no laws that hold universally. Little is predictable. Humans think, particularly about research, the researcher, the results and then adjust their future behaviour. Yet there are continuities in research that approach such an agreed 'third world' through building on previous work to establish a solid core of knowledge. An example is the relation between education and social class differences. This work started with Lindsay in 1926 with a study of educational opportunity in London among children from different social classes (Lindsay 1926). The evidence of inequality and waste of talent was confirmed in 1938 (Gray and Moshinsky 1938). It was elaborated by Floud, Halsey and Martin in a study reported above in 1957. Since then there have been many further confirmations (Douglas 1964; Douglas, Ross and Simpson 1968; Halsey, Heath and Ridge 1980; Fogelman 1983). This work was then used in the development of research into school effects discussed later in Chapter 11. A similar tradition was established in educational research by a succession of school studies showing how the differentiation of pupils by teachers soon produced a polarization into pro- and anti-school groups. This tradition starts with an American classic (Waller 1932), is given its British momentum 40 years later (Lacey 1970) and continues to generate school studies into the 1990s (Abraham 1995).

Many of the contributions of scientistic social research have proved to be invalid, unreliable, an inadequate basis for generalization. Much has been shown to be sexist and racist. Indeed, the pioneering statistical work at the start of the twentieth century was frequently developed as part of the eugenics movement. The criticisms are mostly directed at the way the enquiring, active human is demeaned. This isolated social research from enquiry in the arts and humanities. It also sustained the unfortunate separation of a scientistic social research from romantic, idealist traditions emphasizing that humans made their own history, culture and reality. When that view itself became dominant in the second half of the twentieth century, it was accompanied by the rejection of science as a model and a rather useful if misconceived baby was thrown out with the bathwater.

Macho, mourner, freedom-fighter or thug?

An autobiographical note will help establish my credentials for commenting on research into youth. I was beaten up at White Hart Lane for cheering the Arsenal. My head was split open by a half-brick at the Den. I was first a policeman and then taught in secondary modern schools in London.

The awkward age, the in-betweens, the adolescents are always newsworthy. Psychologists and sociologists have always found this a promising subject. But to fulfil that promise and understand the young requires methods that involve the researcher with groups who often resent intrusion. The development of interpretive research methods owes a lot to these attempts. Stanley Hall's studies of young people pioneered intensive observation in psychology (Hall 1904). In the Chicago School of Sociology in the 1920s a concern with social pathology included the participant observation of gangs (Thrasher 1927). In Britain the interest grew rapidly in the 1960s as the young seemed to become visible, rebellious and cultural innovators. This coincided with increased interest in interpretive methods in social research.

In psychology the early work was biological and evolutionary. Hall observed the young passing through an inevitable period of storm and stress, thus recapitulating in the individual the primitive stage in the evolution of societies. Freud similarly saw individuals going through stages similar to the progress of civilizations leading at puberty to reproductive adult sexuality. In these psychological views collected in the clinic, the sources of conflict lie in the past experience of the individual. Youth is often seen as mourning the lost security of the womb, the mother, the family, even the school. Sociologists observing behaviour in the field, or rather in the run-down areas of town, examine distinctive subcultures. This is a macho world. The understanding of that world has produced a very different picture from the psychological. The young mark out and defend territory. They establish a distinctive way of life. In the affluent 1960s they acted as the cutting edge of cultural change. They served as the freedom-fighters opposing capitalism. Today another picture is being drawn. The researched, usually male, are being left behind in the race for qualifications and hence employment. Their racism and sexism is increasingly seen not as a defence against a hostile capitalist world, but as thuggery.

In 1973, Scharff in London and Willis in the Midlands were independently researching the attitudes of working-class boys moving from school to work (Scharff 1976; Willis 1978). Each researched in inner-city comprehensive schools that had been organized out of secondary moderns. Both observed, questioned, got to know the teenagers. Both report in the language of the boys. Yet the results suggest schools and teenagers that belonged to different worlds.

For Willis, 'The most basic, obvious and explicit dimension of counter-school culture is entrenched, general and personalised opposition to "authority"' (Willis 1978: 11). The 12 lads studied made life hell for the teachers. They derided their studious peers. Their language is pepperd with 'fucking' this and 'fucking' that. To Willis this evidence points to the way working-class kids get working-class jobs. The lads behave in school in ways that equip them for work that will ensure that their subordination will continue. By their own beliefs and behaviour they reproduce the class divisions that condemn them. This isn't just a correspondence between the values of capitalism and those of schools. These lads gain strength as a group by the very behaviour that is leading them to unskilled work.

At the same time, in similar schools, in similar areas in London, Scharff, using similar methods with youth of similar age, was reaching very different conclusions. Scharff's adolescents were also resistant and resentful. But they wanted to get closer to their teachers. They wanted to cooperate. Their anger against schooling is interpreted as a symptom of numbness, a sense of loss at having to leave their schools which, deep down, they felt as 'mothering institutions'. They may have superficially denied the value of schooling, but they were actually 'mourning' their impending loss. Scharff's lads never seem to use four-letter words when quoted.

Now the focus shifts again to the soccer stadium to look at evidence from other interpretive research on the young. The first major enquiry into football hooliganism was delivered to the Minister for Sport in 1968. Between 1948 and 1966 there were only 195 cases of disorderly behaviour reported to the Football Association. But by the end of the 1960s the media were stoking up moral panic and social researchers were combining business with pleasure on the terraces. It is not, however, easy to be a participant observer in such a crowd. At vital moments all hell is liable to break loose.

The fans have been seen as a varied bunch. To Taylor they were the last of the traditional working-class supporters as the game became commercialized and the grounds were improved (Taylor 1969). Clarke also stresses the importance of changes in 'the people's game' (Clarke 1978). The culture of support, passed from one generation to the next, was being ended by the clubs and by safety regulations. For Marsh, as well as Taylor and Clarke, the violence on the terraces can only be explained by reference to a social and political situation in which these fans find themselves (Marsh 1978). It is the erosion of working-class culture, with soccer at its heart, that holds the clue. The game is being made into a spectacle, commercialized, with the fans of the two teams separated, the rich seated and with the crowds kept back from the pitch.

For Taylor, the lad on the terraces was a resistance fighter with the historic task of perpetuating the traditional working-class values of soccer. But to Marsh, aggro, with its ritual, was an outlet for natural aggression. Clarke's fans are compensating for a boring life by a Saturday afternoon release of frustration.

The conflicts in these studies of youth are partly the result of the different questions asked within and between psychology and sociology. They are partly the result of searching for evidence in different places by different methods. Much sociological research is concerned with small deprived groups in inner cities. Much psychology is centred on emotional disturbance among individuals in clinics and hospitals. But there are still alarming differences in interpretation even when similar groups are researched in similar situations. What is observed is determined by the preconceptions of the researcher. In particular much of the research was in the critical, Marxist tradition (Hall and Jefferson 1975). It was divorced not just from psychological research but from both scientistic and interpretive mainstream sociology (Davies 1995). The research was overwhelmingly about young males. It ignored the racism that was rife as the first Black players entered league football. Even more important, it failed to appreciate the importance of the statistics on trends in employment. In the 1990s, a new form of class and institutional discrimination – a crisis of masculinity – was being described (Mac an Ghaill 1996).

The most alarming examples of the way preconceptions determine what is observed and how observations are interpreted came once feminists and anti-racist social researchers started to publish in numbers in the 1970s. This was not just the realization that the gangs, the groups and the individuals were overwhelmingly male, but that they were overwhelmingly sexist and racist. Further, the hypermasculinity, the fascist attitudes to the Black community and the rejection of schooling were increasingly hard to defend in the 1990s. There were also fewer heavy, unskilled manual jobs available. They were more likely to be seen as 'shitwork' than macho.

It is now realized that girls are doing better than boys at every age in school. Women are dominating entry to jobs that are growing while men are often dependent on shrinking occupations. This problem is exacerbated by the repeated finding of social research on young unskilled males that they want real men's work. Here all the researchers agree. But none anticipated the emerging problem of a new second sex, lacking education, unattractive as marriage partners and certainly not either the spearhead of a proletarian revolution or its likely beneficiaries. The Marxist view of the inevitability of revolutionary change as capitalism foundered, placed working-class males in the vanguard of change. The reality was a place in the rear. These young males were indeed a problem. But solutions were not going to come from the immanent collapse of capitalism. The lads were being redefined as cultural terrorists not freedom-fighters, thugs not defenders of worthwhile traditions.

The problem of a new second sex, an underclass without the skills to get and hold a worthwhile job, is not new. Researchers have shown how this group act to aggravate their disadvantage. But it is no help to be romantic. These were not working-class heroes but sexist, racist thugs. The succession of attempts to improve training shows the depth of the problem they pose. There is now a database from longitudinal research that is designed to promote and inform interpretive studies (Banks *et al.* 1991). The attempts to understand how the world seems to this underclass cannot ignore the wider changes in which they become victims. In Chapter 3 the excitement of interpretive research is described. But the intensive, personal, local focus of this work can neglect changes in the economic and political context. Humans construct their own reality, but in a world that is changing and which can be understood only by research with an historical focus.

CHAPTER 3

Interpretive social reseach

The dominance of science as a model for getting to know about the human condition has always been seen as a threat to that humanity. There have always been believers who looked to the sacred, the romantics who looked to the emotions and the spirit, the humanists who objected to any reduction to laws and numbers. Books on the differences between quantitative and qualitative methods tend to oversimplify to numbers versus accounts and hence miss the long history of this dispute about what there is to know and how we can get to know it. Social science did not replace the priest and the prophet, the poet and the author, the dreamer and the jester. There have always been many paths to truth.

Significantly, as the philosophers who saw the promise of applying science to human behaviour were writing at the end of the eighteenth century, so were those who looked to the emotions. Hume in Scotland was a contemporary of Herder in Weimar. The Scot pressed for experimental reasoning, the use of observation to detect the laws in the organization of human relationships. The German rejected this dependence on reason, emphasizing the human capacity to interpret events and build cultures. These two traditions have persisted in social science for more than 200 years. But history here as elsewhere is written by the victors. In the first half of the twentieth century, scientistic thinking dominated in Britain. In the second half, social anthropology came home as the Empire shrank and interpretive traditions become popular.

The two traditions influenced both psychology and sociology as they were established in the twentieth century. While behaviourism, rejecting any concern with the subjective, was dominant in American psychology to around 1970 there were German holistic psychologists such as Kohler and American social psychologists such as Lewin, Rogers and Kelley who continued to research into the thinking human in social situations. In sociology there was also an alternative to scientism in the Chicago School of Sociology from the 1920s, studying their toddling town from the viewpoint of those involved. Translations into English of German social thinkers accelerated in the 1950s. The idea that reality is what humans define as real carried a powerful message for social research. Understanding became the aim of research. So we now go into the field and listen, look and interpret. Here the ethnographer is seeking to understand how the world looks to humans in their everyday lives, in their natural settings. There can be no imposed control. The focus is on the subjective world of those researched.

This interpretive research is guided by the view that humans construct their own view of their world. It attracted feminist and anti-racist researchers because it was a way of examining the responses of the subordinate to the way reality is defined and imposed by dominant groups. The focus on the way groups are categorized and identified also makes it attractive to those with a political agenda. If reality is constructed, then the unequal distribution of power can be used not just to oppress, but to justify the oppression and convince those who suffer that this is a natural state of affairs. Uncovering that means getting close to those involved and letting them tell their own stories.

These interpretive approaches provided important evidence just where scientistic research was inadequate. Emotions cannot be measured but are important. There is loss in the reduction of aspects of human behaviour to numbers. Concentrating on inputs and outputs in a subject such as schooling ignored the processes that accounted for differences which were of most interest to those seeking improvements. Usually the scientistic research provided useful evidence on policy and practice, but to guide not to change them. The research designs could eliminate the chances of discovering the unintended consequences of actions that are so illuminating. Interpretive research is ideal for detecting serendipity because it is in the field, among the human action. The ethnographer's world is a succession of unexpected insights.

The first question hanging over interpretive research is whether it is possible to enter the field without preconceptions determining what is observed. Woods (1985) describes how his best ideas came when walking the dog, listening to music, relaxing. Ideas do not spring direct from observations in the field. The mind of the researcher is 'programmed', 'energized', 'keyed' with ideas from a social science that 'disciplines' the production of ideas. The intention is to study the undisturbed natural situation. The researcher has to be alert to leads that could be important. But just as an hypothesis can guide scientistic research, so ethnography is guided by preconceptions.

The second question arises from the dependence on the researcher identifying and finding the really important clues for understanding how those involved give meaning to their lives. All human activity can be mysterious to an outsider. Entry into a gang, a classroom, a family, a factory can be confusing. Reporting fully on how sense was finally made of this confusion and the meanings of it to those involved eventually recorded is impossible. Reviewers have to take a lot on trust.

The third question arises from the selection of cases. Why did Mead choose Samoa? Why this infant class? The selection is often opportunistic. It's a warm and welcoming place. You have friends who help you obtain access. Any generalization, any claim to be representative is suspect. That doesn't reduce the value of the insights from interpretive research. They help us understand how humans make sense of their world. Those insights are also attractive for those who want to change the world. Now the temptation to generalize increases. Once the account is taken into professional training, into guiding policy and practice, the unique case may be forgotten.

The human subject in interpretive research

At the centre of interpretive research is a human subject defined to contrast with the machine, the computer, animals. This is a thinking and self-aware person capable of sophisticated communication through a spoken written language. Using these faculties, humans have organized complex economic and political systems. They think about their social relationships and their part in them, including being involved with researchers. The lives they lead are meaningful. Those meanings may be disputed by others. Perhaps they seem absurd. But they are valued and defended. Where a scientistic approach, based on methods developed for investigating the physical world, can ignore this rich subjective human world and exclude or control it while experimenting or questioning, interpretive social researchers focus on it. Thus the human at the centre of interpretive research knows a lot about what is going on, interacts with the researcher and can predict what is going to happen next. Now the appropriate metaphor is not of actors playing parts written for them, but of actors constructing their own roles in a drama that they help to write.

This human capacity to make life meaningful does not mean that there is any necessary agreement about the meanings. The human may define the situation in a way that makes life bearable, but researchers and others may find it intolerable. Nor is this a passive relationship. The researcher is being observed by an enquiring, active and equally inquisitive subject. In scientistic research, procedures are controlled and standardized to minimize interaction. In interpretive research the attempt to preserve the natural situation guarantees that it will occur, even when the work is covert.

This intereraction can be seen as both short and long-term. First, both researcher and researched act reflexively. Both influence the research situation. The thinking human gives it meaning. But researchers are also human. They become part of the episodes they are observing. The human, whether researcher or researched, is influencing the research situation. In interpretive research this is acknowledged and used in designing the work. It is assumed that every one will be behaving in a human and hence interactive manner.

In the longer term, social research contributes to the stock of knowledge that we use to understand our lives. Our ideas and evidence are pervaded by economics, psychology, sociology and so on. Concepts such as the market, motivation, social class are in everyday use. As social scientists model the social world, their ideas spread through the media, through the growing number of social science courses and students and become part of everyday interpretations. Hence researchers often meet sophisticated responses. In all cases they meet humans who have usually worked out the meaning of their lives. It is the variety and implications of these that make interpretive social research so exciting.

The tendency to study deviant cases in interpretive research makes this active human subject particularly important. Gangs, drug addicts and those on the fiddle are likely to be physically as well as mentally active. Patrick, after experience of teaching in an approved school, joins a Glasgow gang, posing as a housebreaker. Reflexivity here was perilous. When the gang handed him an axe to join an expected fight, he wisely departed Glasgow for the south. Gangs have their own views on life. Just as there are limits to the control that can be exerted in the psychological laboratory in order to preserve something of the natural, so there are limits on attempts to merge with those researched in ethnography.

It is the importance of not disturbing the natural situation that raises ethical issues. Promising topics are often the most difficult to access. Local Education Authorities will direct researchers to schools that are doing well. Headteachers will protect the teacher who has problems. Hargreaves (1967), Lacey (1970), Ball (1981) and Burgess (1983), researching in schools, taught to help their acceptance. Ditton (1977) becomes a bread roundsman, Henry (1978) a driver, Mars (1982) makes himself at home in the docks. Once the evidence is collected a quick retreat is advisable before any publication. Dockyard mateys tend to be rather sensitive. The need for retreat can be gauged from the titles of these three books, *Part-time Crime: an Ethnography of Fiddling and Pilferage; The Hidden Economy*; and *Cheats at Work*. Publication can hurt the researched. In scientistic research, control can reduce validity. In interpretive research the preservation of the natural situation can produce ethical problems.

The need to merge into a group to investigate a sensitive issue can lead to questionable practices. Homan (1991) describes covert methods that included hiding under beds, masquerading as patients, as Black, as a convert for baptism. The most frequently documented British cases are Homan (1978), Wallis (1976) and Fielding (1981). Homan infiltrated the Pentacostal movement, spending four years studying assemblies. Wallis joined a course on Scientology, withdrawing after a couple of days, but continued the research by interviewing 'apostates'. Fielding obtained permission to interview officers of the National Front, but then observed local groups without them realizing that they were under scrutiny.

The most famous American study using covert methods is Humphreys (1974). The professor from the University of Southern Illinois set out to investigate the 'tearoom trade'. This consists of homosexual activity in men's public toilets. It is one of those delightful statistics that enhance all research reports that 56 per cent of arrests for homosexual acts apparently took place in such 'tearooms'. Today research in public conveniences is not easy to arrange, but Humphreys managed to observe 120 sexual acts in 19 different loos in five parks in his chosen city. Further, he then completed 50 interviews with 100 men who had been observed visiting the 'tearooms'. That took persistence, ingenuity and a disregard for ethics. To obtain the addresses, Humphreys noted the numbers of the cars parking at the loos and then added these to a list of names he was interviewimng for a social health survey. Fifty per cent of those approached cooperated, possibly because they feared exposure after remembering their previous assignation.

Justifiably, the Humphreys' case is the most harshly criticized covert research because of the use of car numbers to obtain an interview a year later. The reasons for such lapses vary. The subject may be important, but negotiated access impossible. Covert methods may be the only way to investigate. The researcher may not even see a problem. In the last 20 years most universities have established ethics committees to check that there are no serious lapses. The public has also learned to detect prying academics. Schools once exposed to research are likely to avoid any more embarrassment. Consequently the maintenance of the natural situation is difficult. Published accounts usually assume that the situation wasn't adjusted by those involved as a response to being researched. But the numbers of social scientists now qualified and the influence of their work mean that responses to research are likely to become more sophisticated.

Finally, the model of the person in interpretive research merges at one extreme with the holistic, the mystical or the romantic. Reality is not just constructed through social interaction, it is wonderful. Now there is not just a rejection of determinism, of humanity subject to laws that can be established through research and used for prediction, but of human reason itself. At another extreme, interpretive research attracts the critical researcher keen to raise awareness and change the world. It is ideal for probing into the way groups identify themselves and feel identified by others, particularly those with power. The motives for researching are varied and not always to add to our stock of knowledge.

This range of interests makes it important to search for motives in published accounts. But interpretive research is difficult to describe and tends to change direction. There is never enough space to give a full account. Atkinson (1984) looks back at his study of clinical teaching for trainee doctors and is struck by the sheer complexity of even such a modest project. The fullest account he gave was 20 000 words in his doctoral thesis (1984). But even that left out whole aspects of the research process buried in files that also contain important topics never reported.

The procedures of interpretive social research

The procedures of those who initially pursued a science of society were mainly to test theories against observations and responses. But the sequence of events in social research is now increasingly reversed. Instead of theorizing and then collecting data to test the theory, the interpretive researcher first gets involved in the field and then theorizes to understand what is being observed. That is not just a return to an earlier version of science as induction. Common to all social research is the acknowledgement that from start to finish, an open mind is impossible. All researchers have preconceptions that affect what they see and how they interpret it. But now the logic behind the methods is that theory should be formed out of observations in the natural situation, not imposed on it in advance. Consequently initial ideas will have to be amended, theories adapted to new situations and researchers have to learn from the evidence they are gathering.

This change in the logic of social research follows from rejecting the idea of a real social world out there waiting to be studied, to assuming that the world is constructed by those involved. Research is aimed at understanding the meaning of that world by those involved, not at discovering laws and hence predicting. The aims of the interpretive researcher remain description, theory generation and the guidance of policy and practice. But now the intention is not to test theory but to develop it from observations in the field. Hence there is no prior specification of the factors that are to be related. Nor can there be any specification of extraneous or confounding factors. If the situation is to be natural it will also be complex and confounding. There is 'progressive focusing' as observation identifies the theoretically significant events. But there can be no planning to identify and control extraneous or confounding factors in advance. They are part of the natural setting.

This exposure of the interpretive researcher to the full complexity of natural situations means that the choice of factors selected will vary between studies. Few will be reporting on similar situations or examining the same key factors. Put another way, the problem of controlling confounding variables in the research design is avoided. But the researcher still has to select in order to focus observations on specific events. Thus what is extraneous and what is central is decided in the field. Even the most complicated situations can be researched. Intimate detail that is beyond scientistic research can be included. It can give a flavour of life's rich tapestry. It is often cheap to organize. It is a powerful way of exposing injustice and raising awareness. Studying behaviour divorced from the thought behind it has become increasingly hard to defend. But penetrating that thought is not easy and the selection involved is personal, can be idiosyncratic, is often political and always difficult to make fully public.

Interpretive social research has the four key features that follow.

The research is in natural settings

It is not easy to preserve the natural situation while it is being researched. Even where the work is covert there can be disturbance. A stranger has joined the group. Researchers can miss the comments when they leave the room. Why do they take so long in the toilet? Why do they take a notebook in with them? Isn't he a bit old to be wearing jeans? Why won't she ever come shoplifting? The presence of a researcher can raise fear or anger. Patrick (1973) participated in his Glasgow gang for four months. Within that time only 12 outings were made. Was he really accepted? Few outings seemed to have been more than fleeting. Surely many would have been at their most interesting as the night went on? Flight was soon deemed necessary. Had the gang already guessed that this approved school-teacher was not what he claimed?

It is also necessary to assess how natural the setting really was. In many school studies the researcher taught to minimize disturbance. But teachers only guess at the real world of children. An adult's presence is enough to disturb. Further, the researcher is often an occasional visitor. Teachers reading an account of their school by an ethnographer can justifiably query validity and reliability. Is this account, based on a few visits arranged by me, by someone who knew neither the children, the teachers or the curriculum, really entitled to publish as a true account? Why is the account any more valid than mine when I have spent years getting to know this situation and am a part of it as a genuine participant observer? How do we know that another researcher would reach the same conclusions? Isn't it like the inspector's report based on chance observations – but worse because inspectors are at least experienced professionals?

McNamara (1980) describes three aspects of this 'outsider's arrogance'. The data are suspect. The meanings attributed to children and teachers are problematic. The researcher's theories can ignore the alternative theories used by the teachers. McNamara was vigorously counterattacked by Hammersley, one of those criticized (Hammersley 1981). He pointed out that McNamara provided no basis for the validity of the alternative explanations. That merely confirms that there is no way of deciding which is valid. There are many versions of events in natural settings. Confounding factors in one can be the key to understanding in another. That is the inescapable conclusion of the interpretive stance. Reality is what we, researcher and researched, define as real. There is rarely agreement.

The research is open-ended and flexible

Scientistic research is planned in advance. The techniques used are often standard. They are piloted to detect weaknesses. Deviations from the design are to be avoided. But the interpretive researcher selects the issue, the site and the group, negotiates access, but doesn't select techniques or define the issue in any binding way in advance. Burgess (1984) discusses cases where leads are followed up and others dropped, new key informants are adopted and others neglected. Such switches are not just possible, but anticipated. The danger is of continuous distraction. There can be a feeling of being overwhelmed by the wealth of information available. Hammersley (1984) starts by observing and recording in classrooms but soon pays increasing attention to chat overheard in the staff common-room. A project approved by the Inner London Education Authority as a mapping of the spread of mixed-ability grouping first became a study of classroom practices and, running out of money, a study of tensions among the research team (Davies *et al.*, 1985).

The flexibility adds to the surprises, the snags, the fun of this style of enquiry. The setting can be exciting. The unexpected is always round the corner promising new discoveries. The views encountered are often alarming. Changing an experiment or survey during implementation would break the link to the model behind the methods, destroy the logic in the methodology and make any aggregated numbers meaningless. Changing the sample in a survey to focus on a more interesting group would be judged as outrageous. But it is the interesting case that matters in ethnography. The aim is not representation but understanding.

The focus is on the meanings of those researched

The skill of the interpretive researcher is in detecting and drawing out the private meanings of subjects. This accounts for the emphasis on involvement. The groups studied are often infants, or the hurt, the oppressed, the resentful. Infants faced with researchers such as King, kids faced with Corrigan or Woods are looking up at six foot of social scientist. Rapport may be difficult to establish given that gap. Further, few of us are as youthful-looking as Patrick (1973) or as enthusiastic at joining in rugged street football matches. It's difficult to be unnoticed in a school when you are introduced as 'professor' and my own background in the police ruined one attempt to socialize with the local tearaways when one innocently asked about my flat feet.

It is the variety of meanings reported that makes interpretive research so informative. From *Classrooms Observed* (Nash 1973) to *The Happiest Days?* (Woods 1990) there have been a stream of studies of how children interpret what is going on in school, make life bearable and often frustrate the teachers. This research has been extended to accounts of how reality looks from a variety of viewpoints. These range from small but significant groupings such as Black, gay students (Mac an Ghaill 1994) to numerous studies of women (see, for example, Dawtrey *et al.*, 1995). The former throws light on the problematic elements in the sexuality of straight young men. Feminists have shown the way the world has been structured from a male viewpoint. But be wary. This account suggested that pleasure from marihuana-smoking had to be learned, constructed (Becker 1963). This has been challenged as misleading. The mixture must have been weak. Forget the construction, take a puff and 'wham' (Pearson and Twohig 1975).

Data collection and theorizing go together

The flexibility of interpretive research enables information to be collected and followed up quickly. Thus fieldnotes are essential, not just as a record, but as the source of insights for further work. This is why researchers struggle with tape-recorders, try to transcribe notes, retire to the toilet to scribble. The notes can only cover a few incidents, yet type up into reams of paper. How all this data is read, digested and compressed into an account remains a mystery. Many tapes and typescripts must just collect dust, particularly as the flexibility of this research leads to frequent changes of direction and hence much redundancy.

Increasingly the computer can be used to help organize and retrieve specific information. But it is the perception of the researcher that extracts themes, focuses further work and leads to theories. This 'progressive focusing' can be facilitated by 'theoretical sampling'. Here the researcher identifies a few themes that seem theoretically promising and attends to incidents where they are likely to be influential. This is obviously opportunistic. It is difficult to give an account of the steps taken. The researcher is unlikely to remember when the themes began to emerge. Often the researcher is reading about new ideas and alerted to new themes which are then recognized in the field. In accounts of the way themes are developed there are numerous influences apart from the data itself (see, for example, Fuller 1984). Research sensitizes researchers not just to their topic, but to academic and everyday evidence that seems relevant. Interpretive research can be confusing as well as fun.

Somehow sense has to be made of observations. The notes and recordings have to be made meaningful. The natural situation is rich in data. At some point it has to be organized. The most influential strategy for analysing information collected is grounded theory (Glaser and Strauss 1967). The sequence recommended starts with the researcher entering the field alert to the sort of events and incidents that are likely to be relevant to the subject. The second stage is to define and relate these categories by further observations and comparisons. Theorizing and observations go together, the former progressively guiding the latter. Once the categories are clarified the third stage is to produce hypotheses that explain the relationship among the various categories. The fourth stage is to reduce the hypotheses, relate and rank them into a simplified model of the complex reality of decision-making. At each stage there is a further focusing-down on the important features until a simplified model is produced.

The idea of grounded theory is a particular attraction of interpretive research. As data is collected and analysed, themes and hunches that illuminate them are identified in the data. These can then be reinforced by theoretical sampling, concentrating effort on the most promising events. The grounding in specific data means that it cannot be refuted by more data or a better theory. It is valid in relation to the cases in which it is based. That also limits its generalizability and means that 'theory' is defined in a very restricted way. But the main objections are that it is often impossible to identify which data is theoretically important. Even more important, Glaser and Strauss seem to assume that an open-minded linking of data and theory is possible. But researchers of all people are likely to be saturated with theories that determine their perceptions. Hence these are likely to be confirmed or elaborated rather than grounded in observations.

Grounded theory is a promising idea, but difficult to practise. Hammersley (1984) suggests that dredging data to collect the maximum number or ideas is more common. Porter (1984) reports that Glaser and Strauss give insufficient advice on how to sample to develop grounded theory. That does not reduce the usefulness of interpretive research. It does mean that readers of accounts should search for the way the work was done and be wary of any lack of detail, particularly where it seems to be replaced by the jargon of grounded theory, analytic induction, progressive focusing and theoretical sampling.

The question posed in Chapter 1 about the failure of thousands of research projects on the teaching of reading to yield any agreed evidence for use by teachers still applies to interpretive research. Experimental studies, usually comparing 'decoding' and 'meaning' as methods, have always been criticized for failing to take into account how those involved, in and outside the school, saw the process of learning to read. Hence researchers have examined how children see the task of reading, what skills they bring to it, what errors they make, what strategies for learning seem to help. Other research has concentrated on the views of parents and teachers. The intention is interpretive: to find out what reading means to those involved and hence to improve theory and practice.

There has also been at least 40 years of research into the reasons why children, particularly from working-class homes, suffer from poor language development. These range from theoretical (Bernstein 1960) to studies of relationships in families (Wells 1985; Tizard and Hughes 1984). Others have investigated how teachers see this debate (Blatchford, Ireson and Joscelyne 1994). But disputes rage on. In 1996 Her Majesty's Inspectors criticized reading standards in London schools. There was a vigorous counterattack by the three local authorities concerned, concentrating in particular on the number of non-English speaking children in the schools (*Times Educational Supplement* 17/5/96: 19). Later in the year the Inspector's report was attacked by the London Institute of Education. By then, the dispute, described as an 'Audit of War' in the *Times Educational Supplement* (25/10/96: 18) had become bitter, involving not only a battle over the Inspector's support for phonics, but apparently personal and professional issues over inspectorial criticisms of Institute staff. The *Observer* further reported the dispute (26/10/96) and this provoked a response from the Institute (*Observer*, 3/11/96). This correspondence was also reported in *Research Intelligence* (Mortimore and Goldstein 1996). This is an area of inconclusive research, but strong feelings.

The interpretive researcher at work

The grip of scientific research was illustrated by reference to research on strippers (McCaghy and Skipper 1970). They depended on close observation, but also insisted on measuring the artistes and comparing them with more- or less-endowed women in the general population and in girlie magazines. But description leaves important questions unanswered. How, for example, did the strippers feel about the men in the audience? How did they view their own involvement? To answer such questions the researcher has to be in the action, among the customers. But that eliminates some researchers. Some scenes are restricted to men or women, the young or old. Patrick looked half his age, was a useful if dirty footballer and could pass as a young delinquent. Becker was a pianist and could access the drug scene, even if the advice to him after his article was published was to change his dealer. The setting determines who can research, and how. Many may be able to pass as a teacher, even as a docker, but few as a stripper.

Yet more than 20 years after McCaghy and Skipper, here is 'The Reflexive Self through Narrative: a night in the life of an erotic dancer/ researcher' (Ronai 1992). There are significant differences across this generation gap. Ronai is a women. The research doesn't lapse into measurement. It uses a technique described as a mix of participant observation and systematic interactive introspection. That means that she was central to the action, in contact with the customers and interpreting not only their actions but her own.

Ronai danced to finance her first degree. In 1987 she was dancing again to gather data for her Master's thesis. Her professors supported her as a researcher/dancer and were sympathetic to the problems encountered. Ronai carried out the interactive introspection while table-dancing in bra and panties, or topless. In between dancing, listening to sex talk from customers and trying to keep their fingers out of her panties, she was analysing their behaviour and her feelings. These feelings, the setting in the club and the actions of the men at the tables, were recorded and then used in the thesis.

Interactive introspection under the circumstances faced by Ronai must be difficult. How could you detect your own feelings while dancing on a table? But this is in a book titled *Investigating Subjectivity*. How else could the meaning of such a situation for the dancer be researched? Interpretive social research has opened up new areas of behaviour to study. It is a long way from science as generally understood. Yet Ronai is careful to specify the aims, history and context of the work. The logic behind the methods and the way they worked out are clarified. There is sufficient information for an informed review. Few journalists do that.

The contribution of interpretive social research

For Delamont (1992), research in the field is a pilgrimage. The pilgrims seek enlightenment, they tell stories, they exchange their knowledge for a research degree, a new job, royalties. While it isn't always fun, it beats juggling with figures for laughs. The attraction is that it is about the way people make sense of their world. It tries to take in the thinking that leads to the understanding. This concentration on the person in their natural environment is very close to bird- or gorilla-watching. It is easy to exaggerate the gap between interpretive and scientistic. They share the explicit definition of the subject, the systematic enquiry and the priority to making the whole enterprise public. But here it is the human interpretation of other humans that is both the strength and weakness, not the use of standardized research techniques to produce data that can be processed statistically. Thus there is less chance that results will be divorced from the actual situations which they are supposed to reflect. Interpretive research is more likely to stay grounded in concrete situations.

The cost of this grounding in reality is that results are specific to the case investigated. It is not a sample representing a population. Generalization is liable to be misleading. That is a major disadvantage for psychologists maintaining their scientific status. In March 1995, *The Psychologist*, the bulletin of the British Psychological Society, published a series of articles on qualitative research. These were revisited in January 1996 (Morgan 1996). There was some agreement that it was sometimes better to analyse even a single case than large samples. Scientific description did not necessarily require large numbers. The aim of psychologists should be to understand and that could not be done through experiments concentrated on behaviour, eliminating the subjective and taking place in artificial conditions. But the snag in interpretive research was the difficulty of replication, of repeating the enquiry. This was the basis of science, but impossible with the flexibility central to interpretive research. There could never be enough information published for anyone to repeat it. Those involved would in any case have changed as a result of the first experience. As long as the title 'science' is to be used, interpretive research lacks the necessary reliability.

The second contribution of interpretive research has been to move from 'taken' to 'made' issues (Seeley 1966). Scientistic research is expensive and often depends on funding by government or a large organization. The brief is 'taken'. Such research has often been radical in its findings. The emphasis on social class as a determinant of opportunity was reinforced in this way. But the problem was still that of the policy-makers. Why was there so much wasted talent? How can it be reduced? Interpretive research can often help researchers 'make' issues. Feminists, for example, have raised fresh questions about the education of girls. How do they see the curriculum? What assumptions are made in schooling about sexual identities? The 'making' of these subjects exposed very different features in the education of girls and boys, previously concealed by 'taking' problems that did not differentiate by gender.

The third contribution arises from the focus on meanings. The subjective world of outsiders, of minorities, of the oppressed are often an eye-opener. Here research overlaps with investigative journalism. It can be a powerful lever for change. If life looks like that from the streets, from the old folk's home, from the training scheme, then the assumptions behind policies and practices should be challenged. This is to see the social world as a network of meanings that often contradict, are always changing and should be the bases of policies.

The problem for those who use interpretive research to build theory or influence policy and practice is that they have to depend on the account being both full and frank. The former is unlikely. The most complete accounts of research-planning and implementation have come in retrospective studies, often years after publication. They are also written by the researchers themselves. In *Inside a Curriculum Project*, the project team and teachers comment on my account (Shipman, Bolam and Jenkins 1974). This resulted from disagreements over my draft for publication. Their comments turned out to be the most valuable parts. They show how the research looked very different according to where you were around and in the project. Such disagreements are common. The publication of Bell's account of the Banbury study was accompanied by so much hassle that Bell's co-researchers would not waive their rights under British libel laws (Newby 1977b).

In some cases it is possible that the researchers only obtained a partial understanding of events. *The Rules of Disorder*, a study of trouble in school, describes a power struggle between teachers and pupils (Marsh, Rosser and Harré 1978). The pupils were seen as trying to establish power in the classrooms to protect themselves against affronts to their dignity as humans. But while the teachers are seen as part of the problem there is no account of their views. Nor do the views of the pupils seem to have been checked. Some of their statements suggest they were wise to the answers that would suit the research. Nor is there enough evidence to see the school as an organization, in a context, or how frequently the researchers visited to obtain the information, and how this was done.

It is the latitude enjoyed by the interpretive researcher that enables the profound meanings of those studied to be revealed. The subject and its location will be decided in advance. But even the fullest accounts give little idea of what happened in the field to get to the intimate detail. Autobiographical accounts tend to be self-justifying. Interpretive research is concerned with human understanding. But in denying the legitimacy of scientistic methods, its supporters can also jettison the basic justification for all research: that the planning, procedures, preparation of results and conclusions should be made fully public for review.

PART TWO

Techniques for Collecting Information

The choices within research design

Most discussion of choice within research is concerned with sampling. But at all stages – from first thoughts to final conclusion – choices are continuous. In fieldwork in natural settings the unexpected is always around the corner. But even in apparently straightforward social surveys Murphy's Law holds. Some snags are anticipated through careful pilot study, through training, through supervision. Others are managerial. Ambitions have to be tailored to costs. Other problems arise as the work progresses, with emergencies, especially illness, and when time and resources run out. To illustrate this, here is an account of a large-scale follow-up study of reading standards organized within the Inner London Education Authority (ILEA) in the 1960s and 1970s. This was used as the basis of further studies of influences on attainment and formed the basis for much of the early work on school effectiveness in England.

Following recommendations for positive discrimination in the 1967 Plowden Report, the Research and Statistics group (R and S) of the ILEA produced a 10-factor primary and a 12-factor secondary school index enabling the Authority to rank schools according to the measured deprivation they faced and to fund them accordingly. Included were indicators of social class, one-parent families, housing stress, large families, poverty and recent immigration. R and S also organized the testing of children at age 11 in English, mathematics and verbal reasoning to enable the ILEA to balance the intake into secondary schools, and collected the results of public examinations.

In the late 1960s, steps taken under the 'war on poverty' in the USA were worrying policy-makers in Britain. The decision to fund schools on the basis of the deprivation they faced was one response in the ILEA. Little, then Director of R and S, initiated a longitudinal study of reading attainment of all children born between 2 September 1959 and 1 September 1960. They were first tested for reading in 1968/9 and the programme was repeated for this cohort as they went through primary and secondary school in 1971, 1973 and 1976 (ILEA 1969, 1972, 1975, 1977). Questions were asked about the organization of schooling and attainment at entry to secondary school; the results were related to the social background factors in the indexes described above.

The information from this survey helped the ILEA to fund its schools in line with its policy of positive discrimination, to assess standards in schools and to decide on practices and policies. The evidence was used to press the Authority's Colleges of Education for a restoration of the teaching of reading, to establish specialist teacher centres and to raise concerns about the position of the children of unskilled workers and of recent immigrants (Little and Mabey 1973). The evidence that it was social class rather than the proportion of immigrants that was the major factor in attainment was used to advise against bussing and to establish limits to the policy of positive discrimination (Shipman 1980). The data was also released to academic researchers including the *Fifteen Thousand Hours* study (Rutter *et al.* 1979). Many of the researchers were also involved in the ILEA research for *School Matters* (Mortimore *et al.* 1988).

This was privileged research, within a large local education authority with its own staff of researchers and statisticians. The input, school context and output data that was available was unique. The testing at age 11, the collection of social context data and examination results came from more than 800 primary and 200 secondary schools. Yet at every stage choices had to be made. As these are listed it has to be remembered that no other group of researchers could call on these resources or negotiate directly with politicians, administrators, inspectors, head-teachers and teachers. Yet planning was always a compromise. All the parties to negotiations knew their education service, had their own teacher's union or academic advisers and could predict the flak that would fly if results were poor. Technical design issues rarely delayed the work for long. The blood on the carpets of County Hall came from negotiations over access to schools, the time and effort asked of teachers, the sensitivity of the information requested. Always there was trade-off. Research had to be shown to be worthwhile for all those involved, particularly the children and their parents.

The ILEA needed basic descriptive data to run the education service. But it also required evidence on standards and the many factors that influenced them. The researchers had to guess what evidence would be needed in the years to come and press hard for permission to plan, because of the time needed to deliver the evidence in time to influence policy. But the research was also data-driven. The social background information, transfer test scores, examination results and details on school organization were already available in the research group who collected, analysed and distributed it. This database was mined in anticipation of future needs for information. Again, that judgement of what would be needed involved difficult choices, not only over trends detectable from available data, but over likely political and professional developments and the cost-benefits of choosing this rather than that as a priority for research.

The Literacy Survey was a major effort to meet the need for information of a large local education authority. At each stage more choices had to be made. Enquiries and complaints peaked around test time. For example, each test of reading had to be cleared through many committees. No subject produces such heated debate. The choice of test or mix of tests, their suitability, the time they took to complete, the conditions required, their standardization, the scores they yielded had to be discussed. In 1973, selecting a test for the 13–14-year-olds proved difficult. Finally the NFER EH2 Reading Comprehension Test was chosen because it had been recently restandardized. But this turned out to be on children attending West Suffolk schools. While this met the criteria of NFER, it was difficult to convince the ILEA that it would be a fair comparison. Agreement hinged on the use alongside the EH2 of the NFER SRA Test which had also been used in a parallel form in 1968 and 1971. But the West Suffolk children had scored below the national average which had therefore to be taken as 101. With an ILEA average score of 98.0 the explanation was complicated in an area where banner headlines in the national press always arrived on time.

Across the years of this research the political context changed fast. The teachers were increasingly unwilling to provide social background data. Margaret Thatcher stopped the collection of data on immigrant children on the DES Form 7 (i). Fortunately the information was already available on this ILEA cohort, but such a large-scale study with such detail has not been possible since the early 1970s. The policy of positive discrimination that required data on social background was being phased out. The pressure on schools from DES national surveys increased. Teachers became less willing to cooperate. As professional and political attitudes changed, so did the priorities for research. The concern with social class in the 1960s and 1970s as underlying issues of race and sex seemed outdated in the 1980s. Choices are made in contexts that change rapidly. The last major English study of school effectiveness was organized in the ILEA in the 1980s (Mortimore *et al.* 1988).

In the ten years of this research there were a succession of difficult choices over the definition of cohort, research design, tests, background data, response, statistical treatment and reporting. Most of these issues were not technical. On the phone, in correspondence, at committee meetings, during informal discussions dealing with complaints, enquiries, the press, decisions were made about what was valuable, what was practicable, what was likely to become valuable, what was available through contemporary academic research, what could be released to researchers wanting access, what should be abandoned or pursued. The final reports to the ILEA Schools Sub-Committee were brief practical summaries of ten years of negotiation where technical and political considerations coincided. That coincidence occurs in both scientistic and interpretive research and lies behind the technical chapters on methods which follow. The choices made always change the research design. To publish all of them in major studies is usually impossible. Research is rarely fully public. Peer review is consequently limited.

CHAPTER 4

Samples, cases and response

Research always involves choices. The funds, time and energy of the researcher are always scarce. In scientistic research populations have to be sampled, questions pruned, demands on the researched minimized. In interpretive research decisions have to be made over where to concentrate resources, when will be the most convenient and rewarding time to be observing, who are likely to be the key informants (Ball 1993). Choices are never easy. Schools, for example, have compliant and difficult classes, confident and nervous teachers. The children may settle down comfortably in September, but can get edgy in the bad weather of February. Everyone knows that the deputy head is the key to keeping order, but is hostile to academics who want to pry.

One choice facing all researchers is whether to select samples or cases. This is an essential step in the restriction, the definition, the limiting of the scope of research. A sample implies representativeness and the more this is a concern, as with government agencies feeding information to policy-makers, the more careful the sampling has to be. But many selections are made to illustrate, understand, develop theory or raise awareness. Interpretive researchers tend to reject sampling as scientistic, the basis of often misleading statistics, but still have to select where their case study will be situated. Here there is no intention to be representative, although the temptation to generalize will still be strong. Probability-sampling allows the researcher little scope to pick and choose, but cases allow choice to be made in the field. Further, all the complexities of sampling can be of less importance than the response obtained in determining the limitations of the results achieved. Above all, research is often reported without enough detail for the reader to know how or why the choices were made.

The choice between sampling and choosing cases depends on the purpose of the research and the resources available. Governments require reliable descriptive statistics. Thus the Census aims at 100 per cent cover, but also includes 10 per cent and 1 per cent samples to collect more detailed data and to produce trends across decades (Dale and Marsh 1993). Market-researchers aim for representative samples, but here the individuals are picked by the researchers on instructions provided by the office and the probability of any one person being picked is unknown. Interpretive researchers examining the way identities are constructed are likely to select a group particularly affected by the issue under review. Each method of selection has advantages and snags. For example, policy-makers need sampling for representation, but generalization to the population removes the evidence from its local context. Case studies keep the evidence in context, cannot be used for generalization, but are consequently of value to practitioners. Thus Stenhouse (1980) pressed for case study in education as a way of bringing the maximum support to teachers and to avoid exploiting them in the search for abstracted, decontextualized academic knowledge.

Types of sample

Probability samples

A sample is selected to represent a population. In probability-sampling the chances of any individual being selected is known. The data collected can be treated statistically and results stated as probabilities. Hence the relationship between variables such as race, class and sex or measures of school organization on the one hand and attainment measures of pupils on the other can be stated in terms of the mathematical confidence, such as 99 in 100, or 95 in 100, that the relationship discovered was caused by genuine differences, not by the sample chosen. That probability is dependent on the characteristics of the sample in relation to the population. Probability samples appear under the titles random sample, systematic sample, stratified sample, cluster sample, stage sample. Because the sample is identified in advance it is possible to calculate non-response, whether because of failure to find or unwillingness to cooperate. Hence steps can be taken to increase response by postal follow-up or visit and to compensate for the loss.

The key feature of probability-sampling is that judgement about selection is not left to the researcher once the sample is drawn. A common term for this is random sampling because each member of a particular population is given an equal chance of selection, However, lucky dips are rarely used. It is more common to take a systematic sample from existing lists such as the electoral register, or school or medical records. These choices are not random, but the chance of being selected is known. Those born on the 5th, 15th and 25th of each month, for example, provide a 10 per cent sample.

Probability-sampling does not guarantee representativeness. It can be rotten but random luck to select only millionaires in a sample for studying income distribution. It is small consolation that the chance of this happening can be calculated. Large samples reduce this kind of mischance, but are expensive. The usual procedure to minimize such risks of a maverick sample is through stratification. The population to be sampled is broken down into smaller, more homogeneous groups before sampling. Thus a box of 100 marbles, 10 of 10 different colours, could be sampled first by 'stratifying' them into 10 boxes of the same colour. Then one from each box could be selected. The 10 per cent sample would be representative. The chances of a fluke selection of a few colours only is reduced in advance. This accounts for the term probability sample rather than random being used. It is a known not an equal chance of selection that is arranged by first categorizing by class, sex, income and so on.

It is often necessary to be sceptical about the use of the term sampling. It implies that a study is representative and may be used for generalized conclusions. But the question 'representative of whom' is important. Is it representative of those who always send back questionnaires in this girl's magazine? Or those who can't resist phoning their views to the BBC after a broadcast debate? The greatest blunder in survey history was the 1936 Literary Digest Poll predicting that Landon would defeat Roosevelt. This was a postal questionnaire from a sample drawn from the telephone directory. In 1936 that eliminated poorer, Democratic Party voters. Size means little in sampling. Over two million voted. Yet Roosevelt won by a landslide. *The Hite Report on Love, Passion and Emotional Violence* is commendable in containing an essay on methodology (Hite 1991). One hundred thousand questionnaires were sent to clubs, to organizations across the USA and to anyone who wrote in after seeing plans for the survey. With 127 questions such as 'Describe the time recently you were most happy with your lover, most joyous', the 4500 who returned the questionnaire were likely to both have time on their hands and an exhibitionist bent. The implications of a response rate of 4.5 per cent are discussed later. But Hite does give the reader a full account of sampling methods. Where it is missing it's safest to be wary.

Judgement samples

Judgement, purposive or quota samples are all aimed at selecting individuals, groups, organizations that are representative of a target population. The judgement about who or what to select for study, unlike probability-sampling, is ultimately left to the researcher in the field. This eliminates non-response. The researcher goes home once each quota is full. The price of this flexibility is that levels of confidence and hence the statistics based on these should no longer be calculated. Further, the discretion left to the researcher leaves doubts about selection. This is purposive because it can serve the aims of the research. Reliability is relaxed.

In quota-sampling, used by market researchers, nobody knows the probability of you being stopped by a tired researcher on a wet Monday morning. The aim is to collect 'quotas' defined by age, sex, income bracket and so on to give representativeness. The researchers are given a list with numbers in categories defined by age, sex and so on. Lurking on a street corner, one of them approaches a likely looking passer-by who seems to fit the quota of middle-class married woman aged between 30 and 50. Interviews continue until each quota is completed.

In practice quota-sampling gives reliable results with experienced interviewers. It is also cheap and does not depend on having lists already available from which a sample can be selected in advance. The problem here, as with all judgement samples, is the dependence on the researcher and the cooperation of those approached to fill the quotas. The use of volunteers to form a sample is particularly hazardous, though very tempting. The reader is right to suspect that those who come forward are probably not representative. The Kinsey Report on human sexual behaviour remains a classic (Kinsey, Pomeroy and Martin 1953). A campaign was organized to interest clubs, families and other groups. Quotas, in the form of specified groups, were then defined. But despite a final sample of 12 000, a minority of quotas were filled to Kinsey's satisfaction. The first volunteers were found to include the sexually active, aggressive, exhibitionist. Reluctant volunteers had to be pursued. But those were tough times for homosexuals and others branded as deviant and despite the care taken to check respondents and fill the quotas, doubts remain about whether this is really a representative study of sexual behaviour in the human male and female.

Judgement samples often lack even the prespecification of quotas. They can depend on returns from magazine or newpaper articles, or appeals following broadcasts. An example is *The Hite Report on the Family* (Hite 1994). This is based on 3000 completed responses, 50 per cent from the USA, 35 per cent from Europe and the rest from around the world. The questions were distributed through selected magazines, for example, *Amazon* and *Corridor* in Oxford and Cambridge in England, *Elle* in France. Respondents were asked not to give names. The research methods are described as a mix of Sociology, Psychology and Cultural History, together with innovations from feminist methodology. Eighty questions were asked, many containing multiple subquestions such as 'When you were very little, around three or four, can you remember what it was like being close to your mother?' The book contains an appeal for volunteers for future Hite research. Given the essay-type answers and the number of questions, any sample would be defined by stamina as well as reading habits.

The titles given to judgement samples indicate their attraction and dangers. In addition to judgement and quota samples there are convenience, opportunistic, snowball, purposive, typical samples. All indicate the discretion left to the researcher. Snowball-sampling, for example, involves obtaining the next respondents from those already interviewed. This lack of control can produce a biased sample. But that is balanced by the absence of non-response. In both cases the reader should look for the care taken over avoiding one or the other.

Theoretical sampling

One popular way of developing theory is to base it in closely observed data (Glaser and Strauss 1967). Grounded theory sounds solid. It is a key to developing theory through ethnography, the intensive study of small groups in their natural setting. The data guides the development of theory and in turn the latter guides the next phase of data collection. The sampling is directed at the apparently theoretically significant. This therefore leaves the typical or representative as a lower priority.

The problems with grounded theory arise from this priority to the advancement of knowledge through concentration on the theoretically interesting. Hence the common annoyance when researchers publish accounts that seem to bear little relation to the situation known to those who granted access to the research. Further, researchers often find it difficult to detect the data that really is theoretically significant. Observation and interpretation are liable to be so run together that researchers may be 'seeing' a very different reality to that seen by those participating. Meanings have been imposed rather than detected. This abstraction may eventually advance social science, but it can also be seen as the exploitation of those researched.

There is no necessary superiority in any form of sampling. Scientistic social research reducing behaviour to variables that can be related statistically depends on probability-sampling. But this is expensive, open to non-response and above all artificial. Judgement samples are often suspect because they are comprised of volunteers, but that may be all that is required. The key to the quality of all samples is their relation to the aims of the research and the care taken by the researcher, including taking care to make the bases of choice fully public. Market-researchers and pollsters before elections can make mistakes, but they usually get reliable results within narrow margins. A lot of research is not aimed at generalization, but at understanding the way we live together in specific circumstances, at trying out new methods, at developing theory. Once again, what is always necessary is to give the reader enough detail to 'see' the sample or cases and why and how they were chosen.

The relation of sampling to the aims of the research links this technical issue to the logic, the methodology, discussed in Part One. Sampling is one part of the way research is thought through, aimed at producing valid and reliable knowledge within limited means. *The Hite Report on Love, Passion and Emotional Violence* reported above was based on large numbers of volunteers writing in response to a widely distributed questionnaire. Would more valid evidence be collected by interviewing a small sample? The more intimate situation could lead to refusals and inhibit responses. This sensitive subject has been so investigated. O'Connor (1995) randomly sampled 71 women from the records of five general practitioners in North London and intensively interviewed 60, concluding that such interviewing was possible to organize and produced frank answers. There is usually such a choice of sampling method. But the decision can be arbitrary or unexplained.

The list of actual samples that follows shows the variety in selection. Probability and judgement samples are often combined, A school is chosen for convenience, but classes can be sampled at random.

Observations can then be made of children sitting at the four corners of classrooms. Large surveys, for example for the Department for Education and Employment, will often be selected in stages. All schools can be stratified by size, type and region and a random sample taken in each of the consequent categories. Then pupils can be sampled within the selected schools by date of birth to give the required numbers. The sample is now representative of the nation's schools, but the numbers tested, observed, interviewed are in thousands not millions. A parallel narrowing-down occurs in interpretive research with cases or small samples. As the research progresses there is a concentration on important issues or theoretically interested features as they are detected. All research involves choices, whether made in advance or during the work. The reader needs to question whether those choices for the particular sample or case can account for the evidence presented.

Cases and case study

The popularity of case study, particularly in studying schools, rests on the promise that such research will produce useful insights, particularly for teachers. Cases are also popular in interpretive, ethnographic research where the aim is to understand behaviour in natural settings and to find how identities and meanings are constructed. Now there is often one school, a class or two, a small group of pupils, a gang. There can be no claim to be representative. These are cases not samples, designed to find out how particular people make sense of an issue, to develop or test theory, to illustrate a point, to guide practice. Choices are still made and there will still be absentees, refusals, the sullen and the eager. For Stenhouse the use of cases is recommended because it forces the researcher to interpret situations, use judgement, and arrive at a promising course of action (Stenhouse 1980). Unlike research based on samples it keeps attention on contexts, never extracting variables from the conditions in which they arise. It is therefore very suitable for aiding professional practice.

A very well-documented case is the study of Bishop McGregor School (Burgess 1983). Looking for a PhD topic, Burgess meets education officials, attends meetings of teachers, gets the feel of local schooling. Then a stranger introduces himself as the headteacher of Bishop McGregor School, gives his phone number and invites Burgess to visit, despite being told he is speaking to a researcher from the University of Warwick. At the visit Burgess is given lunch, meets staff and students. Few researchers are so lucky. But headteachers who volunteer their schools for research by sociologists think they have little to hide. The judgement to accept was by Burgess. It resulted in a candid and thorough account, including the reasons for accepting the offer and of the methods used.

By the 1970s ethnographic, interpretive research based on the observation of natural situations had commonly replaced scientist experimental and survey research as the way to valid knowledge in sociology.

This rapidly became popular in the study of schools. The result was a number of doctoral theses and research reports usually described as ethnographic case studies (see, for example, Pollard 1985). Case study was also useful to illustrate the social construction of reality (Berger and Luckmann 1966). This has been particularly fruitful in investigating the incidence of sexism and racism and in seeing how identities are constructed and imposed on minorities.

Case study had another practical advantage. It was small-scale, required few resources and took the researcher straight into the action. It became popular with interpretive research and shared its rationale. If research was to understand human behaviour it had to study it in its natural settings, hear it in the language of those researched, theorize about it from the evidence collected. In education, for example, the 'teacher as researcher' movement used case study as a way of accumulating useful knowledge for professional reflection and hence the improvement of teaching. This is, however, another move to use research primarily to raise awareness. It raises once again the objection that research is about the accumulation of knowledge – not criticism of it – and hence that the methods should not be confused (Hammersley 1993).

The difference between cases and samples therefore is not just that the latter are designed for generalization and abstraction and the former designed for reflecting on practice in context. That is important for the reader assessing how far evidence can be generalized. But there can also be a difference in the perceived relationship between researcher and researched. Abstracting evidence, reporting it in academic jargon, ignoring its potential for helping those who provided the access, is exploitation. In the Inner London Education Authority in the 1970s there was a section of a Research and Statistics Group devoted to negotiating access to schools for researchers and trying to get a report out of them after the work had finished. Only a minority fulfilled this part of the contract to research in London schools. Many cleared a research proposal and then tried to carry out another. Few reported back to the schools, even as a courtesy. Research can be a very selfish exercise.

Finally, sampling and the selection of cases can be combined. A sophisticated example can be found in the '16–19' initiative funded by the Economic and Social Research Council (Bynner 1992). This employed a variety of research methods based within a large-scale follow-up study. In four areas – Swindon, Liverpool, Sheffield and Kirkaldy – 800 15-year-olds and 800 17-year-olds were sampled from school records and asked to complete questionnaires in 1987, 1988 and 1989. At the second stage the samples in each area were boosted by another 500 as mobility had reduced the sample size to 4800 from the intended 6400. Response rates for this core sample were around 80 per cent (Bynner 1992).

The core, questionnaire study was supplemented by interview-based research and ethnographic studies, both using the core sample and the available results. Seven more research projects were funded to examine issues and groups not part of the original survey. A number of comparative studies in Europe were also funded from separate sources. Ten universities in the United Kingdom were involved and to date over 500 papers have been published. This research was itself a continuation of the *Young People in Society* programme funded by the Social Science Research Council in the 1970s (Beloff 1986). The sample of two cohorts aged 15 and 17 each followed-up for three years gave a total age range of 15 to 20 and data on changes across time. The associated studies have provided evidence on the way young people have responded.

Response and non-response

The need to focus on non-response arises not so much from the numbers, but from the danger that the reasons for refusing or for not being available for selection may be related to the issue being researched. Research on alcoholism can be weakened if the non-response has resulted from reluctance to pursue those who are frequently inebriated, or disgust that some groups could contain those with such a vile habit. It is legitimate for researchers to ensure that the sampling of place and time includes just those of interest. If every alcoholic is in a pub there is no point in sampling heavy drinkers in the street. But readers need to know this. The time of day, of the week or month or year, the weather and so on can also make a difference. This can be controlled in random or probability-sampling, but the danger increases as discretion to choose who and where to question or observe is left to the researcher in the field. Thus the judgement sample, the quota sample is suspect unless the office or the research director trains, supervises and checks that instructions are being followed. Without that the sample is liable to be friendly and cooperative and not representative. Case studies are not usually intended to be representative, but the basis for selection and for omission is still needed for assessment of the evidence by readers.

There is often too little information published on the procedures used in sampling or the selection of cases for possible bias to be assessed. But the conditions under which the evidence was collected can often be imagined. In Charlotte, Mecklenburg County, North Carolina, social scientists researched the community reaction to a prosecution following the showing of a film judged to be obscene (Linz *et al.* 1991). First contact was made by random-digit dialling on the phone. Those answering were told that the research meant them watching and evaluating a film. Three hundred and eighty-eight did not refuse at this stage, but 104 said 'no' when they heard it was X rated. The remaining 284 were sent a pre-film questionnaire. One hundred and twenty-nine turned up to see the film and completed a second questionnaire. Twenty of these were shown a 'control' film, without any explicit sexual content.

There are gaps in this report. The reader doesn't know how many people were phoned at the start. The reduction from 388 to the final 129 took place as the volunteers came to appreciate the nature of the task. Were the final 129 particularly prurient? Were the non-responders puritan, too busy or just forgetful?

Here are examples of response rates for a variety of researches.

The 1991 Census

Planning started in 1981. The first test of response was in 1987 with a dress-rehearsal in 1988. The Census was followed-up by a validation survey to check details and responses. England and Wales were shown to have a population of 49 million. The shortfall was about 1 million, with young and old adults underrepresented, particularly in London (Dale and Marsh 1993).

Government surveys and committees

The General Household Survey has a typical response rate of above 80 per cent, with about 2 per cent not contactable and the rest not wishing to take part (Office of Population Censuses and Surveys 1982).

The Warnock Committee

This only achieved a response rate of 56 per cent for special schools and classes and 48 per cent for ordinary schools. The low response was probably because the questionnaires were sent out in the summer term as teachers were about to go on holiday (Warnock Report 1978).

Postal questionnaires

While Hite (1994) only achieved a 4.5 per cent response, a more usual figure is 20 to 30 per cent. But there is no way of knowing whether this is refusal because it looks like more junk mail or that you are too busy, lack interest in the subject, refuse to even consider it or are away on holiday. All these lead to non-response having a different meaning.

Large-scale core and linked study

The ESRC '16–19' study outlined above achieved response rates of around 80 per cent using postal questionnaires for those who were contactable (Bynner 1992) and interviewing where there was no return following a reminder. To compensate for the high mobility in the first wave of this follow-up study, a further 500 were added to the sample in each area in the second wave a year later.

Follow-up study

In 1968 the Inner London Education Authority tested the literacy of an entire year group of 29 579 children aged nine and repeated the testing when the same children were 11, 13 and 15. In 1971 there were 24 210 tested, 22 438 in 1973 and 21 122 in 1975. Reading scores could only be interpreted within very wide social class groupings as only 60 per cent of the children of professional and managerial families remained in inner London compared with 75 per cent of children of unskilled manual workers (ILEA 1969, 1972, 1975, 1977).

The high rates of response in government surveys are achieved by using large samples and careful preparation, repeated visits or postings of questionnaires, follow-up to see whether non-responders differ from those who responded and sometimes the use of replacement lists. But large numbers do not guarantee representativeness once subcategories are examined. The Assessment of Performance Unit used samples of around 10 000 (DES 1986). But response rates fell as surveys were repeated. In Northern Ireland in 1980 surveys of science attainment for 13- and 15-year-olds had fallen to 70 per cent. With absentees likely to be low attainers and efficient schools likely to organize for maximum response, overall attainment may have been artificially raised. Further, subgroups of secondary school pupils will have shrunk to a size where confidence was reduced.

This problem even occurred in the 30 000 strong sample used in the ILEA Literacy Survey described above. The 30 000 were categorized into five social class groupings, six nationalities and whether they were immigrants or not according to the then DES Form 7(i). Thus there were 60 'boxes' into which the 30 000 were allocated. But the boxes for the indigenous population contained the overwhelming majority. The performance of children of professional/managerial West Indian parents was important to contribute to the debate then raging over the relative influence of social class and ethnicity in attainment. But there were less than ten children in this box. It would have been irresponsible to use these as a reliable sample.

None of these problems arise in judgement samples. The researchers can continue to select until they have the required numbers. In case studies attention can focus on promising practical or theoretical situations. The published results can provide insights but not generalizations. Their strength and weakness is that they remain in context. Further, the absence of non-response is not all gain. It is always wise to consider who was ignored, rejected, why this happened and where. In probability-sampling discretion in the field is restricted. When the researcher is free to choose, the natural situation is preserved, but the unquestioned, the unobserved and the offstage remain a mystery.

The importance of looking carefully at non-responders and those not chosen for study arises from the possibility that they are very different from those who responded or were in the case study. They are a spectre that can haunt researchers just because little can be known about them even where some can be traced and their characteristics noted and compared with those on whom information has been collected. Were the majority who did not answer a postal questionnaire, refused an interview or said they were too busy to be observed, the extremists, the idle, those with something to hide, or those who dislike researchers? Nonresponse is particularly important in sample surveys (Goyder 1987). But it is a problem for all social research.

The mathematical problem of non-response is easily illustrated. If 100 out of 200 respond, and 90 of these answer 'YES', does this mean that 90 per cent are in favour or 45 per cent, a majority or minority? There is no way of knowing unless steps are taken to follow-up to get some idea of the reason for not responding. It is therefore essential for researchers to anticipate and reduce non-response and for readers to be alert to its impact on validity. The Government Social Survey insist that interviewers call when it is convenient and fix appointments where necessary. Faced with refusal there should be some attempt to gauge the reasons and the characteristics of those concerned. But in most research the reasons for not responding are never known.

This problem is avoided in judgement samples where refusals, blank stares and the cheery 'No thanks' are ignored and approaches continue until quotas are full. In case studies selection focuses on those of interest or available for the development of theory, the concerns of practitioners or the emancipation of the oppressed. Here the description of cases is often vague on the lines of 'around 50 aged 16 to 19', 'Four schools and approximately 970 pupils and 57 staff were observed.' An influential study such as Willis (1978) was based on discussions with 12 boys. On interviewing teachers in schools cooperating in a Schools Council Curriculum Project I found that many teachers denied they were in the sample at all. They were, they maintained, 'just helping out'. But they pointed to others, not officially involved, who had played an active part (Shipman, Bolam and Jenkins 1974). Researchers don't always know everything that is going on.

What really went on under the Banyan trees?

Controversy 1 detailed the nature–nurture debate which Margaret Mead was to affect decisively with her study of adolescent girls in Samoa (Mead 1943). The view of adolescence in the 1920s was dominated by Stanley Hall's studies around the turn of the century (1904). Hall was one of the new school of empiricist psychologists, observing the behaviour of young people, building up a model of universal, inevitable rebellion during development. That view rested on the then dominant evolutionary and biological theories that went back to Galton and Darwin. Not only was adolescence a period of storm and stress, but this was a recapitulation in each developing individual of the early stages in human evolution. Each lived through the primitive phases of human life. The alternative, psychoanalytical view of Freud that was published at the same time as Hall described adolescence as the period when the conflicts of infancy were resolved into reproductive, adult sex. This was similarly influenced by the view that the primitive id lay beneath the surface of civilized behaviour. Individuals once again recapitulated the stages of increasing civilization as they matured. Both theories of adolescence had a biological, evolutionary base and saw it as a time of inevitable stress or anxiety as the savage was controlled while the child matured into civilized, normal adulthood.

Into this academic climate of biological determinism stepped young Margaret Mead. She was an American, the daughter of agnostic middle-class parents, born in Philadelphia in 1901 and a doctoral student of Franz Boas (Howard 1985). In 1928 she published *Coming of Age in Samoa*. It proved to be the best-selling of all anthropological books exerting influence at two levels. First, it countered the biological determinism that gave the dominant influence on human behaviour to inherited factors. The untroubled adolescent Samoan experience was so unlike that in Western societies that biology couldn't be determining all human development. Neither could humanity be reproducing a primitive stage of development. So influential was the book that it was used to press the case for cultural determinism, thus replacing one way of seeing humans in the grip of forces beyond their control by another. At the second level the book exploded the current view that adolescence was a time of inevitable storm and stress. The account of the relaxed sexual and social life of Samoan girls suggested that any stress was created by social conditions, and hence remediable, rather than the unfolding of universal biological make-up.

There is little gain in this substitution of cultural for biological determinism. Sociologists came to see adolescence as the period when children were socialized into adult roles. The individual was seen as moulded by social expectations until adult status was achieved. Hall saw adolescents moving to civilized adult normality. Freud saw them as moving to normal adult reproductive sex and Parsons (1951), the most prominent functionalist sociologist of the 1960s, saw them as being socialized into normality within the social system. In none of these cases was there much room for individuality or for the adolescent to influence their future.

The question that Mead set out to answer was 'Were the difficulties due to being adolescent or to being adolescent in America?' (Mead 1943: 12). The current psychological view in the 1920s was that 'rebellion against authority, philosophical perplexities, the flowering of idealism, conflict and struggle' should be ascribed to physical development. Yet as an anthropologist Mead saw attitudes as dependent on social environment. The answer to her question 'Can we think of adolescence as a time in the life history of every girl child which carries with it symptoms of conflict and stress as surely as it implies a change in the girl's body?' was a firm 'No'.

Mead was 23 when she arrived in Samoa in 1925. She stayed for nine months, mainly in a government school whose female students were the respondents used in the study of adolescence. In her biography she confesses to knowing little about methods, to knowing what to look for but not how and of feeling despair at the situation. There is a cautious Appendix on methods in the book. The limitations of the interviews, the description of the social structure of the nearby villages, of a questionnaire and of the psychological tests used in Samoa are listed. But Freeman has collected together evidence to show that her account of Samoan life was 'fundamentally in error' (Freeman 1984). This was partly because of her inadequate knowledge of the language. It was partly her dependence on respondents who may have been teasing or deceiving her. Above all it was through slack control over her own search for evidence that would confirm her view that adolescent turmoil was missing and that sexual relations were casual. To Freeman, Mead was guilty of exampling: gathering up data to support her thesis and ignoring that which did not fit.

The objection of Samoans to Mead's work was the starting point for Freeman's investigation. *Coming of Age* is an affectionate account of Samoa, but for a people who prized virginity in females it must have seemed odd that Mead found so many of her respondents remembering casual lovemaking under the palms. So must the picture of Samoans as a gentle, uncompetitive people. Having seen Samoans playing rugby football against Tongans it is difficult to accept Mead's picture, just as it is difficult to accept that a small-scale society could be organized to accept unfettered sexual relations among adolescents.

The most telling criticism of Mead's work is that she may have accepted evidence from secondary and suspect sources. Central to her view that free lovemaking was expected among adolescents is her explanation of how this is reconcilable with the presentation of proof of female virginity at marriage. This proof is demanded by the 'talking chief', the spokesman of the bridegroom. Mead leaves this unexplained in *Coming of Age in Samoa*. But later, she solves the problem by stating that where the bride is not a virgin, chicken's blood is substituted. Freeman reports that Samoan chiefs were outraged by this account. Mead obtained this information, not from Samoans, but from one Phoebe Parkinson, who, when she gave it, had not been in Samoa since 1881, some 50 years earlier, having only then spent two weeks in a Samoan village. She had never been where Mead did her fieldwork. Furthermore, Freeman maintains that Mead elaborated this account in later books. Certainly in her autobiography, *Blackberry Winter* (1972), she seems to confirm the hearsay nature of the evidence that the bride who was discovered to have lost her virginity before marriage was punished, not for her promiscuity, but for not bringing an adequate supply of chicken blood to the ceremony (*Blackberry Winter* 1972: 178–80). As Freeman states, this completely misrepresents 'the attitude of the dignified and punctilious Samoans toward one of their most sancrosanct traditional institutions'.

It would be wrong to accept Freeman's criticisms without question. He has been criticized in the South Pacific for painting too violent a picture of Samoa. Furthermore, Mead's account of Samoa remains a remarkable achievement given the prevailing views of adolescence in the 1920s. There are accounts of Samoa that suggest that young people there face similar problems and opportunities for sexual experiment as their peers in the rest of the world (Holmes 1974; Ritchie and Ritchie 1979). Above all Mead made the general public aware of the variety of ways in which societies were organized and in which behaviour is manifested. She may have been careless of facts, indifferent about details, but she made a lasting contribution to bringing justice into the lives of women. Biological determinism had provided a reason for avoiding action to ensure equal opportunities for women. Mead used her work and her influence in good causes. But however influential, it has been challenged as unreliable.

There is an irony in this charge of unreliability in Mead's fieldwork. She wrote at least three major works on anthropological methods (Mead 1977). In one of these she details the care that needs to be taken to obtain a sample of respondents that represent the complete cultural experience. Yet in the search for a crucial piece of evidence to complete her case she was apparently willing to rely on hearsay from someone who was neither in the sample nor even involved in the culture studied.

There is little doubt that adolescence is a time of rapid, often radical, physical and social change. Biology and culture play a part. In retrospect, however, the evidence of Hall, Freud and of sociologists such as Parsons is too certain, implying universality and uniformity, where the anthropological evidence, however flawed, suggests variety and resilience. Many contemporary views of adolescence have not moved far from storm and stress. Instead of this being caused biologically it is seen as the product of expectations by both parents and the young themselves. The images behind these expectations are pressed in the mass media. The image of the sloppy, rebellious adolescents of the 1980s isn't far from Hall's storm-tossed or Freud's sexually anxious youth at the turn of the century. What has changed is the perceived role of the adolescents. At the start of the century they were passive, seen by social scientists as swept along by biology, physiology, sexuality. Now they are given an active role as culture-users, adjusting their behaviour according to their image of themselves. At least they have been accorded their humanity. This view also removes any inevitable period of stress. Some may go through adolescence serenely. Others do not. Mead's contribution confirms this at the level of societies. Social anthropology is an antidote to a Eurocentric view of the world.

The criticisms of Mead are a warning that interpretive social researchers attempting to gather information on the way people see their world in their natural setting can be misled. Sometimes the researcher can be intentionally deceived. Increasingly the researched know what the researcher is doing. You cannot argue that social science has been influential without acknowledging that those researched have become more sophisticated. More common are misunderstandings arising from the subtle cultural norms that dictate responses, particularly when one of the parties is a researcher. Thus among the Sioux there are questions that are not asked of men, of young men, of elders (Wax 1979). Only White anthropologists are so rude and responses are carefully managed. Samoans too are polite, but wary when their beliefs are queried. Similar adjustments are the commonplace of interaction between knowing humans everywhere. The more influence from social research, the more that interaction can reduce validity.

CHAPTER 5

Observation

In Chapter 1 the unfortunate case of Blondlot's discovery of N-rays was described. The excitement generated in France was understandable. It was anticipated that X-rays would be followed by a succession of other rays with equally wonderful properties. Blondlot's prestige within the French Academy of Sciences encouraged others to observe, record and apply. There was an additional incentive to exploit this discovery. Around 1900, the defeat by Germany in the war of 1870 was still deeply felt. German science was gaining a worldwide reputation. Röntgen the discoverer of X-rays in 1895 worked at the University of Würzburg in Bavaria. The French with a pride in their past scientific status seem to have seen what they wanted to see. It demonstrates the fallibility of observation, even among those most expected to be thorough in checking its reliability.

The social researcher in a natural setting is particularly at risk while observing. The conviction that reality is socially constructed means that truth is relative. The search for key episodes that will serve as grounds for theorizing further increases the incentive to see selectively. But the selective nature of observation is universal. A Marxist will see class struggle not just in history, but in everyday life. Before critics began to uncover the self-deception in Freud, it was difficult not to have your inadequacies analysed as the consequence of some anxiety about your privates when an infant. To some contemporaries, particularly in academia, the whole world seems to be deconstructing. Fashions change, but our current theories tend to determine what we see.

Ethnography, fieldwork and case study, described in Chapter 3, depend on observation. It is an ubiquitous technique. It is our usual way of obtaining information, requires no necessary instrumentation and is endlessly fascinating. It seems ideal for developing theory grounded in evidence, is unlikely to disturb the natural situation which was the distinguishing feature of these approaches and enables us to detect even the most subtle clues in human interaction. But that ease of interpretation also carries a threat to validity. In the instant between observing and understanding there are miracles of human interpretation, the conversion of observation into perception, into meaningful, contextualized and distinctive knowledge.

This conversion of sense data into meaningful knowledge is the subject of much psychology, sociology and philosophy. The psychologist focuses on the processes in eye and brain that convert sense data into perceptions. The sociologist relates these perceptions to the way society is organized. The philosopher concentrates on how we can get to know what there is in the world. This attention follows from the miracle of human perception. But it is also a warning that observation is interpretation. That applies to researcher and researched. Our observations are instantaneously interpreted by reference to existing beliefs and knowledge. These vary by age, class, race, sex and all the characteristics we wrap together as culture.

There are a range of techniques for observation from the tightly controlled to the unfettered. However covert the stance chosen, the researcher will still be within the group observed. When Patrick fled from Glasgow to avoid grievous bodily harm from his observed gang, he had already influenced it and they had started to view him with suspicion (Patrick 1973). Researchers in schools inevitably disturb the natural situation. While I was researching *Inside a Curriculum Project* (Shipman, Bolam and Jenkins 1974), Jenkins describes my position as initially wallpaper, but my claim to the status as observer soon became a joke among the Schools Council team as I was drawn into planning in both university and schools. Each party to that project, in Schools Council, university, school and local authority saw it as something different and hence pushed for different outcomes. As researcher I was piggy-in-the-middle, exploited as much as exploiting.

The selectivity of observation

Observations are not the result of the senses detecting events out there that look the same to everyone. Our perceptions are structured. We see the world through our attitudes, prejudices, values and through the models in the mind that we have learned. As researchers these models that structure observations into knowledge come from some branch of social science, some professional competence and more general social and political views. Given the extraordinary specialization within social science there will be many models and hence very different aspects will be in focus and the same event will be interpreted in very different ways. There is a delightful contrast between German and American psychologists observing hungry rats confronted by a maze in which food was available at the far end. Both sets of rats learned to traverse the maze. But those seen by the Germans sat pondering the problem in an immobile way until a solution dawned and they threaded their way through. American rats, however, launched themselves hell for leather in a series of bruising trial runs until they learned from their errors. The time taken was similar, the style contrasting. Any student who has puzzled over the differences between Gestalt and behaviourist theories of learning will realize that this ludicrous picture reflects an underlying discrepancy caused by the national differences which seem to have established different frames of reference in the minds of the two national groups which developed these theories.

A more serious if still amusing example of the effects of the expectations of the observer can be demonstrated by Rosenthal and Fode's 1963 experiment with 12 psychology students asked to measure the time taken for rats to learn to run to the darker arm of a maze to find food. Sixty ordinary rats were divided between the students, but six students were told they had maze-bright rats and six were given maze-dull rats, each sample said to be specially bred. Each rat was given ten chances each day for five days to learn that the darker arm led to food.

While there was no actual difference in the maze-learning ability of the rats, the students observed the results that they were led to anticipate by the description of their sample as bright or dull. The bright rats not only became better performers but showed daily improvement, while the dull rats only improved to the third day and then deteriorated. Furthermore, the dull rats refused to start at all more frequently than the eager-to-get-with-it bright ones and were slower to reach the end after they had learned. After the experiment was over the students rated their rats and their own attitudes towards them. Those having 'bright' rats viewed them as brighter, more pleasant and more likeable, and their own attitude towards the rats was more relaxed and enthusiastic than among the six students with the 'dull' sample.

Such effects are not confined to the social sciences, although the frequent use of human beings as subjects of research makes them more prone to self-fulfilling effects. In the natural sciences a researcher can be similarly misled, either by the expectations of colleagues or their own predictions and hopes. Once set to expect a result, scientists in all fields are liable to find their observations biased. This is why controls and repetitions of experiments by others are so important.

The case of Prosper Blondlot and his discovery of N-rays reported in Chapter 1 is a typical example. At the heart of his spectroscopic apparatus was a prism. This was removed by the American physicist Robert Wood, unnoticed by Blondlot, who continued his descriptions of the N-rays he was observing, despite the absence of the lens that was supposed to produce them. It was not, however, just the inventor who saw what he expected to see. Other French scientists were similarly deceiving themselves at this time when new rays were eagerly anticipated.

Styles of observation

Observation is the basic technique for researchers. It is also most likely to be affected by personal, professional and political views. Hence there are difficult decisions at the start of research about the degree to which observations are to be controlled or left freeranging and whether the style is to be participant or detached. Detached observation is possible as in the use of schedules such as that developed by Bales (1950). Small groups, in specially designed rooms, were observed by specially trained observers sitting behind one-way mirrors. Adaptations of this method were used in the ORACLE project (Galton and Delamont 1985). The aim is to maximize reliability by training observers to sample events systematically and stick to the categories of behaviour listed on the schedule.

As the interest in the interpretation of human behaviour has increased, detached and controlled observation has become unpopular. If you are after the meaning of events to those involved, you need to be more like Sherlock Holmes, exercising ingenuity, than Inspector Lestrade following the book. That is the message of Chapter 3. Those who want to interpret social affairs try not to upset the natural setting, and design and redesign their research as new data are collected and stay alert for theories that explain it. Participant observation is the dominant style because it gives the required flexibility.

The complete participant observer merges into the groups studied. Homan (1978) blends into the Pentacostal groups he is studying, as do the sociology students observing what happens *When Prophecy Fails* reported later (Festinger, Riecken and Schachter 1956). In education that isn't so easy. Thus Davies (1982) in her *Life in the Classroom and Playground* is very concerned with the difficulties of really getting to know how children give meaning to events. Adult researchers may think they have found out, but the culture of childhood is well defended. Thus even those researchers who observe while taking the role of teacher may become part of the normal life of the school, but get no nearer the real world of the children. Indeed, the participant role that is chosen to preserve the natural situation may even reduce the chance of finding out what the pupils really think.

It is not easy to illustrate bias in observational studies because replication is not easy. The group or its environment will have changed across time. The participation of a different observer may have its effect. Replication is in any case rare. However, in 1951, Oscar Lewis (1951) published his *Life in a Mexican Village: Tepoztlan Revisited*. This was a study of communities previously studied by Redfield in the 1930s (Redfield 1930). Redfield had seen Tepoztlan as a society in which there was little change, a strong sense of belonging together and a homogeneity among the inhabitants. Lewis, in re-studying the community, was not trying to prove Redfield wrong, but looking for the type of errors that could be made in community studies. To Lewis, Tepoztlan manifested individualism not cooperation, tensions, fear and distrust rather than Redfield's picture of contentment and a sense of community. Later, in 1969, Avila (1969) published another study of this area of Mexico and again refuted the view that change was slow or the people uncompetitive.

It may be that the community had genuinely changed over the period from the 1930s to the 1950s and 1960s. But it may have been that Redfield saw information that fitted into the folk–urban continuum that was his theoretical model. The hypothesis may have directed the observations. Redfield later tried to explain the differences between himself and Lewis (Redfield 1968). He points out that both he and Lewis would have brought their own views into their work, and would have been alerted to see activity that confirmed their very different positions on urban and rural life. Once again this is an illustration of the way 'facts' are created by reference to theory. Where the theories differ, so may the 'facts'.

There are now several accounts of experiences of participant observers in education collected by Burgess (1984, 1985a, 1985b). These confirm that participant observation troubles researchers. Some 40 researchers in these three books expose their concern over reliability and validity. It is an insight not readily available to the reader of the original books and articles, for these only contain brief sections on method. It is not just anxiety about which role to adopt, complete participant, participant-as-observer, observer-as-participant or complete observer, or about their effect on those observed, but about the impact on them. Social scientists enter the field alerted by theories and models. But reality is often a shock and the models often do not fit.

Seeley (1964) working in an American community describes his experiences as a loss of innocence. His sociology came to be seen as a shared illusion unrelated to the reality he experienced. Similarly, Stein (1964) finds that to get insight into his community means detaching himself from his subject. Wolff (1964), going south of the border in Mexico, uses the term 'surrender' to describe the way he became and had to become immersed in the community he wished to understand. The development of interpretive social science has helped prepare for such experiences. Indeed, it was the experiences of sociologists such as Seeley, Stein and Wolff that pushed the subject away from its scientistic stance. But the shock is still felt once you get in a school, a community or anywhere outside academia. Life out there is often beyond rationalization in a model.

There is also a serious ethical problem if researchers 'pass' themselves off as bread roundsmen (Ditton 1977), gang members (Patrick 1973), or watchqueen (Humphreys 1974), in order to get into natural situations. This also raises problems for the reader of the published accounts of the deception. They have to be taken on trust and because each publication makes it less likely that the deception can be repeated, the chances of confirmation or refutation are diminished. The report may have all the veracity as well as the intimacy of a Peeping Tom's notebook.

This issue is complicated by the dilemma that the scientist is in if he starts observing without the consent of the observed or by clandestine means. He is nevertheless a scientist committed to report what he finds and not to conceal information or distort it to protect his informants. This dilemma can be followed in the work of Whyte (1943) on street-corner gangs. Here it was a combination of respect for those who had befriended him and provided the information, coupled with a fear that adverse accounts of them would put the author in danger of being carved up. Whyte's study lasted four years. By the end he was playing an active part in Cornerville society. To his informants he was writing a book. He visited them after publication to gauge its impact. Perhaps this is an indication of the compromise nature of the book. Nevertheless it remains a classic, and its methodological appendix has a full discussion of the ethical issues.

Probably the most fascinating but most morally dubious study was Festinger, Riecken and Schachter's *When Prophecy Fails* (1956). Here the authors and their students infiltrated a group who had prophesied that the end of the world was nigh. The social scientists were fully accepted and even after the world carried on past its predicted end, another observer was introduced to check on the impact of this miscalculation on the group. Recording was done in the toilet, out on the porch or on midget tape-recorders. This was an extreme example, but most social scientists have experienced moments when they have access to information that is obviously private. Publish and be damned can be justified on scientific grounds, but a public conned once is unlikely to cooperate again. Furthermore, social scientists are not exempt from the responsibility to exercise power over others with restraint.

The never-ending nature–nurture debate

A dominant figure in the establishment of both psychology and sociology in Britain was Sir Francis Galton. He was not only the inspiration for the group of colleagues who established psychology, particularly at University College, London, but he helped to organize the Sociology Society in 1903. A major concern of both subjects was the quality of the human stock. The Eugenics Society contained many prominent social scientists until the Second World War (Oakley 1991). Its concern with the problems of declining intelligence, physical health and inherited criminality remained on the social science agenda until the 1960s. The controversy has been driven more by economic and political factors than by developments in social science.

The first stage lasted from the mid-nineteenth to the mid-twentieth century. The Eugenics movement supported the values of male, Victorian colonial policy. White male superiority in intelligence seemed self-evident. So did its inheritance. Galton (1889) wrote extensively on hereditary genius. The models developed and the data collected now seem clearly sexist as well as racist and élitist. Research such as that by Mead reported in Controversy 4 helped to undermine this biological determinism, albeit often replacing it by an equally extreme environmentalism. By the 1960s the evidence on the inheritance of intelligence was under attack. The key point is that once the political context changed, the research methodology, the questions asked, the tests used, the statistical analyses and the conclusions drawn were suddenly challenged. Even researching the subject was seen as sinister.

Today the practical consequences of the Eugenics movement seem obscene. The extreme case is the 1933 Eugenics Sterilization Law in Germany and the 'final solution' of the Jewish problem that followed. But eugenic policies were widely adopted round the world (Kühl 1994). In Britain eugenicists campaigned for the sterilization of the feeble-minded (Sutherland 1984). Five presidents of the American Association for the Advancement of Science served on the advisory board of the American Eugenics Society. Sterilization programmes for criminals and mental defectives were common in North America and Canada. Immigration laws were devised to keep out inferior stock.

Part of the story in education is told in Controversy 7 and the efforts of Sir Cyril Burt to confirm the hereditability of intelligence by collecting data on twins. Few issues have split scientific communities in this way. It did great harm, as children were condemned on the basis of intelligence tests that were assumed to give a single measure of the ability at birth they would live with. Stage 1 came to a close with the political upheavals of the 1960s. By 1969 the publication of evidence that had been accepted as self-evident a few years before was now criticized as racist, sexist and invalid. A typical example was Jensen's article 'How much can we boost IQ and scholastic achievement?' (1969). This defended the thesis that Black children were on average genetically inferior on measured intelligence to their White peers. Burt, Eysenck and a few others continued to defend the 'nature' corner. But by the end of the 1960s, the influence of the environment was generally accepted as dominant, in line with the dominance of policies designed to promote equality of opportunity.

Stage 2 was intensely political. Jensen was accused of supporting the idea of Negro inferiority and of justifying segregation. The publication of a defence of the position adopted by Jensen was reduced to farce. Eysenck, a refugee from Nazi Europe, was accused of fascism (Eysenck 1971). Methodological mistakes bordering on lunacy were suggested and terms like impudent and ignorant abounded. Simultaneously Eysenck was accused of writing in a masterly, persuasive style that could mislead the lay reader (Hudson 1971).

This second stage coincided with the attack on objectivity in social science reported in Controversy 1. Whenever the controversy surfaced it aroused intense emotions. An example can be found in the 1990 issues of *The Psychologist* (Flynn 1989; Rushton 1990). The cause was an article by Rushton that had aleady been published in a similar form elsewhere (Rushton 1987). This was a comparison of the intelligence and other characteristics of Mongoloid, Negroid and Caucasian samples, asking why Caucasians scored consistently between the other two groups. In *The Psychologist*, which incorporates the *Bulletin of the British Psychological Society*, protests came in from individuals, groups of psychologists and whole departments. They objected to the publication. Comments included 'amazed it was included', 'very disappointed', 'primitive'. Given the content this astonishment at publication was understandable.

The anger increased when the editors reported that the article had not been refereed before publication. They admitted it was a serious error, agreed that its content was below the standard required for the journal and promised that it wouldn't happen again. A criterion in future would be that an article should not cause offence. But that only created more fury. Rushton wrote to object to the censorship and the criticism, pointing out that the data had already been published elsewhere and that 'truth must be faced' (Rushton 1990). Other critics of Rushton now wrote to object to the new editorial policy. It was revealed that Rushton had been funded by the Pioneer Fund which had been linked to former Nazi geneticists. Old hands such as Eysenck wrote to accuse letter-writers of McCarthyism. The correspondence is an extraordinary insight into the way this issue continues to polarize social scientists along political lines. It is also a warning that reliance on peer review for publication can break down. Above all, this episode was a reminder that although the steam seemed to be going out of the nature–nurture debate by the 1990s, this was based in a consensus that questions of the inheritance of intelligence should no longer be researched.

Stage 3 is, however, visible as the failure of policies to reduce inequalities becomes apparent. One illustration of this is Controversy 2 where the fate of the unskilled male was discussed. In North America the problem is wide and deep. As labour markets place a premium on qualifications and intelligence, policies to promote equality seem powerless to stop progressive separation into the bright and upwardly mobile at one extreme and an underclass, largely Black, at the other. Attempts to use affirmative action to equalize opportunities are breaking down. Meritocracy hasn't worked. The gap between the best and least educated has widened and the rewards to the former are likely to go on rising while the uneducated find work increasingly hard to get.

The failure of affirmative action revived the nature–nurture controversy. The decisive publication in the United States was *The Bell Curve* (Murray and Herrnstein 1994). This was a revival of 1960s evidence. In America, Asians perform above the norm on intelligence tests, Blacks below it. The bright intermarry and desert the inner cities which decline into a dependency culture that again depresses any chance of children achieving through schooling. Murray and Herrnstein come to conclusions based in evidence that have been controversial across the twentieth century. Brain power is in demand. It is largely determined by nature not nurture. Individual Blacks do get to the top, but on average they score below Whites and Asians and thus tend to get left behind in the competition for well-qualified jobs.

There is still intense controversy over the evidence for intelligence being inherited, unchanging and measurable. None of the issues over differences between races have been resolved. Further, the economic situation is new, but the models of intelligence remain Victorian. Work on them is inhibited by political distaste. In any case, differences within groups may result from inheritance, but that does not necessarily say anything about the causes of differences between groups, which could still come from differences in nurture.

The nature–nurture debate and the factors determining intelligence cannot be kept off the agenda for social research for ever. The consequences of economic and political change should be the business of social research. The impact depends on answers to questions about intelligence. Yet it remains difficult to ask these questions. The irony is that advances in genetics will inevitably force the nature–nurture debate to be reopened. Meanwhile, social researchers work in an intensely political environment that inhibits the asking of even old questions about new issues.

CHAPTER 6

Questions

The central position of the social survey and the questionnaire and inter-view in social research is explained by the need for descriptive data, for views on events, for responses to the pleasures and pain of living, collected in the most cost-effective way. There is a beguiling directness in asking questions and aggregating the answers. Assuming that the ques-tions asked and the answers given are understood by researcher and respondent in the way each intended, the result should be information that is both valid and reliable. But both intention and understanding are affected by factors that may not even be appreciated by both parties.

It is therefore not only the questions and the way answers to them are obtained, but the interaction that takes place as they are asked, read and answered that can be influential. Foddy (1993), drawing on the symbolic interactionist view that humans negotiate shared definitions of their situations as they communicate, identifies four steps to success in asking questions. The researcher must encode a clear question, the respondent must decode it as the researcher intended and then encode the answer containing the information required, Finally, the researcher must decode this information as the respondent intended. At each step there can be problems.

Here is one of 29 questions placed within four carrier questionnaires, completed by 265 people who were then interviewed twice on their answers (Belsen 1981). 'Do you think that children suffer any ill effects from watching programmes with violence in them, other than ordinary Westerns?' The words 'children', 'suffer', 'programmes', 'violence' and the phrases 'suffer any ill effects', 'from watching programmes' and 'other than ordinary Westerns' were all interpreted in widely differing ways. Somewhere along the four steps, intentions and understandings were not shared. Just after Enoch Powell had made a speech about the problems of immigration, *Panorama* sponsored the Opinion Research Centre to ask such questions as 'Would you like to return to your country of origin if you received financial help?' (Jowell and Hoinville 1969). On a wet, cold day in late November in the middle of Walsall, anyone remembering Barbados would be likely to interpret the answers 'Yes,', 'No,' or 'Don't know,' as 'You got the money handy,' 'You must be joking,' and 'Get lost'.

The improvement of the validity and reliability of asking questions is then a major task in social science. A group such as the CogLab at the London School of Economics explores the cognitive and social processes that influence the reliability of social surveys. The findings show why it is that the views of sponsors can affect the responses to surveys they pay for, why surveys come to conflicting conclusions and often fail to gauge public opinion. Apparently straightforward facts can be wrong. What is said may not tally with what was actually done. Beliefs and opinions change rapidly, minor changes in wording produce major changes in response, questions are misinterpreted, answers are affected by questions asked earlier, the order of questions affects answers, opinions are expressed even where nothing is known about the subject (Foddy 1993). Blackburn (1969) reports that within a month of the publication of *The Affluent Worker* (Goldthorpe *et al.* 1968) concluding that 77 per cent of Vauxhall workers at Luton were content with conditions at work and with the management, offices were stormed by the same workers singing *The Red Flag* and threatening to lynch the company directors.

Here is a summary of the planning and execution of the 1991 Census (Dale and Marsh 1993). This was the nineteenth decennial Census since 1801. It took 12 miles of shelving to house the forms and 118 000 enumerators. Planning started as the 1981 Census finished. By 1983 the wording of the questions on ethnic grouping was being trialled. Small-scale surveys were carried out in 1985 and 1986. There were tests in 1987 and a dress-rehearsal of 90 000 in 1988. Training was organized on a pyramid basis. The problems anticipated were the underrepresentation of young and old, particularly in London and the inner cities. The Census was followed by a validation survey. Even with this planning there was criticism of the questions used and a shortfall estimated at one out of 49 million in the population of England and Wales.

Questions about the use of questions

Was there a pilot study?

It is a safeguard to try out questions in advance, although more useful for identifying problems for the researcher than problems for the respondents in understanding the questions (Belsen 1981). The usual procedure is to trial a variety of questions and ways of responding. This is achieved by including questions asking for freeranging views on the issue, on the questions and on the way they are to be answered. A two-stage procedure of open-ended interviewing allowing the pilot sample to express their own views followed by a second stage trialling the questions worded after analysing the first-stage results is often used.

The pilot work on the questions may still leave the respondents flummoxed. The experience of reading a tax return or filling in any official form shows how difficult questions can be even where great care has been taken over their design. Yet researchers have often been reluctant to accept that this problem is inevitable. A good example was the intelligence test. Across half a century a debate raged about claims that the questions used were culture-free. Today there is greater appreciation of the sophisticated way reality is constructed in different conditions and that tests tend to reflect the culture of those who designed them.

Were the possible responses too restricted?

Advertisers play on our vanity. Questions often puncture it. There is threat in being questioned, particularly by a researcher with a clipboard or a tape-recorder. This can affect responses. First, people don't like to seem ignorant or forgetful, so may guess at answers where they really haven't a clue. Second, they may lie to avoid embarrassment. Third, when holding views they prefer to be private they may compromise. Questions about money, sex, hygiene or morality can be threatening. The usual remedy for these sources of possible error is to include 'filter' responses of the 'Don't know,' 'Can't recall,' type, which improve the overall validity of the data collected (Andrews 1984).

The responses to questions can be left open or restricted to a few predetermined categories of the 'Yes,' 'No,' 'Don't know,' type. Precoding answers often leaves respondents perplexed as none seem to fit their views. The psychoanalyst encourages free association. It is usual to have at least seven categories in attitude scales to facilitate statistical calculation. Market-researchers tick into boxes. Feminists encourage exchanges in depth. The researcher chooses whether to categorize possible answers in advance or to allow free response and to categorize later. One constrains and forces often narrow responses; the other retains the natural situation, but leaves the researcher free to interpret the responses to reflect on the subject. The validity can be checked by follow-up discussions with respondents, or by mixing and cross-checking evidence from the different approaches. But there will always be interpretation, whether in structuring reponses in advance or interpreting them after collection. The care with which this is done and its publication is important for both peer and lay review.

Could the environment or the culture have influenced answers?

Naïve in the first flush of positivist fervour to research I used both interviews and questionnaires with students in a training college for teachers. In the group discussions that followed I found they had given me the answers they thought I expected of future teachers, not what they really believed. Abandoning the original study I published the results as 'Environmental influences on responses to questionnaires', a fine example of the art of Texas sharpshooting, drawing the bull's eye around the bullet hole (Shipman 1967). Where the questions are asked or questionnaires completed can also affect results. Using the headteacher's study can produce very different responses to those received after school in a pub.

As serious as a threat to validity is the use of questionnaires across cultures. This is not just a concern about language and questions, but about values, about the meaning of social situations set up during research and about the way both researcher and respondent may construct very different understandings of what is going on. The misunderstandings under the Banyan trees in Controversy 4 are an example. More recently feminist researchers have criticized predetermined, prestructured questioning as manipulative and authoritarian (Harding 1986). They recommend interviewing at depth, focused on feelings and insights. Conventional research can be patriarchal, racist and ridden with social class attitudes.

The questions in tests

The development of tests from the end of the nineteenth century was stimulated by hopes of improving the human lot. It was reinforced by the drive to appoint and promote on the basis of merit not birth. But one century's search for justice can be the next's short-sighted injustice. The balance sheet is still debated, particularly where it concerns intelligence-testing, which received most investment in the first half of the twentieth century. Today there are thousands of standardized psychological tests and their construction has influenced all examination and assessment, as well as popular versions in the media. They help us to categorize, select, diagnose. Even those who reject tests as scientistic have qualified through examinations, trusted because they are controlled, standardized and public. These are the minimum conditions for claiming scientific status outlined in Part One. Above all, standardized tests are carefully planned and justified. They are a useful basis for examining questions that often lack that preparation.

There are tests, such as the Repertory Grid Test, that are designed to allow individuals to construct their own personal way of making sense of their relationships (Kelly 1955). But most are designed to compare individual performance with group norms, or against predetermined criteria. That makes them useful for selection, for ranking, for comparison in the case of norm-referencing and for assessing levels of performance by criterion-referencing as in the case of national curriculum assessment. Research into school effectiveness, into the relative attainments of specified groups, into individual strengths and weaknesses rest on tests and public examinations. They are often hidden under the statistics, lost in publication, abbreviation and republication. They are also the concern of those who observe natural situations, for the actors are in a world organized through such assessments.

Test construction flourished in the last quarter of the nineteenth century, with Galton in Britain, Cattell in the United States, Binet in France. Across the twentieth century test development and modelling human intelligence went hand-in-hand. There have been major scandals as reported in Controversy 7. Yet testing is now an integral part of the modern world, a part of the attempt to introduce merit into the division of labour that started in Britain in the 1850s. In the 1970s testing and public examination were under attack in education. Since then the amount of testing has increased not diminished, particularly with testing related to the national curriculum and the drive to monitor and improve the performance of schools.

As research tools, tests enable large amounts of data suitable for statistical calculation to be accumulated cost-effectively. They make it easy to match individuals and groups for comparisons. But their validity should always be examined. Their face validity, whether they look convincing, can be suspect. Content validity can be challenged if items are meaningless to those being tested. Concurrent validity can be challenged because no two tests will be focused on identical attributes. Construct validity, using actual behaviour for comparison, can be frustrated because the latter can be inconsistent. Finally, predictive validity is often low. The use of intelligence-testing in selection for grammar-schooling was an unhappy example.

Here is a typical test-based study of teacher stress unusual for the care taken to describe the procedures used to collect and analyse data (Punch and Tuettemann 1990). The test used was the General Health Questionnaire (Goldberg 1972) with an alternative scoring method developed to produce a normal distribution more suitable for statistical manipulation (Goodchild and Duncan-Jones 1985). The study shows a very high level of teacher stress compared with the general population and with other professional groups in Western Australia. It also relates this stress to conditions in secondary-school teaching.

There were 789 returns from the mailed questionnaire. Those who sent incomplete forms or were senior masters or mistresses were excluded. That left 574 for analysis. The number of questionnaires mailed is not stated. Did those who respond feel more or less stress? Were those who threw it away more or less stressed? Were the 574 those who had not been promoted? Was that a factor in their stress? The General Health Questionnaire was scored in different ways because Goldberg's original method was unusual, using four choices to stop 'middle users' opting for a neutral, 'maybe' response. The consequences of this are unpredictable. Goldberg also admits that the questionnaire was open to faking and could misclassify people who are only experiencing a temporary crisis or have become used to their symptoms: all conditions familiar to teachers (Shelley and Cohen 1986). Finally, the relationship between school factors and stress may be statistically significant, but 85 per cent of the variance between teachers is not accounted for by the nine school-related factors included in this study.

None of these criticisms necessarily challenges the conclusion of this study that teachers experience high levels of stress. It is in line with other contemporary evidence, suggesting concurrent validity. It is a convincing study using a respected questionnaire. But even with the care

taken over test design, doubts remain. Yet most questionnaires and interview schedules have nothing like the investment made in test construction. The problems in the use of the latter are a warning that the former
may be suspect. All are subject to problems over validity, response and
their relation to the reality being investigated.

The control and validity of interviews

The choice of interview or questionnaire and the form of the questions
used depend on whether priority is given to breadth or depth, on the
resources available, as well as the subject itself, particularly its sensitivity. The interview can be flexible, can obtain precoded reponses, can
probe deep, can be adjusted to circumstances, can increase rapport or
sustain detachment. But the cost may be a reduction in control or an
increase in artificiality. There is often a choice between tight structure,
closed questions and quantitative analysis and flexibility, open-ended
questions and qualitative accounts. Reliability and validity tend to be
incompatible. But both extreme positions, one emphasizing the need for
control, the other the need to preserve the natural situation, require planning, care and the full publication of what was done and why.

The classic case of the way answers can be given as questions are
asked is Pfungst's investigation of Clever Hans, a horse that could solve
mathematical problems, spell and identify musical notes. Van Osten, his
master, made no profit from the act. Experts were baffled until Pfungst,
by carefully controlling the environment of the act, found that Clever
Hans could answer correctly even without the question being asked
(Vogt and Hyman 1959). All animal trainers depend on the ability to
detect slight, even involuntary clues, such as a tensing of the muscles.
Interviewers and human respondents are likely to be just as perceptive
as horses.

Scientistic or interpretive?

The best documented accounts of scientistic interviewing on a sensitive
issue are still the Kinsey Reports (Kinsey, Pomeroy and Martin 1953).
First, the subject was clearly defined as sexual behaviour, not attitudes
towards it. The questions were asked directly to minimize interaction.
The interviewers trained themselves to look squarely at the subject
and to move inexorably from factual background to intimate detail.
Questions of the 'Do you . . . ?', 'How many times?' were fired rapidly,
giving little time to think. Any attempt to brag or to compare with the
performance of others was stopped. There was absolute privacy and no
hint of behaviour being judged right or wrong. Kinsey and his colleagues trained themselves in this quickfire, dead-pan style and learned
the coding system so that respondents only saw symbols being recorded.
They were reinterviewed 18 months later to check reliability. Kinsey

himself carried out 7000 interviews, each lasting more than an hour. He died in 1956. Royalties from his books still support the Kinsey Institute at Indiana University, a research and information centre on sexual issues.

At the other end of the spectrum of research employing interviews on an even more sensitive issue is a study of the pressures exerted by men on young women in sexual encounters (Holland *et al.* 1995b). This study was urgent as the sexual safety of women was threatened by the AIDS epidemic. Ensuring their own safety meant that women had to be prepared to be socially assertive, in control of their own sexuality and, if necessary, willing to lose a valued relationship. The research was designed to examine the pressure exerted by men and ways of empowering women so they could confidently negotiate such sexual encounters.

The research was based on interviews with 150 young women in London and Manchester. These interviews were designed to allow free-ranging responses. Thirty-nine women gave accounts of pressure from men to have sexual intercourse. The accounts collected were then analysed and the use of persuasion, coercion, alcohol and force reported. In ten cases the women described sexual abuse as a child. This emancipatory, empowering research is aimed at producing a model of positive female sexuality from the responses of the women affected. The detached 'Kinsey' style of interview would have eliminated those unrestrained responses. Hence the interviewing was designed to encourage unforced narrative.

These two examples illustrate contrasting approaches to asking questions in social research. The difference lies partly in aims, one collecting quantitative, the other qualitative evidence. But the difference also lies in the social science dominant in the 1950s and 1990s. Kinsey worked when Psychology was largely behaviourist and Sociology positivist. By the 1990s these had changed to mainly cognitive and interpretive respectively. Feminists had by then exposed the male-centredness of previous social research, adding to the attacks on claims to objectivity and supporting emancipatory and critical social science. Further, as the aims of social science changed from explanation to understanding and as the consequent claims for social research became more modest, so did the techniques for collecting evidence.

Are validity and reliability incompatible?

The conflicting assumptions and methods of asking questions increases the need for readers to be given a clear picture of why and how research was organized. In survey research designed to collect data for statistical analysis there may be reliability but little validity if the subject-matter is sensitive or threatening. In interviews designed to encourage freeflowing recall, reliability may suffer from both the licence given the respondent and the scope for interpretation by the researcher. The underlying discontent of *The Affluent Workers* of Luton may never have been uncovered by the interviewing technique used. But listening to tapes of unstructured interviews aimed at preserving the natural situation often reveals leading questions and hints from researchers that are missing from the academic paper reporting the work.

The undermining of validity and reliability in research using questionnaires and interviews can be reduced by careful preparation. The Census and other government surveys are conducted by interviewers who undertake a training programme that includes tests of skills, practice in the field and checks by supervisors. Comparisons of trained and untrained interviewers show that the former achieved more successfully completed schedules, received fewer refusals and reported fewer who had 'gone away' (Durbin and Stuart 1951). Training is usually associated with quantitative surveys. But it is equally important where the aim is to collect spontaneous accounts. It can reduce the interference from an obtrusive, unsympathetic or overfriendly researcher and ensure that time, place, use of notebook and tape-recorder do not affect responses. Thus careful preparation can raise both validity and reliability. This applies in particular to the increasing appreciation of the importance of the social interaction in all interviews.

Who was being interviewed?

Social scientists tend to focus on vulnerable groups not only in the hope of helping them, of changing the system that produced the vulnerability, but also because such groups can tell us important things about the way we live together. But the vulnerable can easily be led to answers in questionnaire and interview. The situation is asymmetrical. The initiative, information and power is with the researcher. This is why feminists object not just to the male language of social research, but also to its patriarchal assumptions. Researchers may be nervous at the start, but soon act confidently. But each respondent comes to a potentially threatening situation. Validity is at risk. Most of us feel uneasy as we enter a room or are button-holed in the street to be interviewed. Groups of most interest to social scientists can be terrified. Minority groups often live with the fear of exposure.

The problems arising from the asymmetry in asking questions are often unpredictable. Children can seize on answers they think are required by the adults interviewing them. They can also act docile and attentive, while being deceptive. They can grab at hints offered to provide some sort of answer rather than using the 'don't know' option. That is a skill that is learned in school. But there the teachers are trained to communicate. Researchers can treat children as rather dense foreigners, inadvertently encouraging the child to play the game and give this apparently simple-minded adult the answers required. Old folk are similarly prone to grab at answers and take the opportunity to have a nice chat. The interviewer struggles to get the questions in against the old person's insistence on discussing the negligence of the local council or neglect by their family.

A researcher such as Mac an Ghaill, interested in researching oppressed groups, has to use a mix of observation and informal discussion merging into unstructured interviewing (Mac an Ghaill 1994). Thus a study of Black gay students in school could focus on their sexuality or on the heterosexual climate in which they work. Any approach is made more difficult by the alienation of all students and their consequent suspicion of researchers. Mac an Ghaill, working as a teacher but researching in the emancipatory, critical tradition, relied on getting to know the students, discussing life histories, collecting accounts and assessing the culture within the school. Any formalized approach would have been fruitless.

Researchers become expert in using particular methods. They write books about them. They are members of specialist academic communities. They are often personally concerned in their subject matter. J. and E. Newson, authors of a series of books on childrearing, have described how this interest coincided with their own parenting (Newson and Newson 1976). An interest developed in whether other parents hauled the baby into their beds as he or she screamed, whether they fed by schedule or demand, whether they read and believed baby-books. This interest in what ordinary people were actually doing as distinct from prescriptions of what they should do and academic treatises on why they do it, led to an offer to allow health visitors to interview for the researchers. From there the work developed into a series of major research programmes.

To get information from the mother, in her home, without distortion, Newson and Newson developed interviewing they describe as an art form. The aim was natural communication between persons interested in childrearing. Tape-recorders were used to enable the intervewer to give full attention to the mother. The problems revolving around control and spontaneity were thought through as experience was gained. My own admiration for the work of the Newsons results from the honest way they have described the evolution of their work in relation to their personal and professional development. The research is on an important topic, the methods were carefully thought through. There are full accounts of how and why the surveys were designed and implemented in a distinctive style. Above all the work has been published in a language that could be understood by those who provided the information and would be interested in it.

Class size in primary schools

Early small-scale studies of the effects of streaming, of the teaching of reading, of the impact of different teaching styles, of the impact of nursery-schooling often reached firm conclusions on the basis of comparisons between groups of children that were immediately influential. Many years and hundreds of research reports later the issues remain unresolved. Increasingly expensive research has uncovered the complexity of what were once seen as straightforward issues.

Nowhere is that early impact more apparent than in research on the relationship between school-class size and attainment. It seems common sense that smaller classes will have higher attainment. They are a priority for teachers. Small teaching groups are one reason why parents pay for private schooling. But this research often made headlines because it contradicted existing beliefs, broke the consensus, was discordant.

Three early reviews of the many, largely small-scale studies all concluded that if there was any relationship, large classes tended to contain children whose attainments in basic skills was higher than that of their apparently more fortunate peers in smaller classes (Fleming 1959; Rossi 1970; Powell 1978). There followed a number of large-scale studies confirming these discordant results. The *International Study of Achievement in Mathematics* covering 132 775 children and 19 000 teachers confirmed that countries with the largest classes tended to get the best results (Husen 1967). The usual response to this early research can be found in the Plowden Report on primary schooling (Plowden Report 1967). Faced with their own survey results that large classes seemed to achieve more, the Committee concluded that reduction in class size should remain a priority.

This early research was crude. The large-scale projects often calculated class size by dividing the number of children in a school by the numbers of teachers, making an allowance for administrative responsibilities among senior staff. Even where class sizes were assessed directly there was an assumption that these remained constant, where in practice teachers often adjusted size to the task in hand. There was only rarely any attempt to look at the way different-sized teaching groups affected children of different ages, abilities and backgrounds. Nor was the teaching style used in groups of different sizes or in different subject areas usually taken into account. Poor attainers may be placed in smaller classes for remedial purposes. The highest attainers may be placed in larger groups with the best teachers. Popular schools attract motivated children and can afford to have larger classes. Smaller classes may encourage individualized methods that are very difficult to organize successfully. The real benefits of smaller classes may come below 20 and the real disadvantages appear above 40. But comparing existing classes usually means that most will be in the 25 to 35 range where differences may not be that significant. The key factor may be the attitude of the teachers involved (Burstall 1979). If teachers adjust to small class size it may make a difference, but class size by itself may not be the decisive factor. Finally, the age of the children may be important. Primary-class sizes have always been above those in secondary schools and there may be important age phases where intensive attention from teachers pays off.

The growing realization that crude comparisons could be misleading meant that researchers became wary of class-size research just as the educational context changed. The movement to a child-centred primary education aiming at maximum individualization of learning was given official approval in the 1967 Plowden Report. Small classes were favoured because they made this individualized learning possible. Since then there has been a rapid change of official policy. The child-centred movement came under attack, culminating in *Education in Schools* (DES 1977a), which described the child-centred approach as a trap for less-aware teachers. From thereon small classes were suspect because they tempted teachers to excessive experimentation.

In the 1990s there is pressure to increase the amount of whole-class teaching. School inspectors in particular swung from encouraging child-centred to recommending teacher-centred learning. Class sizes began to rise after decades of falling. The evidence that larger classes raised attainment was no longer unwelcome to government although still outrageous to teachers. The focus of research switched to school effectiveness. From that research the little that touched class size was cautious. Mortimore and his colleagues in the Inner London Education Authority (ILEA) confirmed that the effects were only marked outside the range of classes sized under 24 and above 27 (Mortimore *et al.* 1988). This research also found that attainment was slightly higher in smaller classes.

Pressing for a return to the class teaching of basic skills in primary schools, Her Majesty's Inspectors argued that reducing class sizes could have a low priority as there was no strong link between the numbers in a class and the quality of teaching and learning (OFSTED 1995). This report by Inspectors has been attacked for ignoring the lessons of class-size research (Day 1996). The Inspectors' report actually says little about whether children would have done better in classes of a different size. It ignores evidence about the teacher stress once sizes increase. The availability of research that seemed to deny that class size was an important factor in the attainment of children was a support for an attack on poorly organized individual and group work and for pressure to return to more formal methods.

The early research pointed the way to better research design, and also to the complexity of the issue itself. It required extensive social engineering. It arrived from Tennessee (Word 1990). This was a large-scale follow-through study. It was genuinely experimental. There were 7000 children aged 5 to 8, in 300 classes in 80 schools followed-up for four years. The children and the teachers were randomly allocated to classes of different sizes. Here for both Reading and for Mathematics small classes did seem to have an impact. Further, this impact was most marked when size was under 20, even more marked under 15, and most effective of all under five. However, the effects remained modest. Nevertheless, this has been influential research. Faced with an unexpected windfall of a billion dollars to spend on education, the Governor of California, looking at the Tennessee evidence, opted for reducing class sizes for the 5- to 8-year-olds to an average of 20.

The reception in Britain was predictable. First, Blatchford and Mortimore (1994) welcomed it as the first genuine experiment, with the necessary randomization to control extraneous factors. However, caution was still necessary. It's wise to wait a little for later criticisms. Even the most sophisticated research may not cover all the complexities that surround even an apparently straightforward issue such as the relation of attainment and class size. Thus questions remained, despite the optimism of Blatchford and Mortimore. How was the sample eroded over the four years? Did the teachers know they were part of an experiment? Did they have an incentive to get the results obtained? What teaching styles were adopted? Were there factors that could have confounded the results regardless of the randomization? An example of such a factor soon came from outside education. In a study of 10 000 high schools in North American school districts between 1960 and 1992, Hoxby (1996) found that unionized schools spent more, had lower class sizes yet had less competition between schools and higher drop-out rates. Somebody is always moving the goalposts.

The really critical analysis of the Tennessee research came in December 1996 (Prais 1996). First the results were challenged by recalculating them on a 'value-added' basis. Now, for Mathematics and Reading class size seemed to have a negligible effect. Second, that effect was achieved at a very high price. A 1.6 per cent increase in scores on the Stanford Achievement Test required a 60 per cent increase in teaching cost per pupil. Third, there was a disadvantage in being in a smaller class in the second year. Did the testers produce this by over-generous marking at the end of year 1? Did the teachers prepare children for the test? Third, and most worrying, 108 children were moved between classes as 'incompatible'. This was done at the request of teachers and parents. Not a lot out of 7000. But that number of children, particularly at one or other end of the spectrum of ability, could account for the small differences.

Blatchford and Mortimore concluded in 1994 that this Tennessee study meant that research into class size and attainment should have a high priority in Britain. Prais reached the opposite conclusion. Such research should stop and resources be given to research on teaching styles, class organization, textbooks, where the cost-benefits were higher. Further, more research and reanalyses will follow. But conclusive evidence is unlikely. This simple issue actually involves many of the problems that account for the unresolved educational controversies in this book.

CHAPTER 7

Variations on the experiment

The experiment is the model of scientific method. It is rarely appropriate outside the psychological laboratory in social research because the control exercised disturbs the natural situation and the use of random allocation to experimental or control groups is usually seen as unacceptable social engineering. Yet it is these procedures that eliminate the influence of confounding variables and enable causes to be separated from, yet related to, effects. The same features of the true experiment that make it such a powerful way of finding the causes of effects, of explanation and hence of prediction, also reduce the validity of the experiment for examining the human condition.

The impossibility of organizing true experiments accounts for the embarrassment of researchers when asked why it is that they cannot be certain whether streaming, or large classes, or progressive methods, or comprehensive schooling, or this or that way of teaching reading actually work, or even whether you can find what distinguishes a good from a bad school. It may be that even if the necessary social engineering were possible, the results would still be inconclusive. Random allocation to this or that school might remove current confounding factors such as social background and attainment at intake, but by the time the results were available everything would have changed, particularly as those involved would learn from being in an experimental situation and may have acted to affect the results. Examples of such flaws in an apparently true experiment on the relation of class size and attainment can be found in Controversy 6.

While true experimentation is rare, there are a range of natural experiments in social research. Indeed, even researchers who are scathing about scientific method are still attracted to the natural experimental situation. That includes comparisons and follow-up studies. In this chapter quasi, correlation, *ex post facto* experiments and evaluations are considered. None of these have the control and randomization that marks true experimentation. Yet all aim at showing how events are related, how one event leads to another, how means achieve different aims. They share with the experiment a concern for the relation between events. Indeed the rejection of scientific method still leaves a concern with causes in social research. Behind the rhetoric that interpretive research is concerned with understanding there are often conclusions that explain how this is the consequence of that, as well as an assumption that confounding, extraneous factors have been excluded by research design.

It is, however, the control and randomization that lead to conclusions about causes that makes the true experiment rare in examining human behaviour in social situations. Researched and researcher interact and learn from each other. That is a long way from the situation in the diagram below. Random allocation to experimental and control sample, tight control over the intervention and testing at start and finish to measure attainment are rarely either realistic, practicable or ethical when the subjects are human. It is possible to allocate volunteers at random in a Psychology laboratory, but that is not a natural human situation. The control means a level of constraint that can not only be objectionable but create artificiality. Researched and researcher are thinking humans who will always interact and interpret and hence reduce control.

The diagram shows the simplest experimental design. It starts with random assignment to the experimental or the control group. That assignment controls all the independent variables, providing the numbers allocated are large enough.

	Observation	Intervention	Observation
Experimental sample	1a ⟶	(cause) ⟶	2a
Control sample	1b ⟶		2b

1a and 1b could be observations of identical empty gas jars. The intervention could be to fill one of these with damp beans. 2a and 2b are observations made after a few days have passed. Any differences observed at the end of the experiment can be attributed to the insertion of the beans. The confidence in this conclusion depends on the control exerted to ensure that all conditions were identical for experimental and control gas jars, apart from the insertion of the beans. Extraneous factors have been controlled. There are many variations on this basic design, but it is the model from which causes can be inferred and predictions made.

The problems of this design with humans as subjects start with the rarity with which random allocation is possible, outside the psychological laboratory. In education it is rare because teachers will not allow existing classes to be disturbed or redistributed to form experimental and control groups. To the disturbance is added the reluctance to confine the experiment to only some of the children. So researchers have to use existing classes in a quasi experiment, thus increasing the chance of extraneous factors intervening. Furthermore, in real life, control cannot be maintained for any length of time. Extraneous factors accumulate as the days go by. Thus the maturation of children in the experiment, or unanticipated external events, can be influential. Where tests are used at start and finish, progress can be boosted by familiarity. Children can drop out of either experimental or control groups. Frequently these educational experiments lack a control group. This 'before and after' design is very common in assessing the impact of a new teaching method or curriculum. But as there is no control, there can be no certainty that extraneous factors have not caused any differences that occur.

The dependence on natural experiments in social research mirrors everyday attempts to explain events. We try to understand the present and predict the future by looking at the past and at trends. We compare events that occur simultaneously and draw conclusions from this co-incidence. We look at an innovation and assume that we can detect its impact over time. We examine current conditions and look back to find causes. This is experimental thinking, incomplete and fallible. In every-day life and in social research there is a concern to find connections, causes, trends. Fortunately the experiment is also the easiest method to question over validity, reliability and generalizability. Most evidence from natural experiments collapses once queried because the complex-ity of the human condition means that extraneous, confounding vari-ables provide too many alternative explanations to the one chosen.

Quasi-experiments

The most common compromise in social scientific experimentation is to use existing groups. In education, for example, there is reluctance to place children at random into classes that will be taught in one way while others are used as controls. This also applies to allocation to streamed or unstreamed, large or small classes, comprehensive or selective schools. Social engineering of this kind is seen as disturbing and unfair. Yet random allocation is the way confounding factors are eliminated. With-out it you can't be sure that something unforeseen isn't influencing the results. Confounding variables cloud the issue when randomization is sacrificed. In studies of schools, that applies particularly to factors in the social background of the children and hence their attainments at intake. An approximation to true experimental design is achieved by matching children in existing classes or schools for age, sex, social class, ethnic mix and so on before comparisions are made after the introduc-tion of some innovation. But there is never complete confidence that there are not unmatched differences between the experimental and control groups which can confound results.

Experimental designs are undermined by difficulties in sustaining con-trol. The researcher departs and the teachers amend the teaching method, the streaming arrangements, the school organization. Many will claim they never really joined but were just helping out. Extraneous factors can add up over time. Children leave and others join. The tests used become familiar with practice. Some teachers will give children special help on these tests. Factors not even considered in the planning turn out to be influential. This is disappointing, but often the intervention, be it a new curriculum, teaching method or management technique, should not be expected to have impact. I once had to refuse to evaluate the impact of £10 000 allocated to the teaching of Asian languages in London schools as part of an Inner City Partnership scheme. Peanuts in, peanuts out.

The relaxation of experimental design can be seen in test-intervention-retest designs. These are once again common sense. They are frequently used in practice. You test children on their times running a mile, then give them a vitamin C tablet once a day and retest a week later. Their times improve and you are on to something important. But there is no control. They would improve as a result of running it at least twice. Many who enjoyed it would have tried it mid-week. Others want to impress and get into training. The worst runners would make sure they were absent second time, thus lowering the average time taken. The reliability of experiments decreases as they leave the laboratory for real situations. Confounding factors intervene and, more importantly, are often not even known to exist by researchers.

Correlation research

Correlation measures the association between two variables. Politicians, inspectors and teachers assume there is a relationship between the resources for education, teaching styles, class size, streaming, school organization and so on and the attainment of children. With fully randomized and controlled experimentation rarely possible, correlation research is often used to confirm or refute these hypotheses. Yet this research has left most of these relationships in dispute. The first correlation studies are exciting and help to clarify the factors involved. The evidence on the relationship between social class and educational attainment dominated the sociology of education across the 1950s and 1960s. The publication of *Fifteen Thousand Hours* in 1979 stimulated studies of school effectiveness studies based on correlating intake, output, processes and output factors (Rutter *et al.* 1979).

With computing, the statistical treatment of data has become more sophisticated. But this does not diminish the arguments between researchers over the validity of these techniques. The technical arguments frustrate those who fund research and have to make policy and professional decisions. Often the funds given to researchers seem to have been used only to produce articles criticizing someone else's work. The disputes over a complicated issue such as school effectiveness summarized in Controversy 10 also ignore the quality of the data that has to be used and which is collected by busy teachers not by the researchers. Those who fund and use research want decisive results even where the subject is complicated. The researchers are in an impossible situation. Their results are as controversial as the situation they reflect. Those that simplify are likely to mislead.

There is a final problem with correlation research as it relates variables such as the amount of homework and attainment, or teaching styles and pupil progress. In a true experiment the cause and its effects are determined by the research design. But while homework and attainment are correlated, which 'causes' the other? High attainers will find homework more rewarding. Doing more homework can raise attainment.

Reversing the assumed direction of causality doesn't necessarily lead to nonsense. Bedwetting children soon become anxious. Criminals soon become unemployed. Children bring up parents. Low attainment lowers self-image. Disease soon leads to poverty. Effective schools attract efficient headteachers.

Ex post facto *experiments*

Ex post facto, or after-the-event research designs are once again an everyday way of approximating experimentation. Here, an outcome is noted and related to some past event or trend. In the ambitious early days of Sociology the grand narratives of Comte, Marx, Durkheim and others started with an analysis of emerging industrial societies and traced human history back to formulate laws or stages of development. This *ex post facto* reasoning is universal. It is bread and butter for historians and palaeontologists, used in everyday reasoning and basic to social science. We all understand the present by tracing events back to the past.

Ex post facto experiments are exciting but can have little validity or reliability. They are first steps in building models, developing theories. A search through history, a reconstruction of trends, thinking over possible relationships soon produces apparently original hunches. But the events have happened. They are beyond the control of researchers. They are already history. Confounding factors are forgotten. The causes identified could never have been used to predict. There are countless other factors that could have contributed to the event and these are often beyond recall or study. History and much social science is written by the winners. *Ex post facto* research is, however, about real situations. It can relate factors in new, brilliant ways. *Das Capital* is the result of *ex post facto* experimentation amid the facts and figures found by Marx in the British Museum. It is a triumph of human ingenuity and scholarship. It is also a warning that limitations increase with the ambitions of authors.

Evaluations

Evaluation is another universal activity, ranging from the experiment with random allocation to experimental and control groups through illuminative evaluation based on participant observation to the everyday comparison of the effectiveness of two washing powders. This sounds easy. But once again there are difficulties in measuring effects and ensuring that confounding factors are not interfering. The rarity of decisive evaluations in education illustrates the problems. Since the establishment of the Assessment of Performance Unit in 1974, there have been a succession of quangos set up to monitor standards in schools.

But we still have little idea whether standards in schools have risen or fallen. Nor has 150 years work by Her Majesty's Inspectors. What is now better known is the complexity of that question.

Evaluations are compromised art. Art because each requires a tailor-made, imaginative design. Compromised because researchers usually have to do the best they can as the innovation is usually designed elsewhere and running before evaluation is considered. The art of evaluation is the adaptation of research designs to produce 'maximally useful' evidence within a specified budget (Cronbach 1987). It is a lucky evaluator who has influenced the intervention to ensure effective evaluation. In 40 years of research I cannot remember being involved in the initial planning of a programme before being invited to evaluate it. That is why natural experiments are common and true experiments rare. Researchers have to compromise.

The initial teaching alphabet (i.t.a) was one of the best-funded evaluations of the teaching of reading. It was evaluated against traditional orthograhy (t.o.) (Downing 1964). This was used as a Controversy in the first edition of this book in 1972. Despite all the funds available from the i.t.a. foundation, a second evaluation by Downing that included random allocation to i.t.a and t.o. reading groups, 17 other evaluations and a review of all the evidence (Warburton and Southgate 1969), the conclusion was that more research was needed. That common conclusion follows from the inevitably compromised design.

The Schools Council, established in 1964, funded evaluations of many of the 100-plus projects it sponsored. At first, a conventional test-intervene-retest design was used, sometimes with comparison with a control group. Curriculum evaluation then moved to specifying objectives and measuring the effects of intervention by assessing how far these had been achieved. The problem here was that curriculum developers were reluctant to specify measurable objectives or puzzled by what this meant. Even where teachers accepted the objectives, they soon replaced them with their own. By the 1970s, the reaction against scientistic research had spread to evaluators. The fashion shifted to illuminative evaluation. But that was overtaken by the need to evaluate the national curriculum after the 1988 Education Act and the demand for performance indicators and the monitoring of the performance of schools.

The influence of the controlled, randomized experiment continues in social research. It promises certainty. But only in behavioural Psychology can the methods of physical science be approached, and then the control exercised trivializes the relationships examined. Yet once that control is relaxed, claims to explain and predict have to be abandoned. Correlations cannot sort out the direction of influence. *Ex post facto* research cannot separate the key from the extraneous factors. Evaluations are usually inconclusive because aims and the innovation tend to be both vague and implemented in uncontrolled ways. Nevertheless, evaluations, *ex post facto* research and correlation studies have produced a wealth of insights, hypotheses and above all introduced realism into innovations where ambitious claims have been made. Showing that complex situations are rarely open to improvement by simple inter- ventions is a perennial task for social researchers.

Finally, the technical difficulties of design should not conceal the problems in the data available in most experimentation outside the laboratory. However sophisticated the statistical treatment, garbage in, garbage out applies. When researchers depend on busy teachers and administrators to supply test and examination scores, social background data and indicators of school organization, much data will be missing, some intentionally. Further, the reasons for this will often not be known. At the Auld tribunal examining the William Tyndale case, the crucial evidence was attainment scores of the children in the school compared with the averages across the Inner London Education Authority. But when numbers were low in the relevant school classes and absences high, averages would be misleading. The evidence was made available but the researchers persuaded the tribunal that it should not be used. Researchers do their best with the data they receive in correlation, *ex post facto* and evaluation designs. Sometimes they have to fight to stop garbage going in and coming out smelling of roses.

Experimental and experimenter effects

The laboratory experiment and the collection of data that is used in quasi-experimental and correlation research are open to the subleties of social interaction. This is inevitable in the former. In the latter, pupils, teachers, administrators, examination boards and researchers, have also interacted and interpreted. Experimental effects arise in responses to being involved within an experiment. Experimenter effects arise from the influence of researchers on their subjects. These are closely related to similar effects in observational and survey research. Further, just as the former can be sources of grounded theory, so effects within experi- ments have produced important insights into human behaviour.

The classic study of the effects resulting from being involved in an experiment was at the Hawthorne works of the General Electric Company in Chicago between 1924 and 1927 (Roethlisberger and Dickson 1929). These studies started by experimentally manipulating the material con- ditions in work to gauge the effects on productivity. It was noticed that even when conditions worsened, productivity increased. The methods and the logic behind them have been severely criticized (Carey 1967). There seems to have been managerial pressure to raise productivity. Two workers were dismissed for being hostile to the experiment (Bramel and Friend 1981). But the explanation launched the human relations approach to management and gave social science the Hawthorne or experimental effect. The workers responded to being involved, to being observed, and this was more powerful than the material changes introduced.

In the Hawthorne experiments an extraneous variable was identified as a powerful influence on behaviour and hence as a useful management tool. But the true experiment depends on control. This is difficult even with rats in a maze. They may seem to have learned which of a line of flaps releases a pellet of food when pushed, but may actually have sprinted down the corridor flicking every flap as they passed until one delivered the goods. Humans are even more skilled. As the researcher settles them down, explains what they are expected to do, eyes meet, muscles twitch and all the clues used by Clever Hans, multiplied by human skill, give the subjects clues to how to respond to please or annoy the researcher. Rapport is essential, but it opens the way to mutual influence.

Working with Jacobson, a school adminstrator, Rosenthal, an expert on experimenter effects, elaborated the Pygmalion effect (Rosenthal and Jacobson 1968). If experimenters can exert accidental influence in the tightly controlled experimental situation, teachers should be in a powerful position in the classroom to affect pupil performance intentionally. A smile could raise attainment. It improved self-image. The impact was dramatic. In the Inner London Education Authority, the Research and Statistics Group had to urge caution as politicians pressed for the scrapping of pupil records in schools in case these damaged the self-esteem of those who were doing badly.

The concern among researchers was the small number of children who gained, the small gains, the later deteriorations. More children deteriorated than gained (Thorndike 1968). There was criticism of the tests used and the way results were analysed. The teachers involved did not seem to have taken the experiment very seriously. Once the data was released to other researchers, slipshod design and implementation, inconsistencies and the overdramatization of results were reported (Elashoff and Snow 1971). Nine efforts to replicate the Rosenthal and Jacobson experiments failed. However, few read the *American Educational Research Journal* and Pygmalion effects passed into the folklore of teacher education.

Burt rumbles on

In 1974, Kamin published an analysis of Burt's statistical work, concluding that it was not worthy of scientific attention (Kamin 1974). Two years later Oliver Gillie alleged in the *Sunday Times* that Burt had fabricated data (Gillie 1976). Since then accusations of fraud have appeared regularly, alongside the occasional defence. Here the focus is less on whether Burt was guilty or innocent than the implications of the case for social research. We will probably never know the truth. It lies hidden in the attempts of an old man to keep providing evidence to support the case for the heritability of intelligence as this came under increasing attack from the environmentalists in the latter half of this century. It is an important reminder of the need for research to be made fully public and exposed to criticism.

Burt lived from 1883 to 1971. He published his first academic paper in 1909, was knighted in 1946 and went on publishing to his death. There was also a consistent theme running through his work. Intelligence was inherited and this, not any environmental factors, largely predetermined future intellectual capacity. A typical interpretation of this view for teachers states a 'A child is born with a certain quality of intelligence which is constant through life. This capacity cannot be increased in any individual, but certain rare illnesses may cause it to be diminished' (Dukes and Hay 1949). Fortunately, even if psychologists believed this, fewer teachers did and parents very sensibly saw it as nonsense. But its pessimism hung over British education for most of the twentieth century.

The authoritative source on what happened is Hearnshaw's biography (1979). He delivered the address at Burt's memorial service in 1971 and was asked to write the biography by Burt's sister. As he wrote, the accusations appeared. Reluctantly Hearnshaw concludes that there had indeed been fabrication and falsification of evidence. Burt must have added to the numbers of identical twins used to assess the relative effect of inheritance to build up the sample from 21 in 1955 to 53 in 1966. The papers by Miss Conway and Miss Howard were probably written by Burt and a paper in 1969 tracing standards from 1914 to 1965 must have been fiction.

The response of the psychological community is documented in the *Bulletin of the British Psychological Society (BPS)*, particularly the 'Letters' section (*Bulletin of the BPS* 1976 to 1980). At first, Burt's peers took sides. The Society remained neutral. But by 1980 the evidence was overwhelming. Following the 1980 Annual Conference, a Supplement to the *Bulletin* announced the Society had concluded that 'There now seems no reasonable doubt that Sir Cyril Burt perpetrated a fraud in that he fabricated data and that is inexcusable because it offends against the principles of science' (*BPS* 1980).

The correspondence in the *Bulletin* has continued into the 1990s. Sometimes it has centred on trying to find Miss Conway and Miss Howard. They probably were real people picked out as authors by Burt. But there is no evidence that they ever did the research. Second, there have been vigorous counterattacks (Joynson 1989). These suggest that Burt didn't fabricate data, but retrieved it from work done decades earlier. The picture of this eminent man searching through old papers stretching back into the 1930s, to build up a sufficient sample for statistical calculations on the situation in the 1960s is, however, even more worrying than the possibility of outright fraud. These counterattacks produced another upsurge in correspondence in the *Bulletin*, including attacks on Hearnshaw (*BPS* 1992). Members asked for the Society to reconvene a symposium. But the Council was now cautious, saying that in the light of greater experience there was no longer a corporate view (*BPS* 1992) The campaign under the title 'Burt Recidivus' had achieved its goal, even though Hearnshaw and other critics remained adamant that the case against Burt was overwhelming.

The present state of this personal tragedy is that articles and books are appearing with titles such as 'Sir Cyril Burt: last casualty of the Cola War or the first in the battle for political correctness?' (Ward 1993) or Cyril Burt: fraud or framed? (Mackintosh 1995). The damage from the extreme version of the heritability of intelligence has been done. But it cannot just be left as an unfortunate episode resulting from the attempts of an old man to support the theory that he helped to construct and had made him famous. That ignores the crucial point. How could this happen in a scientific community which is assumed to guarantee the validity of its work through the informed scrutiny by friendly-hostile experts? What happened to peer review?

Whether Burt started to fabricate data in 1909 (Kamin), 1943 (Hearnshaw), or on his retirement (1950) there was a long time in which his peers remained silent, particularly as Kamin maintains that every article from start to finish lacked the detail expected in a scientific paper and that the statistics presented were barely credible. The answer starts with Burt's age. He was a Victorian. Like most of his contemporaries he was influenced by the Eugenics movement. The genius behind this movement in Burt's youth was Sir Francis Galton, Charles Darwin's cousin. Burt met Galton as a neighbour while a young man and like many of his generation used him as a model. He was McDougall's first student at Oxford. He knew Spearman who pioneered the model of intelligence based on a general 'g' factor that was fixed at birth. He worked with Karl Pearson who pioneered correlation as a statistical tool. This was a group of bright men, with bright relatives and friends, pressing for the improvement of the human stock and seeing intelligence-testing as an important means for achieving this.

The modelling of intelligence, its testing and the application of this evidence to education gave Burt great authority. Nor was it undeserved. Burt used his great influence to improve the education of the less able in a lifetime of service to government committees and as educational psychologist for the London County Council between 1913 and 1932. He was a powerful man, intellectually and physically. He had extraordinary energy. This led to posts that enabled him to dominate the psychology of education. He chaired boards of examiners, sat on appointing panels, advised the growing body of educational psychologists in local authorities. Above all, he edited the *British Journal of Statistical Psychology* and sat on the editorial boards of many other journals. This enabled him to publish when he wished, without refereeing. It probably enabled him to plant articles praising his own work, and led to protests when he changed work submitted for publication. Significantly the criticisms when they came were from an American and a journalist. The only British contribution to the exposure was from Clarke and Clarke (1974).

Why did it take so long for the cries of anguish from parents that the intelligence of their children was not fixed at birth to be heard? The human waste that resulted was criminal. In the case of the claim to have achieved cold fusion on a bench-top described in Chapter 9, it only took a few months for replications to be organized and for the scientific community to demand that research diaries be produced for scrutiny. In social science there is still a lot of research that is published, but produced in private.

In Burt's case his working life was spent jotting ideas and calculations on paper and storing these in ever-growing piles in the office and then at home. The mysterious increase in the number of identical twins across the years, the sudden appearance of statistics showing a long-term decline in attainment, can be seen as the results of an old man scrabbling around among piles of old papers and piecing together an argument to support the case he had promoted all his life. I still have boxes of mysterious punched cards, audiotapes without dates, pages of calculations whose origins are beyond me. Improved data storage may mean that the consequent confusion will be avoided in future, but to ask a social scientist for research diaries would seem a very strange request to many. Nor is replication possible in most cases. The research setting and the interaction can never be recalled in any but the most artificial laboratory experiment.

The response of the *BPS* to the Burt case was first to delay making a decision. Then they reluctantly confirmed fraud. Faced with a counterattack they maintained they could no longer take a view. This isn't cowardice. It isn't possible to be decisive when the issue is human research into human behaviour. Social research involves researcher and researched in interaction, interpretation, learning. Even retrospective accounts can give only the researcher's reconstruction and that is an inevitably favourable interpretation.

The Burt case is yet another confirmation of Popper's insistence that there should be no deference in science (Popper 1945). The pioneers in an academic subject are rightly honoured, but later often derided as the next generations demolish their early work. But behind the argument about Burt as fraud or framed were the 11-plus failures, the secondary modern schools, the advice to teachers that intelligence was fixed at birth. This hopeless picture harmed generations in Britain in mid-century and without the deference shown to Burt and others it could have been avoided.

CHAPTER 8

Reinforcing the evidence

It is easy to miss the involvement and excitement of the researcher in written reports. This often appears in autobiographical, retrospective accounts of how the work was done, but these are often folktales, with the researcher as hero and the procedures as quest (Atkinson 1996). In practice, during the initial thinking, design, implementation and analysis of results and publication, researchers are focused, alert to ideas and events that seem significant. This involvement ranges from intense reading round the subject, discussion with anyone interested and awareness of relevant events around them. Simultaneously they exclude factors not deemed relevant. The published account is the product not just of a clearly defined research act but of inclusion and exclusion over time.

The published account of research consequently does more than describe what was done and what was found. It locates the work into the context of related theory and evidence, recent history, policy and practice, often in a shorthand by the use of references. Frequently the article or book collects other work together and draws new messages from it. Anecdotes, incidents and statistics are added. The effects of this selectivity are the subject of Part Three of this book. Here the concern is with the use of documents and other sources in the light of the accumulated evidence from historians, literary critics and postmodernists as well as social scientists on the problems of using texts and other sources as evidence. Just as observation, the asking of questions and experimentation are affected by the unequal relation of researcher and researched, so the relation of author, context and text affect the way evidence is documented.

Triangulation

In a court of law, a jury is presented with evidence from expert and lay witnesses using a variety of forensic, documentary and observational sources. In everyday life we cross-check, believe that two heads are better than one, seek second opinions and other points of view. In social research this is labelled triangulation. It has been further elaborated into time, space, person, respondent, datasource, researcher, theoretical, methodological, partnership, team, multidisciplinary, reflexive and no doubt many other triangulations (see, for example, Denzin 1970).

These are all ways of reducing dependence on the one-person, one-model, one-method collection of evidence.

The possible elaborations of triangulation are endless. It is useful as a check on the credibility of evidence but not an insurance against the unreliable and invalid. Nor, if all the approaches are racist or sexist or culture-bound or redundant, is it a guarantee of objectivity. It became popular in the 1970s in research on the curriculum and on school organization, particularly where the primary aim was to help professional practice. Evidence was reported or played back to the teachers and pupils who provided it and the comments were collected. Teachers were also asked to comment on the interpretations of the researchers (Walker and Macdonald 1976). Clearing all accounts with all respondents, however, can lead to endless circulations, discussions and alterations. This can become indulgent, with the method of clearance becoming the major product of the research. Triangulation is an important warning against dependence on single sources of evidence. But even the most straightforward situation can be constructed so that each participant has a singular interpretation of its reality. Sooner or later researchers publish and however hard they try to reflect the range of views, it is their account which appears.

An example of the explicit use of triangulation is the study of Bishop MacGregor School (Burgess 1983). Here ethnography is supplemented by analyses of letters and documents available in the school and from autobiographies and diaries prepared by the teachers. Interviews with teachers then clarified the diary entries. A common triangulation is the use of two or more methods of data-collection and the use of documentary evidence in discussing the published results. It is common to check observations against interviews, to use interviews as a check against questionnaires. A questionnaire is usually designed to probe the same topic from different directions. An attitude scale will have many questions focused on the same trait.

Triangulation is a reflection of the difficulties faced by social research in producing valid and reliable evidence. Observations of the effect of increasing the pressure on the volume of a gas with temperature constant are unlikely to differ significantly. But in all but the most controlled laboratory experiments, social research involves human subjects and human observers actively interpreting what is going on. Triangulation became more important once social research moved into the field. Controversy 5 illustrates the ease with which alien situations can be misunderstood. If the aim is to change the world rather than to study it, the sole view can be confidently stated. But triangulation is an acknowledgement that social research is rarely decisive and that confidence is often best established by collecting and presenting a number of viewpoints.

Documents and references

Papers from the 1970 Annual Conference of the British Sociological Association changed the sociology of education. They were published and republished (see, for example, Brown 1973). But one paper by Bantock was never included. Its theme – that sociology could learn from literary criticism – was apparently judged to be unrelated to the interpretive sociology being proclaimed. Bantock was a right-wing critic of education, and approaching retirement. As an historian he was concerned with the use of texts and in the intervening period his concerns have overtaken social science, mainly through translations of French philosophers such as Derrida. Publication includes and excludes. The criteria for selection can include many other factors than the quality of the work itself.

The need to examine texts for validity has long been a concern of historians. The blunt assertion that history is written by victors remains the basis for most perspectives. But this does not only apply to the hacks and sycophants who flattered their patrons. It applies to the student presenting a thesis for examination, to the author sending a typescript to a publisher and to professional associations selecting papers for a conference. The smoothest career path in academia is pursued by working within an established academic community. But in social science this is often risky. This book is replete with evidence hailed in one decade, derided in the next. *Schooling in Capitalist America* appeared in 1976 and was contradicted by the same authors in 1986 in *Democracy and Capitalism* (Bowles and Gintis 1976, 1986). Its obituary and an indication of the interest created in its brief heyday was published in 1988 (Cole 1988).

Documented evidence is not only an interpretation of evidence at a particular time. It is simplified, translated, summarized, used as a reference, stripped of its theoretical and methodological justifications, applied to new cultures and contexts until it is outdated and placed in the archives. Caution is necessary during the elaboration. Primary sources usually have sections on methods. These can be pruned in books and disappear when compressed into a reader. Open University readers are particularly prone to this pruning. It is revealing to reconstruct the path of evidence from its collection to documentation. Census data is basic, the collection carefully planned, the analysis scrupulous. But it is provided by a citizen, tabulated by another in a way determined by experts who serve government, and interpreted by readers. Juveniles appear in old folk's homes and pensioners in schools. Documentation is a long chain of events open to interpretation and misunderstanding.

The Inner London Education Authority never intervened in the work of its Research and Statistics Branch in the 1970s. As long as basic statistics, evaluations of selected programmes and a flow of useful information were delivered the researchers were left to negotiate, organize and deliver their own research programme. But negotiation meant discussions with advisory and consultative committees, officers of the Authority, teacher unions, headteachers, parents, all of whom had the ear of politicians, pressure groups and the media. Negotiating access, releasing data and preparing the Authority for the publication of *Fifteen Thousand Hours* (Rutter *et al.* 1979) meant hovering like an anxious midwife over the birth of someone else's baby. The book itself went through the normal cycle from instant media headlines, exaggerated political response, academic critique, provision of funds for follow-up, to a place in the history of educational research and the status of 'Rutter' as meaningful reference.

Documents, and the references to them that refute or support an argument, are then live not dead sources. They are themselves interpretations of reality, further interpreted as references. There are three useful cautions over their use. First, researchers, like the police, courts, doctors, teachers, examination boards and so on fit individuals into categories and hence identify them as delinquents, patients, bright or dull. Thus Cicourel (1967) sees records not as a source of information on delinquents but as a way of showing how they came to be labelled as delinquent.

Second, the historian's warning remains important. The great tradition of Marxist historians in Britain have a very different view of the path to modernity than those who write about the great and the good. The Levellers and the Diggers, the Luddites and the Chartists were rarely mentioned in Whig histories of the rise of Britain to Great Power status. The history of the victors, of those with power, of the educated, the literate is inevitably one-sided. This still applies. Those with unpopular views can still find that the way to publicity is blocked.

The third caution arises from postmodernism. Here truth is reduced to interpretation. Authors impose meanings on reality and document these as if they were reality itself. Thus it is necessary to get behind the text, beyond the author, to peel away the rhetoric and fathom the underlying assumptions. Here in the postmodern critique the models, the structures, the systems, the narratives imposed by social scientists and others have to be scraped away. Just as feminists have rejected the idea of objectivity, so the postmodernists debunk the aspirations of social science. Documentary evidence needs to be deconstructed to get to the buried assumptions that can seduce the unwary reader into believing that a final explanation has been presented.

The reconstruction of events from documents

Much social research involves the construction and reconstruction of transactions and organizations from documents as a supplement to new evidence. The shorthand of the reference is used to flash evidence to readers who are assumed to know the body of work referred to or are in a position to consult. But social research also uses documents as a primary source to reconstruct past events and life histories. From the 1920s, sociology at the University of Chicago concentrated on the subjective interpretation of the situation and maintained this tradition until it became dominant elsewhere in the 1960s. The most influential work was *The Polish Peasant in Europe and America* (Thomas and Znaniecki 1918–1920). This book was the subject of five studies of the use of personal documents sponsored by the American Social Science Research Council in 1938.

The story of the letters, autobiographies, diaries, newspapers and court records is a Marx brother's filmscript. They came to the notice of Thomas when a pile of garbage thrown from a window landed at his feet and he noticed and picked up a letter. An advertisement placed in a Polish emigré journal produced offers of more reminiscences about life back in Europe. Newspapers were collected on a visit to Poland. As the First World War broke out, a courier, trying to escape being called up for the army, abandoned more documents as he fled. Polish immigrant societies documents in America and court records were added to the accumulating piles. A long autobiography was added. Blumer, looking at this data, concluded, rather kindly, that it was inadequate (Blumer 1939). This hardly mattered. Thomas admitted that he and Znaniecki were 'indisputably in the wrong' to give the impression that the book was founded on the data.

Gottschalk, Kluckohn and Angell (1945) looked at the use of these documents as historians. Were they authentic? Were the sources of information reliable? Was the evidence credible? Were the witnesses informed and honest? Did they report accurately? Was there corroborating evidence? How did it relate to other relevant evidence? Once again there was doubt about both reliability and validity in this case. To an historian it all looked very vulnerable.

The doubts of the evaluators about the documents has not, however, diminished the influence of this study. The reason can be seen in another evaluation by Dollard (1935). His concern is with the way sense is made of material, on the way it is pieced together until it is meaningful. Here Thomas and Znaniecki developed the idea that reality is what people define as real. That insight has become the major assumption in sociology as the emphasis swung to interpretation, to understanding, to the construction of reality. The documents used were a hotchpotch. But they were approached and organized by using a model of the way humans make sense of the world around them that has survived decades of scientism and now flourishes.

Many other Chicago classics have stood up to re-examination years after publication (Plummer 1983). Shaw's Jack Roller, a mugger, was interviewed by Snodgrass up to 50 years after his life history had been published (Shaw 1931; Snodgrass 1978). Sutherland's *Professional Thief*, Chic Conwell, was also interviewed long after his history had been written and he was presumed dead. He turned out to be an articulate, entertaining and shrewd man very capable of writing accounts of his crimes (Sutherland 1966; Snodgrass 1973). The authors were inevitably hustled, but the thieves confirmed the validity of the accounts published.

These life histories established Chicago as the centre of a distinctive style of social science. The studies of neighbourhoods and urban life have remained influential. But life histories and the use of documents are a minor interest in social research despite the insights gained.

Documents, used with discretion and triangulated against other sources, can provide important evidence and those who have lived through important events are usually very willing to describe their part in them. Goodson, for example, has located curriculum change into its context by relating interviews to histories of curriculum change (Goodson 1982). It is too promising an approach to be left to historians and journalists.

Statistics as indicators of reality

Statistics are convenient summaries of behaviour, of changes and of the relation between events. But there can be a big gap between them and the reality they represent. They are the product of a series of interpretations that convert complicated behaviour and attitudes into simplified form. For example, the Home Secretary pronounces each year on the annual statistics of crime. In September 1996 they showed rises, particularly in crimes involving violence. But this was placed into the context of two years when the number of crimes seemed to have fallen. But the British Crime Survey carried out every two years by asking a sample of people whether they had been victims showed a rise not a fall from 1993 to 1995.

These statistics are typical in being determined by the actions of harassed officials using categories that rarely fit the human behaviour under review. Criminal statistics start with the police and depend on crimes being reported. But this in turn depends on the public and police policy as much as criminal activity. For example, across the period 1993 to 1995, reporting was affected by the tendency in high-crime inner-city areas for property insurance to become too expensive for many people. For those who ceased to insure, the incentive to report crimes against their property fell. Further, police were often too busy to respond to and record minor break-ins. Some crimes receive publicity: their reporting increased and consequently criminality seemed to have increased. Police start a campaign against mugging or burglary and the crimes recorded rise. They have to meet new targets for reducing crime and the number recorded falls.

There is also no necessary connection between the number of crimes, the number of criminals and the impact on the public. One criminal can commit 100 crimes or 100 criminals one each. Police can concentrate on stopping street crime and hence neglect housebreaking. Every public outrage affects the distribution of the scarce resources available to Chief Constables. The statistics that finally appear are the product of changing policies, interpretations from the bobby on the beat up to Scotland Yard and the Home Office. Similar events account for disputes over any set of statistics, however official. While a station constable, I ejected a woman four times when she came in to complain of being beaten-up by her boyfriend. The fifth time I was not on duty and my relief decided to proceed. Some months later I was reprimanded as the accused went down for a three-year stretch. It is on such judgements that statistics are built.

The same problems with statistics can be found in education. Years spent serving on committees of the Schools Council, the Assessment of Performance Unit, the Records of Achievement Steering Committee and the Schools Examination and Assessment Council were a merry-go-round. Every new committee faced the difficulty of converting the attainments of individual pupils into statistics that reflected the performance of teachers and schools. That is a difficult task, discussed in Controversy 10. It isn't easy to identify the contribution of the school by some measure of the value added, rather than relying on output measures that reflect intake and social background factors. To take account of all the factors that contribute to attainment in school means collecting more data than anyone is willing to provide – and even with that provided it can still produce statistics that may approximate the complexity of the factors involved but does not yield the simple answers wanted by those who make policy or implement it.

Statistics are nevertheless essential because they are often the best we can do to get simplified pictures of the human condition. The Big Mac index, basing the real value of currencies on the price of a burger in different countries, suffices as a ready guide. Economic statistics never predict accurately, but they are still indispensable. But official and other statistics can construct as well as reflect reality. This is why questions on ethnicity are controversial when they are prepared for the Census. It is why women struggled to remove categories such as 'housewife' from surveys. In the 1960s, scores on intelligence tests were used to categorize children. Those scoring 50 or below were classified as 'ineducable idiots'. Statistics label and typecast as well as simplify.

The way statistics are collected, analysed and presented should always be remembered. This is a human and fallible process. It is also wide open to slight adjustments that can produce important changes in the picture presented. The Government Statisticians Collective have described how figures are produced inside the bureaucracy of the Government Statistical Service (1993). Massaging is arranged through changing the definition of terms, the extrapolation of trends, adjusting figures to affect indexes and manipulating the boundaries of categories. Figures carry authority and consequently attract a lot of political attention.

It is this power of statistics that makes them so suitable for supporting an argument. But like social science itself they both reflect the social world and help to structure it. Criminal statistics give some idea of the state of public order. But they are also used by politicians, the media, criminologists and people in the street to influence the debate over how best to maintain that order. Assessments and league tables are powerful instruments in pressing for educational change. In just the same way researchers use statistics as supports for evidence and also to reinforce the arguments for change. Their validity, reliability and strength as a base for generalization still need to be questioned. That is often difficult, for statistics are reductions of complicated human transactions to figures through a series of calculations and interpretations. To clarify the relationship of figures to the reality they reflect is in many cases impossible for the outsider. But that is the case with most research. It is usually impossible to provide the reader with sufficient information about what was done and why. Thus it is time to move to Part Three and to examine the way social research is made public.

Personal, Professional and Political Influences

Suffer the little children

Children are awkward subjects for social scientists. As long as it could be claimed that the causes of their behaviour lay with god or the devil, expert confidence was boundless. This carried over into social science. Laws of development could be plotted and predictions made. Children were ideal subjects for experimentation. But in a more secular world and with the switch to an interpretive social science aimed at understanding human behaviour by getting to know it in the terms used by those involved, there is a problem. How can we understand children? For those who argue that only women can study and understand women, Blacks understand Blacks and so on, it seems insuperable. Participant observation is still going to be intrusive. How do you interpret the babblings of babies, the fancies of infants? Perhaps it is best left to the poets? Yet advice proliferates.

The confidence of the behaviourists who ignored the meanings behind the behaviour they observed led to advice to parents in the 1920s and beyond that was often obscene. Across the years, on the advice of experts, children have been separated from their parents, thrashed, restrained and mutilated by often well-meaning adults. I was myself snipped of my tonsils, adenoids and foreskin at an early age. My mother fled with me from Muswell Hill before the doctor, an admirer of Sir Truby King, did any more damage to my private parts. But she couldn't win. We moved next door to a member of the League of Health and Beauty who romped with her children naked around her lawn. I lived my prepuberty behind closed blinds. Any helpless human group is liable to be the victim of experts. Especially when they seem to live in a world of their own.

First, there are opposed conceptions of the infant. They have been viewed as little angels and little devils. For every Puritan stressing that the devil rocked the cradle there was another seeing the child as the best copy of Adam before he tasted of Eve or the apple. For every evangelical warning children to contemplate themselves on their death-beds, in their coffins, in their graves there was a Wordsworth or a Blake expressing their innocence. This romanticism reappears in the writings of Sully, an early Professor of Psychology, the founder of the British Association for Child Study who in 1893 wrote, 'For us today, who have learned to go to the pure springs of nature for much of our spiritual refreshment, the child has acquired a high place among the things of beauty' (Sully 1893: 2).

Second, there has been a continuous concern over the apparent sexual activities of infants. In the nineteenth century masturbation came to be seen as the most frequent cause of insanity through 'debility of the brain'. Thumb-sucking was seen as a closely related substitute for this depravity. The advice was to keep an eye on children in the lavatory, tie their hands outside the covers at bedtime, make them wear sheepskin nightclothes or splints and, if such restraints failed to stop them, resort to stinging ointments and cauterization (Comfort 1967). It was a hard life for the sensual child.

Third, experts swung between recommending emotional warmth and cool detachment, in line with their assumptions about the natural good and evil of their charges. Watson, the 'father of behaviourism' in psychology and an influence on Truby King, the dominant influence in the interwar years in Britain, warned that infants must be treated as adults, never hugged or sat on a lap. Just in case the maid got too friendly she should be replaced after a brief period. 'If you must, kiss them once on the forehead when they say good night. Shake hands with them in the morning' (Watson 1928: 8). I was a child under that regime. By the time I was a father, the advice had been reversed. Parent and child now had to enjoy 'the fun morality', whether it was fun or not. You and she were obliged to be happy. Note too that girls had suddenly joined humanity.

Hardyment (1983) traces five stages in this advice. From 1750 to 1820, nature and reason, represented by Rousseau and Locke, competed as guides for literate parents and teachers. From 1820 to 1870, mothers not philosophers were in command – at least in the middle classes. From 1870 to 1920 science and sensibility took over, influenced by Sully and the Eugenics movement. From 1920 to 1946 growing superior children dominated, with Watson and Truby King the major influences in America and Britain. From 1946 the emphasis was on spontaneity. This has also been described as the era of the 'fun morality', based on interpretations of Freud and Piaget and popularized by Spock (1963). Now you had to enjoy parenthood. This division into periods is inevitably crude but it does relate childrearing practice to developments in psychology. Hardyment (1983) wisely sees her history of childcare not as a substitute for books on how to do it, but as their antidote.

Advice for teachers changed in line with that for parents. From Sully at the end of the nineteenth century, psychologists have promised a science of education. But the evidence was inconsistent and changed rapidly. Training, learning by rote, punishment to inhibit bad behaviour, rewards to promote the good were based on behaviourism. The influence of McDougall persisted into the 1950s and modelled children as driven by instincts which often had to be repressed and always had to be directed. By the 1930s Freudian ideas were entering teacher-training and repression was seen as dangerous. The very privileged went to progressive schools where inhibitions were removed. A.S. Neill, the most famous progressive headteacher of this period, was psychoanalysed by Reich who is famous for founding Orgonomy which still

survives with its *Journal of Orgonomy*, its American College of Orgonomy and its support for Bioenergetics and Radix. Here the concern is
with achieving orgastic potency. Summerhill must have been fun. As
must Malting House School, described in Chapter 9. Here, from 1924 to
1927, Susan Isaacs, influenced by Freud, developed ideas which she later
introduced into teacher-training at the London Institute of Education.

Here then is the ideal subject for social scientists wanting to influence the human lot. Large numbers of parents are confused and worried
about the new arrival. The proud grandparents are only too keen to give
advice. 'Feed when it cries.' 'Feed by the clock.' 'Cuddle it if it cries.'
'Let it cry.' 'Ensure that its feet are flat on the ground when sitting on
the potty.' 'It's wetting the bed because you've repressed it.' The mix
of folklore, religious belief and psychology persists. There has never
been a Golden Age. The history of childhood is littered with the dis-
gusting (DeMause 1974). Every book seems to put forward conflicting
views. It is a rare opportunity for fame and fortune. Watson's *Psychological Care of Infant and Child* sold over 100 000 copies (Watson
1928). Spock's *Baby and Child Care* had sold over 15 million copies
by its 148th printing in 1963 and was still going strong.

There is a final warning about the way we have made children suffer
through dogma. It will not stop. The Orkney child-abuse cases were
still unresolved as this revision was written. Barbara Wootton (1959),
reviewing the report of the Younghusband Committee on Social Workers,
pointed to the glib way they accepted that rapid advances in the social
and behavioural sciences had made it possible to provide a better service. To Wootton all that could be put into a lecture on human needs,
motivation and behaviour, the areas where advances had been assumed,
were disconnected fragments from psychology and obvious truths that
sensitive and intelligent people have always known. The article is titled
'Daddy knows best'. At least much of the paternalism has since been
exposed.

CHAPTER 9

The author in time and place

The key questions in Chapters 9 and 10 are about the intentions of authors and whether they provide enough information about what was done and why to allow the reader to review. If the work is under the title of social science or research, authors have an obligation to provide sufficient information to enable that review to take place. If the intention is to raise consciousness the reader should still be able to review and hence there should still be sufficient information to allow this to happen. That accounts for the questions in the Introduction to this book. It is legitimate to reject the relevance of validity and reliability, but the reasons for this should be made clear for the reader, particularly if the intention is to raise awareness of the distortions in existing beliefs and practices. Any enquiry may lead to important knowledge. But the assessment that determines credibility depends on the provision of information. Withholding it places the work among the arcana, the secretive, that have so often been the basis for the very authority that is being attacked.

The rejection of the idea of value-free social science came late to Britain and the United States in the late 1950s and 1960s. To Mills (1959) it had enabled abstracted empiricism to dominate social research. To Gouldner (1962) value-free social science had led to moral indifference. Fact-gathering had served governments, but ignored important political issues. Marxists have long emphasized that knowledge is constructed along social class lines. The attack on value-free social science has been extended by feminists and anti-racists. There is now general acceptance that reality is indeed constructed socially and much research is directed at understanding that construction, or exposing the injustice involved. Thus research ranges from description to prescription and authors from the dutiful servants of administration to outraged protesters. The reader has to rely on the published account and is rarely in a position to know the personal and political motives of the author.

There is another rarely discussed feature of authors that can affect publication. They usually work in universities and colleges that are assessed on the amount of work published. Careers also depend on getting into print. It can be an inexorable pressure and can result in shoddy work. But this pressure is exerted on authors who are also excited by writing, keen to influence, anxious to add to the public good. Most publications soon disappear into archives. But reputations are made, classics are recognized and anything in print can bring a glow to the author. It is therefore tempting to boost the product and forget the reader. Limitations can be concealed by the conventions of reporting. Peers, often a small group of specialists, know more than enough to agree on credibility. But the language, style and referencing make this impossible for anyone in another discipline or interested in the application of the evidence.

The author

One of the unfortunate legacies of science after Newton has been the magisterial style of reporting research. This is didactic dead-pan, developed as a way of silencing critics by suggesting that the knowledge presented was discovered impersonally, not the product of our human and hence fallible ingenuity (Watkins 1964). The result of not revealing autobiographical detail forces the reader to guess how the ideas were generated. Further, the jargon makes it more likely that its further interpretation will be distorted. The conventions of reporting do not just make peer review difficult. To Medawar they mean that the scientific paper is a fraud, suggesting that research starts with an open mind and the collection of facts and ends in revelation (Medawar 1964).

In the natural sciences didactic dead-pan restricts the numbers who can engage in peer review. But they are well organized for rapid and often decisive peer review. Their methods and subject-matter also make the replication of experiment possible. In the social sciences replication is impossible unless the subject is trussed up like Anthony Hopkins in *The Silence of the Lambs* and about as unnatural. In all social research the human complexity of both researched and researcher makes autobiography even more important than in the natural sciences. Yet the same conventions are applied by authors and the jargon pastes over what really happened in the research, even where the intention is to understand real-life situations. Reporting fully is in any case difficult. Thus in observations of natural situations there has to be radical abbreviation for reporting what went on and it is often impossible for a reader to do more than guess what might have happened in that pub, among those trainees, in those toilets. Yet this information is essential for assessing evidence that may be used to guide policy and practice.

The announcement and demolition of claims to cold fusion took only a few months (Huizenga 1993). Pons and Fleischmann announced room-temperature nuclear fusion on 23 March 1989. Four watts out for each one in from a bench-top, test-tube experiment was a sensation. The researchers spoke to a world conference on 12 April 1989. On 13 April 1989 the US government instructed 12 national laboratories to replicate the experiment. On 11 July 1989, Huizenga's panel, formed to advise the US Secretary of Energy, reported that the experiment was not convincing. In little over two months there was a decisive evaluation. On 30 May 1992 the Professorial Board at the University of Utah voted against retaining Pons and Fleischmann on its staff. That doesn't mean that cold fusion is impossible. Pons and Fleischmann remain at work.

It is impossible to envisage a social scientific case that would create such a furore. The American Sociological Association's programme committee, established to find out why the sudden end of communism in Russia and Eastern Europe was not predicted by social scientists, inevitably concluded that there should be another committee set up (American Journal of Sociology 1995). The retrospective studies of social scientific classics in this book show unreported evidence that could have altered the results, but nothing in social science could match the impact of the reluctance of Pons and Fleischmann to make their research diaries public. But no such check would be possible in most social research. Fieldnotes would be too personal to be critical evidence. Further, very few social researchers seem to bother to write them and those that do are reluctant to let them be reviewed (Broad and Wade 1982: 78–9).

The difficulties over peer review when humans are involved as subjects can be illustrated from biology and archaeology where most of the documented scientific frauds have been detected (Kohn 1986). The most fascinating case is Piltdown Man. The remains were discovered in 1911 by an amateur, Charles Dawson. He dug up more skeletal bits and pieces in 1913 and 1915. The key to the evolution of man seemed to have been found. The support of experts such as Smith Woodward seemed to confirm *eoanthropus dawsoni* as the missing link between ape and man. The remains were sent to the Natural History Museum in London.

There were a few odd things about this discovery. Dawson was an amateur. After he died in 1916 nothing else was found despite much shovelling. None of the discoveries ever seem to be of women, suggesting Victorian and Edwardian male sensitivities. In 1948, however, new techniques showed the Piltdown skull to be not more than 50 000 years old. Then bits were shown to be of different ages. Staining and filing were detected. The jaw was shown to be from an orang utan (Weiner 1955). The implements and fossils found nearby were also found to be frauds. A 'who dunnit' started that continues unsolved today.

The finger was first pointed at Dawson. But he would have needed help. Spencer (1990) saw Sir Arthur Keith as the culprit with fame as the spur. Other possible culprits are even more interesting. Sir Arthur Conan Doyle, whose Sherlock Holmes would have been useful in solving the mystery, has been suggested as the villain. So has Teilhard de Chardin, the French philosopher and mystic. Certainly they visited the site. By the 1970s another theory emerged. Experiments on forging human remains were found in a trunk in the Natural History Museum belonging to Martin Hinton. Had he tried to get his own back on Smith Woodward by planting the forgeries and leading Dawson to them? The plot thickened – but then the trunk seems to have been lost.

The importance of the Piltdown Man case is in showing not just that some eminent scientists are dishonest and others gullible, but that personal and professional pressures cannot be ignored in research. Somewhere in the Piltdown case there was jealousy and hatred as well as ambition. Even more predictable was the acceptance of evidence because it was expected. These eminent men were not exposed to public scrutiny until they were all dead. The dead-ends of all science, natural and social, occur when scientific communities are closed. The players in the Piltdown saga were all gentlemen with ideas of loyalty and honour that today are difficult to understand. Their disputes were private affairs. Yet exposure to scepticism is a price researchers and authors have to pay, alive or dead. That is the lesson Karl Popper taught us (Popper 1945). Closure is not only the enemy of science, but of a democratic society.

Pressures on the author

Authors are under pressures that can influence the way research is reported. Personal ambition is reinforced by enthusiasm to share the excitement of research results with others. Pressures from employers to publish drive them on. But they are also constrained by the specialized groups who research in the same area, who will perform the authoritative peer review, who hold the keys to approval and preference. They are also influenced by publishers and by the few who referee their work for publication. Getting into print is not just a matter of telling it as it was. The account is selective because space is limited, reference to related work is expected and there are anxieties about the response of the great and good and from the political, religious and social beliefs that enter our interpretations of what we have researched and written. It is all very well Popper saying that we should publish without deference, but in a book like this the threat of libel is real.

The most telling evidence of the way publication can conceal as well as reveal comes from retrospective critiques of classic studies. The *Polish Peasant* study described in Chapter 8 turned out to be based very loosely on the documentary evidence that was itself the result of farcical adventures. The results of the Hawthorne studies on which human relations models of good management were based seem to have been the consequence of removing those workers from the sample who did not seem to respond to warm human relations. In a third classic, the Lewin, Lippitt and White experiments on the responses of children to different leadership styles, one of the original researchers has described how he and his fellow researchers gave their all to their democratic but not their authoritarian or *laissez-faire* roles (Lippitt and White 1965). This experiment took place as the menace of Hitler was at its height and support for democracy would be expected. The researchers may have affected the work habits of the groups involved by their acting in the experimental roles they adopted. Fifty years later Spock was still using this experimnent to emphasize the benefits of a democratic environment for raising children because it encouraged self-discipline and cooperation (Spock 1989).

The critical post-mortems on these classic studies came decades after publication. In each case the authors seem to have been influenced by the political and economic climate in which they were working. Only when that climate changed was there the critical examination of the way the researchers came to their published conclusions. It is unlikely that only studies that have become classics were flawed. Nor were the researchers necessarily aware of the influence they were going to exert. These have remained stock references for more than half a century, apparently undiminished by criticism. They were outstanding contributions to social science. But their survival can only be the result of their support for the paramount values in Western culture.

However, there have been dramatic changes around and within social science and social research. Social scientists have responded with remarkable agility. The political collapse of communist states has weakened the Marxist interpretation of human history, culture and structure. Other metanarratives such as structural functionalism have been largely abandoned. Others such as globalization are now being promoted. Behaviourism has lost its dominance in Psychology and the attacks on psychoanalysis and particularly Freud's part in it have proliferated (see, for example, Grosskuth 1991; Masson 1992). But all these pale besides the growing influence of feminism and anti-racism. That impact has been described in Controversy 1. The problem may not be the pressures undermining the detachment of researchers and authors, but the assumption that social research can ever be objective, given the evidence available of class, racial and gender bias.

A look through my own writing in the 1960s and 1970s is consequently embarrassing, not just for the models used and the confidence that social research could be objective, not just for the emphasis on social class and the neglect of race and gender, not even for the use of 'he', the exclusion of women, or their invisibility in written accounts, but for blindness to the way reality was constructed and hence researched from a male perspective. Today it is legitimate to argue the case for objectivity as a goal against those who see all research as an attempt to persuade or raise consciousness. But yesterday's social research was male-centred. Tomorrow it will be shown to have some other bases for bias. Authors work under the spreading shadow of their own redundancy.

Some idea of the pressures on researchers can be gauged from a collection of retrospective accounts written to tell it as it happened (Shipman 1976). Lacey, starting out on the work that resulted in *Hightown Grammar* (1970), was advised by some colleagues to take a detached view of schooling, while others pressed him to take the lid off the grammar schools. John and Elizabeth Newson show how the birth of their own child focused their attention on childrearing as a topic. Douglas feels the weight of data from his longitudinal study bearing down on him as he selects what to publish. Ford looking back at her study of comprehensive education sees herself as having floated a counter-rumour because of her disgust at the replacement of one form of injustice in education by another that was more subtle and tenacious. Dale, seriously ill, trying to make up for lost time and to remedy a series of disasters, nearly falls under the wheels of a horsedrawn brewer's dray.

Some idea of the immediate pressures on researchers and authors can be gauged by asking questions about the work reported from conception and design, through implementation to presenting results and conclusions. Why pick this topic, model it this way, base it on the work of this academic group, choose these methods, this sample, that context, that evidence, that way of presenting and analysing results, interpreting them and drawing conclusions? Some answers may lie in the text. Others may be found in the introduction, the conclusions, the biography on the rear cover. If it's an article in the *Journal of Orgonomy* it will favour bioenergetics or orgastic potency. There are more than 100 titles in the helpful *Overcoming Popular Problems* series published by Sheldon Press, ranging from *Beating the Blues* to *Coping Successfully with your Irritable Bowel.* Family Systems Theory sounds academic, is referenced to works in psychology, but ends with 'Yearning for God – Bliss' (Bradshaw 1988).

Finally, the pressures on authors intensify as publication nears. Everything becomes relevant to the forthcoming work. This book, that newspaper contain related evidence. Personal and professional developments confirm or refute the forthcoming publication. Colleagues are bored, librarians stretched, computers burn out. For some, writing becomes a drug. They become entrepreneurs, with a staff to help them churn work out and even to set up publishing firms. It is addictive as well as professionally rewarding: a rare combination. For the reader it is a warning. It may be written in academic dead-pan, but it contains much personal investment. The detective work to review it has to go beyond the text itself. Few authors provide enough clues.

Researchers and authors follow conventions that conceal as well as reveal, include as well as exclude. It is safe for the winners of the Nobel Prize for the discovery of the double helix to publish an account of the close and exciting race to get into print before their rivals (Watson 1968). But short-cuts, the use of pipe-cleaners and inspired guesses are unlikely to impress PhD examiners. Significantly, the most amusing, critical and unconventional guide to doing social research has come from an established researcher who has published widely (Delamont 1992).

Researchers are always under pressure. It is often difficult to resist. Somehow or other those sponsoring research usually seem to get the results they want. The Church of Scientology International hires an independent research agency to question those who had bought a copy of *Dianetics: The Modern Science of Mental Health.* Seventy-nine per cent said that 'Dianetics changed my life,' and 90 per cent that it 'helps man improve his potential' (Church of Scientology International 1992). In the 1960s there were two surveys of religious education in schools in Britain, each using samples of around 2000. One of these, for *New Society*, concluded that 90 per cent wanted religious instruction in schools to continue. The other, for the British Humanist Society, concluded that there was no real expression of support for the retention of religious instruction in schools (Shipman 1988).

In research funded by the American Medical Association (AMA), Wiggins and Schoeck (1961) reported that the old were in good health, energetic, independent and secure within families and communities. This supported the case of the AMA against free medical care for the aged. Examination of this research showed that it had been loaded to produce these results and that non-Whites in particular were under-represented in the sample (Cain 1969). Ironically, Wiggins and Schoeck were the authors of *Scientism and Values* (1960) a book which warned against doctoring research results to boost its credence.

In some cases careers, funding and publication are in the gift of those in authority. This applies in all societies, but can be lethal in totalitarian regimes. From 1929 bourgeois elements in science were under attack in Soviet Russia. In 1936 the Medico-Genetical Institute was closed and Lysenko branded fellow biologists as deviationists. Hundreds were arrested and Vavilov, the leading Mendelian Russian geneticist, was arrested, sentenced to death and died in prison in 1942, the year he was elected to the Royal Society in London. Lysenko was honoured until the damage to Russian agriculture could no longer be tolerated. By 1963 Mendelian genetics was being openly discussed and after Khrushchev resigned in 1964, Lysenko was dismissed.

This disaster was a consequence of Russian leaders interpreting Marxism to dictate the rationale and direction of all science. No criticism of the official line was allowed. The harm done by sealing science off from international contacts was realized once the effects on agriculture and plant-breeding were realized. The overt pressure on science is heaviest in totalitarian regimes. It also occurs in democracies. American scientists suffered under the McCarthy witch-hunts in the United States in the 1950s. Around contemporary social research, social biologists are unwelcome and it's a brave social scientist who gets involved in the nature–nurture debate. The key to progress is open discussion and an unwillingness to defer to authority. But the price paid by the non-conformist can be high.

Pressures from the author

It is never satisfactory for readers to have to guess why this was selected, that excluded, but beyond seeing that Smith was male or female, holds a doctorate and works in X university there are often no more clues published. A few know that Smith led student revolts in the 1960s, wrote tirades against capitalism in the 1970s, joined the Conservative party in the 1980s and is currently the most reactionary referee and examiner in social science. A fictitious case, but it illustrates the difficulty for most readers when faced with an apparently authoritative work. The author knows the strengths and weaknesses. A few colleagues know why the work has a particular slant. Other readers have to guess. Publication is asymmetrical and hence never fully public. Even those refereeing an article or book, reviewing as peers or conducting a doctoral examination, have only the information that the author puts into print or volunteers in discussion. A lot has to be taken on trust or obtained from those who are in the picture.

This book contains many examples of influential research, ranging from classics to the trivial, which have later turned out to be flawed. They were reported so that readers had no chance to assess validity or realize that the aim was to make them aware that there was something rotten that needed exposing. The ease with which an author can boost research evidence has increased with the proliferation of publications. A few words tapped into a computer produces the necessary references. Those supporting the evidence can be selected. The often unsuspecting reader has been faced by apparently convincing evidence that culling criminals, sterilizing the unintelligent and controlling breeding across ethnic groups is the way to improve the human stock (Kühl 1994).

Fortunately the rapid increase in the number of journals published has provided space for exchanges in print between authors and critics. Here is one exchange consisting of four articles, all in one issue of *Educational Psychology* (Olssen 1993; Schwiesco 1993). Olssen starts by attacking educational psychology as pseudo-science because of its attachment to individualism and positivism. Schwiesco's criticism of this is that educational psychology is not overwhelmingly positivist, that Ollsen relies on the semi-coherent ramblings of a few French poststructuralists already past their sell-by date and that the subject is not a sham. In the response that follows, Ollsen thanks 'Joshua John Schwiesco' and says that he has completely missed the point. The main point made was not about positivism but individualism. Ollsen claims that he didn't write that educational psychology was a sham. His position was not poststructuralist, but a mix of Gramsci and Foucault. Schwiesco was given the last word in this exchange and it is blunt. Olssen is just plain wrong, having misunderstood both positivism and individualism and their connection in methodology. By the miracle of modern communication these exchanges are in one issue of a journal and between academics in the universities of Otago NZ and Reading UK.

The serious point here is that a similar exchange of insults could be arranged over any article, provided the editors know who is for or against. This rough and tumble is the stuff of academia. Printed peer review is often a polite dead-pan shorthand, full of thanks for the care taken over the review, spelling out forenames, scrupulously avoiding libel. In senior common rooms the references in print to ontological and epistemological inconsistencies are reduced to saying the article was rubbish. Often others will join the fight, to serve as seconds, or try to referee. Nor are such fracas unproductive. Once the gloves are removed there is more of a chance for outsiders to see not just limitations but the passion with which opposing views are held. It is by attempts to refute that leverage is exerted on established dogma. Feminists and Blacks had to undermine a social world defined by White, middle-class males. Working-class leverage remains weak, but the protesting voices are occasionally heard (Lynch and O'Neill 1994). If this book goes into a fifth edition it will become even more of a blow for the wrinklies' construction of reality.

This passion among researchers accounts for the intensity of the debate over the possibility of objectivity. Those who feel strongly want to change things. Research is an opportunity to do this while engaging in an addictive 'mental golden journey' (Delamont 1992). Few activities offer such a chance to combine to search for knowledge, to exert influence and to have fun. The serious side is that social research is important within the training and practice of professionals as well as providing many of the ideas that influence the way human affairs are discussed and decided. Authors never know when their tentative ideas about child abuse, false memory and so on are going to cause tragedies.

The first impact of researchers is on those studied, whether through questions, interviews, tests or observations. Many schools have been identified and harmed by researchers publishing without sufficient care over preserving anonymity. The majority of the 12 'Rutter' schools in inner London were identified by the press within days of publication. Other researchers, given access to inner-London schools, sensationalized their publication by changing the focus from the subject originally cleared. This provided one motive for writing this book in the 1970s, while I was Director of Research and Statistics for the Inner London Education Authority.

The open expression of feminist and anti-racist hopes of using research to raise awareness of injustice has been refreshing. In the 1960s, Ford's expression of her socialism in studying comprehensive schooling was a rarity (Ford 1969). A contemporary collection of articles on feminist research has the emancipatory motive up-front (see, for example, Holland, Blair and Sheldon 1995a). The convention in scientistic research, copying the style of the physical sciences as far as possible, concealed the human motives of both researchers and researched. Very often these were as critical and emancipatory as any feminist research. But the intentions were kept private and the conclusions needed careful reading to detect the subtle switch to prescription.

Finally, research rewards the researcher. Getting into print is essential for a successful academic career. Publication massages the ego. Living in the stockbroker belt, I find it safer to say I am a researcher than a sociologist. Being first in print has long motivated scientists. Disputes between Hooke, Newton and Huygens, between Cavendish, Watt and Lavoisier, between Davy and Faraday are part of the folklore of science. The race for the structure of the DNA molecule shows that the importance of being first survives (Watson 1968). Determination paid off by publication in *Nature* on 30 May 1953. There is less likelihood of any such breakthrough in social research. Consequently first publication is often in a book not an article. Hence the author goes direct to the public and the media, not to academic colleagues. This avoids the peer review and refereeing involved in publishing in a learned journal, but results in headlines and later, often dramatic, critical reviews from a variety of contrasting viewpoints.

Publication can hurt some people and help others. It can produce unexpected consequences for professional practice. It can influence the way people think. This varied and often unanticipated aspect of research makes it even more important to be open about its limitations. The uses made of evidence on intelligence or maternal deprivation, Marxism or cultural deprivation, Keynesian or moneytarist economics, had costs as well as benefits. The duty to publish so that an informed review can take place is a condition for any research under the title of science. It also increases the chances that evidence will not be stretched beyond its elastic limits as it is taken and applied by professionals and into everyday understanding.

The author in context

Authors inevitably generalize from snapshots of a changing context at a particular time. Those snapshots are taken from a specialized position. The date of publication, the country of origin, the specialism of the author can all be important clues for assessing the limitations of the published work.

The date of publication and of references in the text are readily available clues to possible redundancy. Books and journals stay on library shelves, on reading lists, beyond the point where they have been overtaken by events or overwhelmed by critics. McDougall's *An Introduction to Social Psychology* was published in 1908 (McDougall 1908). Its 31st edition was reprinted in 1963. It was on my reading-lists when I took a Postgraduate Certificate of Education in 1957, although its theme – that men were driven to act by instincts – did seem odd to a recently graduated sociologist. The emphasis on 'men' was marked in most of the readings. A recommended *An Introduction to Teaching* in 1952 differentiated the sexes as follows: 'Little boys are full of energy, mischievous in an open and whole-hearted way. They are destructive and noisy, lacking in imagination and sympathy.' Little girls on the other hand are described like kittens: 'delightful creatures, so graceful and playful. They have the most engaging ways and even if sometimes they are a little shy at first they make very attractive friends' (Barnard 1952: 28). Writing that today would get you arrested. Barnard continues to describe boys as more logical than girls with more developed powers of reasoning and abstract thinking. Professors of Education are of their time and place.

Even recent books soon become redundant. The introduction may give the date of completion. That can be long before the date of publication and years after the end of the research. Fieldwork for *Social Mobility and Class Structure in Modern Britain* started in 1972 (Goldthorpe, Llewellyn and Payne 1980). The manuscript was completed in 1978 and it was published two years later. A normal span from starting research to publication was Lacey's *Hightown Grammar* (1970). Based on fieldwork between 1963 and 1964, an article appeared in 1966 and the book in 1970. Foreign work requiring translation can be further delayed. Most of Durkheim's work was only published in English in the 1950s and he and Weber remain forever young as students reference them to the latest translations in the 1990s.

Social scientists are alert to the inevitability of change but, being unable to explain, cannot predict. Hence the decade between researching and the published work appearing on reading lists can make them look silly. Many were left blushing around 1990 when the USSR imploded. But so was I when functionalism was demolished in the 1960s. Postmodernist attacks on metanarratives, even more recent exposures of the fascist past of postmodernists, historical studies of Freudian and Jungian analysis, the attacks on Burt reported in Controversy 7 are only examples of the way social science moves inexorably on. The criticism that demolishes here also confirms there. The fittest generally survive. Science gains its authority from exposure to attempted refutation by critics. That can hurt.

The problems raised by time passing are exacerbated by generalization across cultural and national boundaries. The influence of the United States is powerful here because of the strength of its social science, the shared language and the takeovers of publishing firms to utilize an enlarged market. American psychology students willing to take part in laboratory experiments form frequent samples for generalizing to universal human behaviour. The meanderings of French intellectuals are applied to Anglo-Saxon pragmatics. A glance at any bibliography will show how reference is made regardless of cultural differences. In the controversy over school effects that ends this book there is evidence from countries all over the world with very different arrangements for schooling. Yet it is often mixed together as if context could be ignored.

Finally, the grouping of social researchers into scientific communities, networks and specialisms produces another basis for problematic generalizations. Becher (1989) has described these as tribes occupying territories of knowledge. As with all tribes they induct newcomers, protect their territory and mark it off by using a special language. Yet in print, particularly when the knowledge is applied to professional training or the wider human condition, the tribal lores are often combined as if their often very different assumptions and models could be ignored. The reader is consequently left without any way of appreciating the rationale behind the different special contributions. No coherent assessment is possible. Yet friendly but searching criticism is necessary by all readers. It is the basis for any claim by researchers to be engaged in social 'science', whether the aim is to study or to change the world. It is a safeguard against uncritical acceptance and the application of ideas that can later turn out to be invalid.

The publication of Piaget

Jean Piaget lived from 1896 to 1980. He was a biologist interested in epistemology, asking how we came to know and think. His doctorate was on the molluscs of the Valaisian Alps. Most of his life was spent as Director of the Jean-Jacques Rousseau Institute in Geneva, working on the development of the human mind. He maintained that this work had no direct lessons for education. Yet his work was used to justify child-centred, particularly Froebelian, ideas in Britain and was a major influence on the Plowden Committee Report on *Children and their Primary Schools* (Plowden Report 1967). The explanation of this anomaly lies in the way his research was used to recommend to teachers that young children learn, but should not be taught.

Criticisms of Piaget started to appear in the 1970s (Bryant and Trabasso 1971; Donaldson 1978). Since then his methods and their logic, his results and conclusions have come under fire. By the 1980s Piaget's research was being condemned as of no relevance to the classroom, the curriculum or to learning (Papert 1988). As Piaget had denied that it should ever have been seen as having that relevance, an examination of how his name became synonymous with progressive primary education follows.

There were problems in interpreting Piaget. He had a very difficult writing style. He spoke and wrote in French. When he lectured in England in the 1960s he spoke in French and with only a few notes. Summaries of his talks are prefaced by apologies for their incoherence (National Froebel Foundation 1961). The difficulty in interpretation enabled translators and simplifiers to insert their version of Piaget's findings. There was delay while articles and books were translated into English. Summaries of the work were then produced for psychology students. There was then further summary and simplification for application to education. Finally there were simple booklets designed for teachers in training. In the 1960s a Piaget publishing industry flourished.

Here are the dates of publication of Piaget's work on number. The research starts in the 1920s, is reported in journals and only 20 years later appears as a book in French. It takes another 20 years to reach the education of teachers in Britain in a very simplified form. By this time psychologists were beginning the research that was to expose the flaws.

1 *Le Developpement des Quantités chez l'Enfant* (Piaget and Inhelder 1941)
2 *The Child's Conception of Number* (Piaget and Szeminska 1952)
3 *New Light on Children's Ideas of Number* (Isaacs 1960)
4 *Mathematics in the Primary School* (Ironside and Roberts 1965)

By the early 1960s there were at least three books on Piaget for psychology students in England (Peel 1960; Lovell 1961; Flavell 1963). These were still unsuitable for students taking a rushed course in education. There followed a remarkable proliferation of books with titles such as *Piaget for Teachers*. Ten were published in the period 1965 to 1975, mostly by the National Froebel Foundation (NFF) (Shipman 1988). There were also handbooks published by Routledge & Kegan Paul in conjunction with NFF and books on Piaget in the Routledge Students Library of Education series. Inevitably there was loss in this translation, simplification and application. When this output is added to the thousands of brief interpretations inserted into books and articles on education during this period, the weight placed on Piaget can be appreciated.

Piaget's claim that his work was not intended to inform the practice of teachers is difficult to support given the size of the industry that grew while he was still active. But there is no doubt that the sublety of his ideas on epistemology and human development was violated. A glaring example was the way stages of development were defined by age to help teachers. This led to gross oversimplifications about the need to delay formal teaching. But I don't read French, I am dependent on translations and I am now assessing the applications to teaching 30 years after they were written. The national curriculum, its assessment, and the emphasis on formal class-teaching are a context from which the ideas of the 1960s seem a romantic dream.

The National Froebel Foundation played a major part in linking the work of Piaget to the ideas of child-centred education. By the mid-1950s comments on the relevance of Piaget's work were appearing in the *NFF Bulletin* (Isaacs 1955). Piaget lectured on children's thinking in London for the Foundation in October 1960 (*NFF Bulletin* 1961). At this stage the Foundation was very active, with local, regional as well as international branches. In 1960, Lawrence, the Honorary Director, wrote to *The Times Educational Supplement* offering the NFF as a clearing-house for collecting and distributing information on Piagetian research in Britain (Lawrence 1960a). Six replications of Piagetian experiments were reported in the *Bulletin* later that year (Lawrence 1960b).

The major adaptations of Piaget to support Froebelian ideas came from Nathan Isaacs. He was born in 1895 and had run a successful business importing and exporting metals. He was married first to Susan Isaacs the psychologist – and ironically a critic of Piaget – and then to Evelyn Lawrence, the Director of the NFF. He wrote four of the ten booklets for teachers published by the NFF in the 1960s. Isaac's major theme was that only 'living learning' was viable. Children learned by exploring, organizing and integrating. Classroom or 'twilight' learning was not just wasteful, but demeaning, likely to put a child off education. This view was shared by Froebelians and will be familiar to many teachers of primary-school children today. The support gained from a particular interpretation of Piaget is fully acknowledged as follows: 'We can obviously say for a start that the significance of Piaget's work must be greatest for those of us who believe in progressive education' (Isaacs 1955).

It was the Plowden Committee, looking at primary schooling, that gave the Froebelians their opportunity. They were represented on the Committee by Brierley, the Principal of the Froebel Institute. The evidence submitted on behalf of the NFF by Isaacs was firmly based in Piaget. Here is one typical passage. 'The fresh argument, however, is that through Professor Piaget's penetrating work on the basic nature of human learning, these principles are now placed on a massive new foundation of psychological support' (Isaacs 1964).

Despite the Committee's admission that Piaget is difficult to understand, he 'appears to most educationalists in this country to fit the observed facts of children's learning' (Plowden Report 1967: para. 522). Other evidence produced for the Committee particularly on language and on the importance of social class factors was acknowledged but then ignored. Throughout, the emphasis is on discovery, readiness and the stages of development. 'Mental stages follow as a sequence,' (para. 23). 'Until a child is ready to take a particular step forward, it is a waste of time to teach him to take it,' (para. 25). 'A great majority of primary-school children can only learn efficiently from concrete situations, as lived or described,' (para. 521).

The emphasis throughout the Plowden Report was on learning not teaching. Children progressed from an initial logical incapacity to a capacity for logical thinking through stages. They had to be 'ready' for learning. Isaacs in his submitted evidence was only prepared to consider conventional teaching by the age of 12 or 13. Plowden's support for middle schooling was seen as a way of delaying the formal teaching of secondary schooling until the children were ready. Twenty years later formal teaching was being recommended for infants.

By the 1960s Piaget's research was being replicated, extended, applied, compared across cultures. Psychologists described themselves as Piagetian. With Jerome Bruner, Piaget dominated educational psychology in the 1960s. The 'Jean and Jerry' show made academic reputations worldwide. The criticisms that followed made even more. Advancing or retreating, the great carry others along. Unfortunately the overenthusiastic and uncontrolled use of Piaget's work resulted in a rejection of his enormous contribution to the study of the way knowledge is constructed. The epistemology went down with the simplifications. Meanwhile the education of young children moved from formal to informal and back to formal. Researchers benefit from change, teachers are confused by it and children can be the losers.

CHAPTER 10

The publication of research

Publication links the often private world of researchers to the public who are influenced by it. The many incentives to get research results into the public domain have resulted in a proliferation of publications, catering not just for many different readerships, but for the contrasting needs of authors. They range from refereed journals with queues of authors hoping for the prestige of inclusion, to others that provide an outlet for the excluded. My career depended on articles in refereed journals. Books paid the mortgage and supermarket magazines provided pocket-money. Publication is used as a major criterion for judging both academic productivity and quality. The two may overlap, but the range of journals and books in which research appears is wide and getting wider. Let the reader beware.

The refereed academic journal usually has an editorial board and referees who are established leaders in specialized subjects. But editors can wave-through articles that are later condemned as inferior. At the other extreme are the popular books and magazines that may use the insights from learned journals but usually after several stages of simplification and adaptation, and often without attribution. In between are thousands of journals publishing original and derived work, with and without refereeing. There are books that range from first publication of important research through collections of readings that are several stages removed from the original, to popular accounts of professional and everyday issues containing often gross oversimplifications.

The gateways to publication

The contrast in the purposes served by different publications can be gauged by the way academics submit articles to refereed journals and are approached by book publishers to write for them. An article in *The British Journal of Psychology* or *The British Journal of Sociology* can be the making of a career. Acceptance by the referees and editors means that it has survived peer review. It may now influence further research, be applied to professional practice, be replicated and elaborated. An English example was Bernstein's article 'Some sociological determinants of perception' (Bernstein 1958). It is still debated today and over 40 years it influenced not only the sociology of education, but the training of teachers.

Book publishers also use referees. But now sales have priority. There is also the same variety in subject-matter from the first appearance of often dramatic research results to applications to professional and lay practice years later. Authors may have good reason to go straight into a book rather than via a journal. The impact on the intended audience can be greater. An article submitted to a journal is refereed. Publication may take a year or more from initial submission. While waiting there are likely to be contributions at conferences, seminars and informal gatherings. The gains are that the referees, academic and professional peers will assess the work over time. First publication in a book means instant public impact. The media may take it up and widespread public attention is assured. The losses are that academic criticism, when it comes, will be instantaneous, often ill-informed and lack the protracted review that follows publication in journals. Books have limited space for methodology. Bennett's *Teaching Styles and Pupil Progress* (Bennett 1976) and Rutter's *Fifteen Thousand Hours* (Rutter *et al.* 1979) were both quickly followed by intense criticism that drew further attention to the authors. However, for a book, any publicity is good publicity. You cry all the way to the bank.

If work has been subject to refereeing and peer review, confidence in it rises. But this friendly–hostile criticism that follows publication and establishes credibility is ironically itself largely private. One insight came in letters to *The Psychologist* following the publication by Rushton (1990) reported in Controversy 4. Among these were complaints that the review process must have been flawed. The editors should resign. The honorary editors wrote to explain that this article had not been sent for review. A serious error was admitted and they offered their resignations. In future all articles would be refereed. No article would be published if it was likely to cause offence. That started another protest. Rushton objected to the apologies by the editors for his article and to the censorship, pointing out that the data had previously appeared in other journals. Even critics of the original article now wrote to complain of the proposed editorial policy. The correspondence was closed in January 1991.

It was extraordinary that such a controversial article was not refereed. However, peer review is often difficult to achieve. Referees are often slow to give a verdict. They may be august, but they will have a viewpoint that can block the chances of the innovative or contentious getting into print. An article such as Rushton's is particularly difficult to referee, not only for its political sensitivity, but because it is derived from another. This was in *Acta Geneticae Medicae et Gemellologiae* (Rushton 1987).

The difficulties in publishing sensitive evidence continue to embarrass. In January 1996 *The Psychologist* advertised *The g Factor*, a book to be published by Wiley. In June, Wiley placed another advertisement in *The Psychologist* to announce that they had withdrawn the book because it contained assertions that were repellent. In the September issue there were letters ranging from complaints about carrying the advertisement in the first place, about lack of information and that there had been an attack on academic freedom. The editors' response was that they had no responsibility to give space to an issue just because it had been headline news in the national press. Once again this journal had made space for an exchange of views in the best tradition of broader peer review.

Variety in publication

The importance of peer review in determining the status of research evidence and the many different groups of readers who will carry out such reviews means that there will be conflicting assessments. Different groups of readers will often be reading very different accounts of the same research. They will do this across years rather than months, particularly when the evidence is important for professional practice. New research reported in a seminar paper receives instant appraisal and often useful tips from discussion. Much later, that evidence, simplified and applied, appears in a popular book, stripped of information on its methodology, missing the cautions of the researchers and often without the criticisms that will have been made in the intervening years. Here is an example across a short timespan. 'My central thesis is that human physiological development represents a self-fulfilling prophecy: our children become pretty much what we expect them to become, whether our expectations take the form of hopes or fears' (Church 1973).

The source of this rather optimistic claim is Rosenthal and Jacobson (1968). The problem is not just that the original has been oversimplified, but that in the five years between 1968 and 1973 critics had exposed serious flaws in the original. The timespan between original publication and applications to practice can stretch across decades. That is the case in the classics described in Chapter 9. Lippitt and White's experiments in the 1940s are still used to support the case for democratic leadership today. More common is a lag across years as a seminar paper is published in an academic journal after refereeing. It is adapted for journals with a wider professional readership. A book appears a couple of years later. References to it then appear in other books. It is abbreviated for a reader. Popular books take aboard a simplified version of the main ideas. At each stage the evidence is condensed and stripped of further context.

Here are two extracts illustrating the way rewording to avoid using the word 'variance' has increased the determinism in discussing the development of intelligence. First, Bloom summarizes his own research on the early development of human characteristics. 'By an average age of about two, it seems evident that at least one-third of the variance at adolescence on intellectual interest, dependency and aggression is predictable (Bloom 1964: 88). Second, van der Eyken adds even more certainty. 'With intelligence, the rate of development is significantly different. One-fifth of the adult level is achieved in the first year of life, nearly half by the fourth birthday, and about 80 per cent by the age of eight' (van der Eyken 1967: 15).

Across the decades adaptations and simplifications can distort evidence, remove original cautions and stretch it beyond its elastic limit. That happened to the research evidence of Piaget described in Controversy 9, despite his protests that his work was not intended to guide practice in education. This is annoying for researchers who not only see their work progressively distorted in print, used to recommend practices of which they may not approve and reinforcing fashionable professional advice, but also see their name used to add prestige to policies in which they had no voice.

The consequences for reports of research in this simplication and adaptation is particularly unfortunate as book publishers are not keen on lengthy chapters on research methods. Along the trail from seminar paper to book there is likely to be less and less of the information necessary to review validity, reliability and generalizability. The worst offenders are often books of readings. These are popular with publishers because they can be up-to-date and cover a lot of ground. They are the set books of most Open University courses, and are used extensively across academia because the work of abbreviation has already been done by the editors. In Open University texts the problem arises from the careful selection to support a case. This is often flagged in the text by square brackets indicating the addition of words to the original and by three dots where substantial deletions have been made. But outside these flagged changes the selection is likely to have removed just the sections from the original that gave the reader some chance of assessing credibility.

The time across which adaptation takes place means that the simplified version in secondary sources is liable to be incorporated into advice for professionals in training after the original work has been shown to be flawed and new work has overtaken it. That was the case for Piaget's research as it was adapted to support child-centred education in the 1960s in Britain. As Bernstein's 1958 article in *The British Journal of Sociology* was reproduced in books on education and introduced into teacher-training, the author had moved his work beyond its early formulation and was himself under attack for having supported the concept of cultural deprivation by defining a restricted working-class language code just as others were celebrating its riches, particularly in Black communities.

The conventions of publishing

Researchers can publish in journals or books that have very different readerships. All can have lengthy periods between presenting the typescipt and seeing it in print. Both outlets may use referees. The choice is usually decided by considering the intended readership. A journal article is likely to be read by a narrow but knowledgeable group, academic or professional. A book can have a wider appeal. In all cases there are conventions of format and style to be followed to make it suitable for the intended audience. The referencing and attribution have to be settled. More latitude is expected when the content is a synthesis or application of existing knowledge. But such secondary publications still have their conventions and potential authors usually take the easiest path to publication by following them.

Boosting the case

There are many ways, often employed without any intent to deceive, to make a case look as strong as possible. It is conventional in preparing a thesis, article or book to concentrate on the case for and underplay the opposition. A thesis is written with an examination by experts in mind. They will know the conventions and be able to detect omissions and query whether they were intentional. Articles in journals are also written in anticipation of informed criticism and easy detection of the short-hands and clues that point to the bases for the selection of the evidence presented. With books and popular journals with a wider professional or lay readership the conventions can make assessment difficult for just the groups who have least knowledge of the author or of the academic conventions. There are, however, a few techniques that are easy to detect.

Supercharging

This boosts quantitative research. The sequence of technical aids from punched card and knitting needle, calculator to computer have made it easy to manipulate data. This has reduced the effort needed to search for relationships between variables. It is impressive to read that results were significant at the 5 per cent level. But that only means that the possibility of the statistics presented having occurred through the chance of selection are five in 100 and hence how likely it is that a second and subsequent sampling would produce the same results. But the replication to check this is usually impossible in social research and always unrewarding. Yet if there is data on hundreds of variables from a single sample, many are likely to be related at this level of significance. Further, samples often have non-response large enough to make the data garbage. Even apparently precise data such as examination results can have results so clustered around an average in a normal, bell-shaped distribution that even a small change in the boundaries can produce dramatic differences to the statistics. No amount of supercharging can remedy a shaky base.

There can be a supercharging problem whenever figures are reported. Variations on the 'fully–only' technique are common. Differences are described as 'fully X per cent' to boost a relationship, but 'only X per cent' to downgrade it. 'Twenty of the samples were selected for detailed study' usually means that the remainder looked unpromising. 'Typical results' can be the best and 'correct within an order of magnitude' means that it was more right than wrong.

Window-dressing

This is found in the reporting of all research and is facilitated by conventions. The impersonal reporting style conceals both the insights and the human errors, the sequence of events that led to the research and the personal history of the researcher that accounts for the initial interest in the subject. Jargon may be a shorthand easily understood by academic colleagues, but outside specialist journals it can bamboozle. Window-dressing in qualitative research where the involvement of the researcher is in interpreting activity in schools, social work, business and so on is often insulting to those involved. Practitioners rely on participant observation to understand their work. But the language of ethnography, analytic induction, grounded theory and multiple strategies suggests that valid interpretation is arcana gained by the researcher after a few hours in the classroom or factory, beyond the perceptions of those who have spent years there.

The menace of window-dressing is that the bright display may conceal obscurity within. The words are not only technical, but can suggest explanation as well as definition. To suggest that Blacks fail at school because of low self-concept merely transfers the problem from schooling to whatever is supposed to cause how we see ourselves. The fallacy here was exposed by pointing to the high Black self-image that was needed to survive in White society. What was needed was good teaching not psychological hunches (Stone 1981). Concepts such as achievement motivation and cultural deprivation don't explain, but label. After a few years other labels replace them.

Referencing

This alerts fellow specialists to a range of related work, instantaneously positioning the work for their review. Reference by a single name can convey a lot of information. But it can also mobilize support and give the impression of powerful backing. Some references, in their day, become mandatory. The latest French *savant* on postmodernism, the likely external examiners of a doctoral thesis, the referees of the relevant learned journal, the leading lights in the subject of a book are essential. It has even been found that there is a correlation of 0.96 between references to the chairperson of doctoral committees and success in the PhD examination (Oldcom 1960).

The referencing game can start with a dedication to the memory of Bertrand or Maynard. You throw in references to the advanced seminar at Harvard. A computer search will add some obscure source such as the *Revista Iberoamericana de Seguridad Social.* Brown and Smith sound like amateurs compared with Raskolnikov and Skavar. The Vienna School sounds more impressive that the Department in Birmingham. 'Participants at the recent congress in Bokhara will confirm' neatly places the reader outside the jetset. 'Personal Communication' establishes the author as well-connected and is impossible to check. The gold-card reference was found in an address to the *Better Schools'* conference organized by the DES in 1985. In the printed version it turned out to be 'Guzzetti, B.J. (1983) A Critical Synthesis of School Effectiveness Research: Implications for Dissemination.' Paper presented to the Rocky Mountain American Educational Research Association, Jackson Hole, Wyoming (mimeo) (DES 1985).

There are many more ways of boosting evidence. Description becomes prescription. Concepts, which are abstract and usually tentative ideas, are reified, made concrete and certain, as they are applied. There is a particular temptation when research designed to test and advance theory is used to guide practice and policy. In the 1970s, the 'new' sociology of education was concerned with the way the school curriculum acted as a control over the distribution of knowledge to different groups of children. It was exhilarating stuff. But it was soon part of teacher-training. If knowledge is the ideology of particular groups, the school curriculum is merely the arbitrary selection of those with power. There is a lot in this argument, but its application to reading, writing and mathematics didn't do much to spur teachers on to raise basic skills. Bernstein's work in the same decade had equally distorted practical results. External examining revealed future teachers convinced that working-class children were 'linguistically depraved' while their lucky middle-class peers employed 'elaborated syntaxis'.

Publishing secondary material

There is never enough direct evidence from research to satisfy the urge to know. Hence professionals in education, management, social work and so on create a market for articles and books that takes what evidence is available and amalgamates and applies it. The majority of published work, including this book, is of this secondary kind. Inevitably there is a threat to validity and of excessive generalization.

Exampling

This is the most common method of using evidence to support a case. It is always easy to find cases that support an hypothesis. That was why Popper insisted on the tougher test for evidence of standing up to attempts at refutation, falsification (Popper 1959). A subject often becomes topical as social conditions change or through legislation or developments within social science. School and society in the 1950s and 1960s, the curriculum in the 1970s, school effectiveness, evaluation and management in the 1980s, the growing realization that gender and race had been neglected across these decades, all increased the demand for publications that could inform students and teachers. This was not just fashion. Attempts by government to improve schooling often created the demand. A little evidence had to go a long way. But it was always easy to find examples that confirmed.

Exampling is the most frequent as a new subject promises large sales. The sudden demand for books on school management in the 1980s was met by a combination of biographical accounts by headteachers, empirical studies of the ways schools worked and borrowing ideas from the latest management gurus. The results may have provided insights, but ten years later these books seem more pious than realistic. Many of the firms used as examples from business have since gone bankrupt. The succession of borrowed buzzwords soon made the books redundant as Richard Covey, Tom Peters, Charles Handy and so on moved quickly on to publish their next idea.

Decontextualization

This is the attempt to borrow ideas and apply them without considering the consequences of ignoring the original context. We now know that Freud could not bring himself to believe that daughters describing sexual abuse by their fathers were telling the truth. His definition and diagnosis of hysteria was a cover-up (Masson 1992). Yet Freud's ideas were borrowed and applied in education. Susan Isaac's account of her work at Malting House School in Cambridge became compulsory reading for students in training at the London Institute of Education where she later worked (Isaacs 1933). It remained on booklists into the mid-1960s. The pupils were often bright, sometimes disturbed children of university dons. From the book they seemed very concerned about their penises or lack of them. Nudity seems to have been encouraged. Little girls enviously watch the boys urinating. It seemed laughable to the PGCE students in the 1960s and even more so today. In its context, interpreted in its Freudian model, it is an important and liberating book. Applied to inner-London schools 30 years later it was hilarious.

There is another common form of decontextualization in books for teachers, social workers and so on. The behaviour of children cannot be neatly explained here by Psychology and there by Sociology or by reference to specialism within each. A book on behaviour in school will draw on insights from subjects and specialisms that are based on very different assumptions about human motivation. Yet those insights are often combined to recommend good practice. If humans are driven by instincts or by forces buried in the subconscious, it is absurd to combine evidence based on such models with other evidence based on the human as scientist, or as constructor of their own reality, as God's children or the work of the devil.

Simplification

This is the inevitable consequence of having to translate social science into practice. That translation is both common and easy. It is why Little Red Books, Black Papers and White Papers can contradict and coexist. It is why there are hundreds of books on the teaching of reading, with research evidence supporting each, coinciding with a concern over reading standards in school that has persisted for 50 years. The advocates of phonics, real books, reading for understanding and so on can produce convincing cases. So did the advocates of the initial teaching alphabet (i.t.a.) in the 1950s. Some 2000 schools were using it by the late 1960s (Moyle 1968). Today it is a rarity. In schools, teachers sensibly use whatever method seems to help individual children or the class as a whole. They take individual and group differences into account, but the quest to impose the 'right' way persists.

In practice all social research is a simplification. The human condition is complicated and has to be modelled and hence simplified before it can be researched. That applies to both scientistic and interpretive social research. Both rest on hunches derived from explicit or implicit models. Nobody enters the field with an open mind. The human world is simplified before it is investigated. Hence the evidence produced is also restricted. Further, if this restriction, definition, delineation is not intentional, explicit, planned and spelled out for the reader, the simplification from the inevitable – if unplanned – selection may be missed. That is why so many innovations have failed in action. The complexity and unpredictability of human behaviour in pratice can bury the best of intentions and the most promising of reforms in theory.

Fancy, fallacy and fraud

The fanciful, fallacious and fraudulent are to be expected in any human activity. Broad and Wade, looking across the whole scientific enterprise, concluded that it was not the odd apple that was bad, but that the whole barrel was infected (Broad and Wade 1982). The reasons for this, the pressure to be first, the convention that the research should not be reported as a human but as a natural, given activity, and the temptation to seal the boundary between science and lay outsiders to maintain status, are even more apparent when the subject is the human rather than the natural world.

Fancy

This takes the published account beyond the research itself. Broad conclusions follow narrow results. Small samples lead to generalizations to populations. *Learning to Labour*, discussed in Controversy 2, a gripping account of the sexist, racist, uncouth and uncaring attitudes of a small group of school-leavers, explains how working-class lads get working-class jobs (Willis 1978). This is explained by reference to the social class system, to the alienation, the cultural hegemony present within capitalism. But this is Willis writing not the lads speaking. This is a common and fanciful transition in the reporting of interpretive research. The lads, and increasingly the lasses, are described as apolitical, unaware of being exploited, living for the present, yet are then transformed by the writer into makers of their own culture and even the vanguard of the proletariat.

All examiners of doctoral theses compare recommendations and conclusions against results, results against methods, methods against their logic, aims against outcomes. That scepticism is a safeguard against the fanciful, a warning to the researcher that modesty is required and that a lack of information to facilitate the critical review will be seen as suspicious. It's understandable to want to change the world, but the fancy-free should be left to artists.

Fallacies

These occur within research designs and the interpretation of results. In social science the most important are psychological fallacies where data on individuals is used to reflect on social structures such as organizations, culture or class and sociological fallacies where information on such structures are used to reflect on individuals. The two disciplines are concerned with the same topics, but start at opposite ends. A sociologist looks at suicide rates and explains the differences between groups, nations, periods by reference to social conditions. Generalizing to individual motivation is hazardous. The psychologist examines individual cases and explains the suicide by reference to personal histories, states of mind. Generalizing to cultural factors is hazardous.

Studies of the effectiveness of schools are vulnerable to such fallacies. The largest study of them all depended on the verbal ability scores of 645 000 children in some 4000 schools in the USA (Coleman 1966). But interpreting school performance from the aggregated scores of individual children on a single test ignored features that were more than the sum of pupil scores. Similar criticisms have been levelled at most of the school studies detailed in Controversy 10 because they lack a model of schooling that would make the statistics meaningful. Other critics complain about the shifting level of analysis. Data on school classes is used to comment on individual pupils. Data on pupils is added-up to a picture of the school. Data is only meaningful by reference to the models that underlie it and these differ both between and within social science disciplines.

Fraud

This is difficult to prove in social research. Much of the work is done by individuals merging into the lives of those they study. Research notes and diaries, even if they are available, cannot provide a comprehensive reconstruction of what went on. Social scientists are not organized to replicate, even in the small number of laboratory experiments where it might be possible. Nor is there any need to organize immediate and large-scale assessment because of the importance of the evidence, as in the case of the claims to have achieved cold fusion.

The case of Sir Cyril Burt reported in Controversy 7 shows how difficult it is to come to a verdict. The attacks on Burt started in 1974 and culminated five years later in Hearnshaw's reluctant admission in his biography that there had been fraud (Hearnshaw 1979). But defenders of Burt counterattacked, often admitting faults because of senility, but denying fraud (Joynson 1989). The British Psychological Society, having admitted in 1980 that there was fraud, yielded to the counterattack in 1992, saw no point in setting up an inquiry and decided that they no longer had a corporate view (*BPS* 1992). This sad case suggests that you can rarely prove fraud in investigating human behaviour because most social research uses methods that cannot be audited. Further, if reality is indeed determined by those involved, or the aim of research is to expose injustice, truth is relative and fraud is what other parties have committed.

The effectiveness of schools

This Controversy asks an apparently simple question. Could research evidence identify the features of schools that are effective even though they recruit from deprived areas? First, this isn't a simple question. Second, there is no certainty that a school with all the features associated with effectiveness in the available research will have higher attainment than a school that lacks more of these characteristics (Gray and Wilcox 1995). Successful schools may work because of unconventional methods. Unsuccessful schools may meet all the criteria. Third, social background factors cannot be treated as extraneous. Gray, Jesson and Sime (1990) estimate that once the differences in intakes were taken into account, the differences in results between schools were halved.

There have always been questions about the effectiveness of schools. It was the subject of the Parliamentary Committee on the Education of the Lower Orders in the Metropolis of 1816. It remained the major concern of the reports of consultative committees and councils in the 1960s and 1970s. Each report included evidence on the strength of the relationship between social background and schooling in England and Wales. Sociologists and historians have documented the waste of talent that resulted (Silver 1994).

The American evidence was particularly pessimistic. The larger the sample of schools studied, the lower was the confidence that there was any impact at all. Coleman's study of 4000 schools, 60 000 teachers and 600 000 children, concluded that there was little impact on attainment from the resources provided (Coleman 1966). Jencks (1973), reworking Coleman's data, confirmed that reallocating resources would not do much to equalize attainment. A Rand Corporation review of available evidence concluded that 'Research has not identified a variant of the educational system that is consistently related to students' educational outcomes' (Averch 1974). The factor that mattered was the social background of the children.

This pessimism could not be accepted by policy-makers. Nor should it have been. Researchers have to simplify. Schools that worked in adverse conditions were soon described in America (Weber 1971) and Britain (Reynolds 1976). These small-scale studies could also refer to characteristics of schools that were beyond measurement. They were optimistic and certain that schools could be organized to be effective, where large-scale statistical evidence had concluded that the school in a deprived area could do little.

The large-scale studies used not just on the measurable, but the available. The research was data-driven and that data was often crude. In Britain, for example, the proportion of children receiving free school meals was used as a measure of social class background. 'Output' was measured by attendance, crime statistics or, at best, examination results. 'Input' was usually a measure of attainment on leaving primary school. Even these crude indicators were only available in a few local authorities, there was reluctance to release them, and most datasets had gaps. Even a few low- or high-attaining absentees could make big differences. So could movement between schools, managed by ambitious parents with bright children.

This early research was difficult to organize. Professional autonomy, often proudly supported by the teacher unions in Britain, made access difficult. Her Majesty's Inspectors' Reports were not published. The curriculum was the concern of each school. Researchers were denied access to schools to assess the quality of teaching. Ideally, school-effectiveness studies should start with a model of the effective school that can be tested against reality. They should then be concentrated on the key features in that model.

Thus school-effectiveness research tends to be weak right where it matters, in lacking direct assessments of teacher quality, methods, hours of work as well as having to use poor input, output and social background data. Further, there are always extraneous factors that could account for the results in different schools. Intangible but crucial features such as school ethos, the climate, the press cannot be measured directly. Above all, schools are complex organizations. Research models have to be simple. There will always be features that account for the exceptions where a school's effectiveness cannot be predicted from the factors identified as important through research.

In the 1970s a second phase of research was forming around a model that included attainments and social background at intake to school, predictions of likely attainment on leaving and on factors within schools that seemed to make a difference. The closed black box of the school was slowly being opened. The change can be appreciated by comparing the stopping by teacher unions of early work on differences in delinquency in schools in the same area of London (Power 1967) and the school-effectiveness studies that followed in the same Authority. Negotiating the 'Rutter' research in London in the 1970s was a major diplomatic exercise. But the pressure was inexorable from central and local government to look for factors that led to effective schooling. It was a decade when researchers joined experts in management, school self-evaluation, record-keeping, the assessment of performance, more rigorous inspection, to improve effectiveness.

Significantly two of the three major British studies were organized within the Inner London Education Authority where its Research and Statistics group stored data on the social background of schools for its primary- and secondary-school indexes in order to fund schools according to the deprivation they faced. It collected Verbal Reasoning, Mathematics and English data at age 11 in order to balance intakes into secondary schools. It stored public examination results. The difficulties of gaining access, information and response outside the ILEA are described in the third study (Smith and Tomlinson 1989).

The publication of *Fifteen Thousand Hours* (Rutter *et al.* 1979) was the first British study to claim that schools could make a difference, despite the influence of social background factors on attainment. It had an extraordinary impact, partly because it identified key factors in effective schools, partly because central and local government was starting to intervene in schooling to try to raise standards. Eventually there was international agreement that at least three factors – high expectations shared among teachers and pupils, strong leadership shared among senior management, and an emphasis on evaluation and improvement – were crucial.

Looking back at the reception of *Fifteen Thousand Hours*, in particular, it seems surprising that only two other major studies resulted. But the costs were high and data difficult to obtain. Above all, the research came to be seen as central to the new drive to provide information for parents, produce performance indicators and organize the assessment of the national curriculum in the 1980s and 1990s. The researchers moved on.

The switch in priorities was seen by academic critics as confirmation that research into school effectiveness had always been managerial, taking the problems facing government, rather than asking the wider question of the role of schools in the unjust organization of society. But it was also an indication that policy-makers had accepted that schools should only be held responsible for the gains in attainment across the years the children were in the school, that schools were only responsible for their 'value-added' contribution. This gave the researchers a further task in the 1990s to show how to collect, analyse and present the results for a school in an informative, fair and cost-effective way (Dearing 1993). The research is proceeding (Jesson and Gray 1991). But so is the implementation of new policies and the latter usually leave the research behind.

This is a summary of a remarkable change in the message taken from research. In the 1960s, social class was seen as the key factor in determining attainment in school, as well as opportunity and lifestyle generally. By the 1980s, the school was taking responsibility for attainment, and gender and race were receiving more attention in studies of injustice. This is only partly explicable in terms of social changes in class structure. It is also affected by fashions in research. Small-scale, interpretive studies could not reproduce the statistical relationship between social class and opportunity tracked across this century in Britain (see, for example, Lindsay 1926). Any attempt to research runs into the political issues involved in the relationship of class, gender and race. The danger is that social class factors will be ignored.

This controversy remains important. If schools can be effective in deprived areas, with intakes of low-achievers, they should be models. But the research has once again shown the complexity of the original question. Attainment at intake to school does not necessarily reflect social background factors. It ignores the effects of different social mixes within schools on children from different backgrounds. Schools might benefit poor children at the expense of the rich, this ethnic group against that. They may do a splendid job for the more able but not for the less able, for girls not boys. Above all, the variations in the attainment of pupils statistically attributable to schools is very small when compared with that contributed by social background. Research into social inequality still merits priority.

CHAPTER 11

The limitations and scope of social research

The ten Controversies in this book illustrate the way issues are conceived, enquiry planned and results published by reference to distinctive research traditions. The emphasis has been on the scientistic and interpretive with the critical always present. These are not just philosophies and consequent procedures. They are convictions held by groups that support members. These are labelled reference groups, scientific communities, disciplines, paradigms, networks and so on, indicating the way members share beliefs and techniques, careers and publications that lead them to distinctive styles of research and publication. Above all, they review and hence validate one another's work. This can get cosy, but rival groups will usually ensure sufficient criticism. This will also come from professionals, practitioners, inspectors, administrators, politicians using very different criteria for assessment and, where necessary, providing support against researchers.

Controversy 10 showed how agreement among researchers internationally produced an influential community publicizing a few key features of the effective school. But school inspectors, management experts, headteachers produced rival versions. The impact of the research in Britain was limited. Initial publication was headline news. But education services were being reorganized and many researchers were funded to help organize measures for school improvement and the provision of information for parents. They often had multiple communal obligations, spanning often conflicting reference groups.

Communal and conceptual influences

The question 'What makes an effective school?' in Controversy 10 is misleadingly simple. Effective for what? Academic achievement? Behaviour? Motivation to go on learning? For all children? Across the years? In the face of contrasting social backgrounds? Regardless of the level of parental support? Given what resources? Researchers have their own definitions. So have policy-makers. Academic communities will also disagree. The answers could just make an unfair system more efficient, further betraying the oppressed. You meet this group and agree that testing has to be easy to manage and results easy to interpret. In another group the impossibility of making a complex procedure simple because of philosophical concerns becomes apparent. There will always be conflicting evidence arising from contrasting assumptions. School-effectiveness research was unusual in the breadth and strength of its communal organization, its specialized journals. It could make authoritative recommendations (Silver 1994). But there were always competing communities holding conflicting views within and outside academia.

In the 1970s, as researchers and Her Majesty's Inspectors were producing evidence on the 'good' school, *Schooling in Capitalist America* was published (Bowles and Gintis 1976). This 'correspondence' theory modelled schooling as a tool of capitalist economies. It was influential in academia because it linked the concern of the 'new' sociology of education with power and control to the proliferating studies of schools and classrooms, showing how economic influences affected the curriculum and education of a majority of children. Just as evidence was published on how to make schools more effective, another academic community was showing how 'effectiveness' really meant the production of an obedient labour force.

The distinction between these groups is mainly that one had taken a problem facing those who organized the education service, while the others were making or elaborating an old issue in a new way. Curiously the respective communities had similar periods of popularity before dispersing into new groupings with new interests. By 1986, Bowles and Gintis, faced with turmoil in Eastern Europe, moved from Marxism to a search for a genuine liberalism through schooling, despite confirming that history was still on their side (Bowles and Gintis 1986). By then school-effectiveness research had also ceased to have the excitement of a breakthrough and was lending its technical expertise to helping government introduce accountability and a market economy for schools.

A division has also persisted between researchers and Her Majesty's Inspectors, even though they have sat and worked together on quangos such as the Schools Council, the Assessment of Performance Unit, the School Examinations and Assessment Council and the School Curriculum and Assessment Authority. Researchers have examined local authority approaches to the evaluation of schools (Gray and Wilcox 1995). They have criticized HMI procedures, particularly for converting judgements into data (Bennett 1987). But in studies of school effectiveness, where cooperation would have been expected, the two communities remained apart.

The most influential study of school effectiveness in Britain was published in 1979 (Rutter *et al.* 1979). Two years earlier Her Majesty's Inspector's *Ten Good Schools* came to similar conclusions (DES 1977b). Their selection of key factors observed as crucial in the making of a good school were effective leadership, a climate conducive to development, an emphasis on learning, policies that were explicit and shared by teachers, parents and pupils. They were identical to summaries of the results of the many research projects that followed (see, for example, Reynolds and Cuttance 1992). Yet these HMI observations were ignored in the research publications. Nor are the surveys of the primary and secondary sectors referenced (DES 1978, 1979). By the mid-1990s this dispute between researchers and HMI had become both acrimonious and personal (Mortimore and Goldstein 1996).

This divide between researchers and school inspectors is not because of a difference in the scale of their work. Rutter studied 12 schools, HMI ten. Nor is it the intensity of the work. HMI full inspections can involve a dozen inspectors working in a school for seven or more whole days and having access to information in the school and local education authorities. There is moreover no confidence among researchers that a school with all the factors they found to be associated with effectiveness will have higher attainment than a school that lacks them. Successful schools may work because of unconventional methods. Unsuccessful schools may meet all the crieria. Gray and Wilcox (1995) take the most common position that the research 'works' in about seven out of ten cases, but good results occur in three out of ten schools, even where the key factors are missing. The research, like HMI reports, is a guide not a blueprint.

Inspectors make judgements. These carry weight. That does make the public disclosure that is central to research difficult. But the Office for Standards in Education (OFSTED) published a handbook containing the criteria for the assessment of schools (1994). They depend on observation. But so do researchers. Both aim at identifying what makes a good school. Both depend on being trusted by teachers. The important differences are that they belong to very different communities. Both may be trying to guide policy and practice. But researchers aim to explain or understand, inspectors to improve. They have very different reference groups. Academia is interested in advancing knowledge. Government is interested in using it.

A striking illustration of the different criteria used by researchers and practitioners came in an exchange over the evaluation of the first British Reading Recovery programme by the head of the Educational Psychology Service in Surrey (Wright 1992). It was criticized for being narrowly conceived, poorly conducted, insufficiently tentative in conclusion and failing to produce useful evidence (Hall 1994). This is typical academic criticism. The criteria are those of research communities applied to conceptualization, research design, techniques and hence the validity of evidence. Wright's response was brisk (Wright 1994). Would it work in Surrey? Yes. Would Surrey children show accelerated gains? Yes. It worked, it was cost-effective, it was the best available. From within a county hall the criteria are pragmatic. Somewhere in a senior common room other academics would comment that the problems lie deeper. The children in the programme were victims of a public education service that, in Surrey, never saw many children of the rich.

The coexistence of theory-orientated researchers containing historians, sociologists and Marxists on one side and policy-orientated reseachers negotiating with administrators, inspectors and teachers on the other, means there will always be conflicting evaluations of research. The publication of *Fifteen Thousand Hours* (Rutter *et al.* 1979) produced a rash of criticisms. Many were technical, but among them were others based on very different ways of conceiving schooling. Why did the research say nothing about the reproduction of inequality, particularly as it was concerned with inner-city schools? Why were factors in the organization of schooling grouped together to emphasize the import- ance of the ethos of the school that was more than the sum of the parts? Why are social class relationships ignored? (Tizard *et al.* 1980). The answers to such questions differ because there are many, not one, peer group doing the review, particularly when the research is intended to affect policy or practice.

The aim of many researchers is to advance theory, to try to under- stand the human condition, including the distribution of power that enables some to pose the questions, others to depend on the answers. There is never an undisputed conclusion. They relish dispute. They work within subjects, disciplines, specialisms, that share and develop distinct- ive views of the human condition. They may aim at objectivity as they research or work to raise the consciousness of injustice. But in all cases they draw on communal support, respond to communal criticism and depend for their careers on communal approval. Their interest is in new knowledge, in changing theories. Fame goes to the innovator.

Researchers, however, often work with those who guide policy and practice. The principal interest now is in helping to guide change rather than improving models. Stable models of the way schools work are required to predict the consequences of interventions. The involvement of researchers in policy-making is usually to advise on the best way of achieving the changes already proposed. They will work with admin- istrators, inspectors, teachers and other professionals. Everyone involved will bring different views of the agenda, refer back to different 'commun- ities'. From 1980 these included the business community as appoint- ments were made to bring market perspectives to bear. The strength of the researchers is usually that they can contribute from theory as well as through their enquiries. But the academic priority to change is usually unwelcome. Policy-makers want stable models from which to predict.

Researchers also tend to work to relaxed timescales. They are spared politicians demanding action now. That often explains the frustration of researchers whose recommendations seem to be ignored. At a review of the final report of a project, the policy has often been moved beyond its terms of reference. The research may be acknowledged as an answer to the original questions, but others now have priority. Above all, re- searchers serving on the succession of quangos planning evaluation, record-keeping, the publication of examination results, monitoring edu- cational standards, assessing the national curriculum, preparing value- added figures for publication, have followed the brief given them by policy-makers, but at a cost in money and teacher time that made their recommendations unrealistic. When it is all over they have increased understanding, helped clarify the issues. But they are one group among many, often challenged by colleagues within academia for taking rather than making problems and often marginal to recommendations that are financially and professionally constrained.

Controversy 6 illustrated this influence of reference groups. From the London Institute of Education, the Tennessee research on class size seemed to demand research in Britain as a priority. From the National Institute for Economic and Social Research such research should be stopped because the Tennessee experience showed that lowering class sizes was a grossly inefficient way of trying to raise attainment.

The technical limitations

Even where there is data that seems reliable, extraordinary mistakes can be made when it is assumed that humans will go on behaving as they did at the time of data-collection. Demographers project populations forward from current numbers. King, in his *Observations on the State of England* in 1696, predicted that it would take 600 years for the population of England, then around 5 500 000 to double. There are nearer 50 million today. In 1938, Charles predicted a population of between 18 and 32 million for Great Britain in the year 2000 (Charles 1938). There are already more than 55 million. It is impossible to predict over the longer term when intimate human behaviour is involved.

The failures to predict added to the attacks on the philosophical basis of scientistic social research. The popularity of interpretive methods rests on both a different philosophy and more realistic ambitions. But the revival of a tradition that dates back to Germany at the end of the eighteenth century is also related to the growth of the social sciences in the second half of the twentieth. Small-scale studies used to make reputations. Doctoral students were approached by publishers with offers to publish their theses. It was great to be a researcher before the competition heated up. In my training as a teacher I was convinced of the value of nursery schooling by Harrold and Temple (1959–1960). This was a study of 42 children from four infant schools, half having had previous nursery schooling. The two groups were matched for intelligence, age and social background and observed by the researchers. Those with nursery-school experience were happier, more self-confident, at ease with their teachers, superior at work in all bar painting and manipulative control, more muscular, socially more confident and had more positive attitudes towards their parents. That they were also more aggressive seemed a small price to pay. Today such a study would be treated with scepticism, not just by social scientists but by the public.

The threat of research

The view adopted in this book is that it is the responsibility of users of research evidence to review it as thoroughly as possible and for researchers to make this possible by full and candid publication. To label something as research has become a universal way of increasing credibility. But this prestige is also a threat. Research can expose. A cosy annual report from a headteacher is converted into a threat by research showing how to report so that intakes are related to outputs and social background. In the days of selection for secondary schooling many primary-school headteachers reported their successes in getting places at prestigious schools without pointing out that this should have been expected from their rather nice catchment area.

Contemporary examples can be found in the presentation of examination results by schools. It is not just that they usually lack detail on attainments at intake, thus giving no indication of the value added by the school, but that the numbers often make it impossible to relate passes to policy over entry to public examinations and to other factors that may determine the averages displayed. A school that only enters those who will get good grades can display 100 per cent success. Schools receiving large numbers into their sixth forms can claim very superior results two years later by relating A-level results to the numbers in the fifth form. When the relative merits of Highbury Grove and Islington Green schools were debated in the *Daily Telegraph* and *New Statesman* in the late 1960s, the battle of statistics moved from comparing 'raw' examination passes to taking into account the number of children in each of three ability bands at intake. Predictably an expert reanalysis, concentrating on children in the top band only, found that both schools were doing better than expected (Gray 1982). Even that reanalysis may have been faulty. Primary-school headteachers in inner London allocated children to bands after being notified of the numbers for each band in their schools. Around the margins of bands many children were placed arbitrarily, or even to ensure that they received a place at a particular secondary school.

These English examples pale beside the extraordinary Cannell controversy in the USA (Cannell 1987). In the 1980s, all 50 states, using nationally normed standardized tests, apparently reported achievement above the national average. Across the whole country 70 per cent of students were told they were achieving above average. The reason seems to have been teaching to the test, but the motives were clear. Once results are presented as research they carry authority. There is a lot at stake. The work has to be left to the teachers. Getting reliable data, even in the more centralized British system, is always going to be difficult. The nearer you get to the way data is collected and collated, the more doubts you have. Meanwhile schools, local authorities and governments get more sophisticated in the way they present results to give a favourable picture. Research carries authority. It informs and benefits education and other services by promoting and disseminating new ideas, new ways of producing and displaying evidence. That is a threat to some, but a boon to others. Making research fully public ensures that the public can interpret and hence influence policies and practices.

The scope of social research

Researchers are usually pragmatic realists, getting on with the job without much thought for problems of what there is to know and how we can know it. They also proceed without delaying long over how the knowledge they produce will be used. Many feel the pressure to research, to qualify, to earn promotion, to support their university, to help colleagues, to pass on research skills. They may be collecting facts and figures, testing and developing theory, guiding policy and practice. They belong to different communities with different interests. Among them will be the politically active who use research as a way of raising awareness, a way of changing the world.

A common feature among this variety will be excitement as evidence accumulates. It is often only when the results are in that their implications are appreciated. Much of the work may be mundane. Most results are predictable because researchers work within disciplines that provide both models and methods that lead to a limited range of evidence and interpretation. But, particularly when it is intended to interpret human understanding, it can be unpredictable. The organization of this school is actually producing the polarization that is its problem. These young women have accepted the identity used by their teachers. This programme is aggravating the deprivation it is intended to improve. These figures suggest that suicide is higher in both slump and boom than when the economy is just ticking over. Then the blood pounds.

Arriving in the Inner London Education Authority at a time when schools were seen to be powerless in the face of social background factors, I was handed a research report showing that Catholic primary schools had higher standards of reading than the rest, but shared similar intakes. I rushed it down to Dr Briault, the Education Officer. His response was terse. Conversion to the Papacy was beyond his authority. Wise, because later evidence suggested that differences disappeared during secondary schooling. Another reformation might have been harmful. However, such lapses were tolerated as long as the Research and Statistics group delivered the numbers that enabled the Authority to resource and administer one thousand schools.

This dependence on description to keep the organization working is shared with those interested in developing theory. It is the basis from which evaluations and hence changes can be made. Simultaneously it is the basis for constructing the simplified models that social scientists use to be able to speculate on the complexities of the world. But little else is shared between these two groups. The academic is concerned to improve models of the real world. Fame comes from changing them. The policy-maker wants a firm base for predicting the consequences of alternative policies. Yet that is precisely what the theorist cannot offer.

The key research activity given these differences is evaluation. This is where researchers are expected to contribute to practice. But even here, the rival attraction of developing theories interferes. From the establishment of the Schools Council in 1964 to the School Curriculum and Assessment Authority, researchers have produced hundreds of reports. Few have provided a basis for action. But evaluation itself has been elaborated. That elaboration has followed the pattern of social research itself, from quantitative studies based on testing or defining objectives to illumination and case study, from bureaucratic to democratic. This elaboration is central to academic enterprise. But a committee waiting for evidence on whether an innovation has worked is irked by a report on the negotiations over who owns the facts collected by the researchers. Especially when they paid for them.

In all cases research evidence carries authority. It is an explicit, systematic, public claim to produce valid knowledge. Its competitors are based in authority that requires faith and obedience, not agreement, among peers. Thus, however mundane, research can shine into dark corners, demystify, lift the cruelty of much folklore and dogma. It can enlighten.

Research as enlightenment

Across a century of sociology the subject has been divided into those seeing humans as constrained by external social reality, those seeing that reality as constructed through human ingenuity and interaction and those attempting to combine both of these conflicting views of the human condition. The most popular compromise today is 'the double hermeneutic' (Giddens 1984). One set of meanings are used by the humans involved to construct the social world. Social scientists study those human meanings and construct their own models. The two sets continually influence each other. Hence the task of research is to get to know what humans know. But the evidence produced and the social science concepts used to interpret the human condition then become part of the everyday lay human capacity for further interpretation. Thus social research is a part of the means whereby the world is understood by those involved.

This view places research within the continuous interchange of understandings between everyday understanding and social science. Thus research is never detached. It has become part of modern life, influencing the way the world is understood by those involved. That places a lot of weight on publication. If research is going to enlighten, to help work out everyday meanings, the researcher's responsibilities persist as evidence is published, interpreted and applied. Jargon is a break in the trust implied in the exchange of meanings.

Behind these possible ways in which research can affect policy and practice lie very different models of policy-orientated research (Weiss 1982). The conventional 'engineering' model starts with the identification of a problem in current policy and of the information needed to solve it. Researchers are contracted to provide this data. It is then interpreted and used to formulate a new policy. The researcher is given a clear idea of what is needed and provides the missing facts. Here there is no confusion in the role of the researcher. The task is specific to a problem, not to advance more general theories. But this rarely happens. The brief is often vague. The problem is too complex. Policy-making isn't a linear progression from problem to solution.

The alternative 'enlightenment' model was first proposed by Janowitz (1972), significantly at the University of Chicago. This is based on observation of what actually happens in policy-making. Researchers are now less detached experts providing problem-solving data, than participants in the policy-making process. The research provides ideas rather than facts about the policy and its likely effects. These are fed into discussions rather than used to solve particular problems.

Given the frequency with which research is apparently ignored by those who paid for it, this enlightenment model is attractive to social scientific researchers, particularly if they are concerned about the impact of both their evidence and the theories behind it. It justifies social research. Similarly, if you have watched your research report disappear into a bureaucrat's drawer, it is comforting to know that the ideas in it will be percolating through decision-makers and professionals. Nor is this wishful thinking. Ideas such as Pygmalion effects, the advantages of destreaming and of applying 'Rutter' to poor schools so influenced politicians in the Inner London Education Authority in the 1970s that in-house researchers had to work hard to dampen down the enthusiasm by pointing to the need for caution because of the frail evidence behind the headline reporting.

The claim that social research enlightens, however attractive, has limits in practice. It has already been argued that there are often school inspectors and others paid to do this. The percolation of research into policy-making may be wishful thinking. Few researchers get that close. Nor are publications necessarily read. Enlightenment sounds grand, but requires a lot of effort.

The importance of the enlightenment model is in emphasizing that the diffused power of research often has more impact than the precise findings on a specified subject. Research is popular because it is generally accepted as the most reliable way of obtaining evidence. It may be flawed, but at least there is concern to justify the methods used, to employ them consistently and to make public not only results and conclusions, but how these were obtained and their consequent strengths and weaknesses. That concern for the logic of enquiry, for design and technique, for limiting conclusions to the evidence produced, justifies the authority of research and its popularity on the supply side. But the demand side is more problematic. The consumer often has to take too much on trust.

Given the claim for research as a potentially solid basis for accumulating valid knowledge, for description, theorizing and guiding policy and practice, what conclusions can be drawn about the conditions necessary for it to merit those claims? The answers lie in the basic features of research spelled out in Chapter 1. Compared with competitive claims to knowledge, it is intentionally restricted in scope, it is carried out systematically, it is made fully public to facilitate review. These features demand modesty, scepticism and honesty not only among researchers, but among the users of research. For that to be possible, publication has to be comprehensible and candid. Those who use research have to be able to assess its credibility, whether qualitative or quantitative.

The modesty should follow from the limitations spelled out in this book. A science of human behaviour has not been delivered. The claim to explain, to discover laws, to predict has been abandoned. Today it is popular to attack positivism – the attempt to apply scientific method to the study of the human condition – as misguided. But it was the basis of the claim to be a science and many of its assumptions and aspirations remain intact. We may no longer believe in a social world that was created, or is governed by laws or out there waiting to be discovered, but we still behave as if this were the case in our daily lives and often as researchers. Even in interpretive social research, where the researcher and those researched are engaged in mutual interpretation, the former will still try to understand what they have observed by imposing their own models. Otherwise there would be no point in being a social scientist. But there are many such models: scientistic, interpretive, critical. These conflicting views of the social world, of the ways we can get to know about these and of the methods appropriate for investigating them, mean that ambitions have to be modest.

The need for scepticism arises from the technical problems in Part Two of this book and from the confusion of method with methodology that so often leaves the logic out of the former. Both the theoretical assumptions that justify using a research design and its suitability for investigating the specific topic tend to be ignored. Consequently the credibility of much research is impossible to assess. For every factual claim there is a counter. Facts turn out to be fiction. Research is often a means to qualification, promotion, prestige, funding, but there is little accumulation of evidence. This follows from the difficulties in replicating research on humans, when the findings themselves change the situation being studied. But it is also because it is often not possible to know how and why the work was done in order to assess it.

This weakness in reporting research has been a repetitive theme in the four editions of this book. In each Controversy in education, issues of major importance raised by research such as school effectiveness, the impact of class size, of streaming, the success of comprehensive schooling, the best ways of teaching reading, the age at which formal teaching should start, remain unresolved. Research raised the questions, fed the debates, but provided few answers. Yet the research in these cases was often well-funded, carefully designed by teams and picked over by critics. Most research reports remain in specialized journals or unreferenced in archives. It adds to knowledge, but even if it enlightens the impact is short-lived.

Thus the last word has to be about the necessity for researchers to make their work public with modesty, scepticism and candour. Assumptions, design, results and conclusions have to be made fully public for peer review. But the peers are not just colleagues. They include those who will follow-up the work and above all those who will *use* it. This wider audience includes the next generation of researchers, those in related disciplines, the media, and above all the general public. If social scientific knowledge affects the human condition being studied, those affected should be given the chance to assess the credibility of the evidence pressed on them. That rarely happens. Popularization carries no academic prestige and usually strips research reports of the little detail they contain. Research can be a powerful influence. It feeds into mass media. It has an increasingly educated population as audience. They require candid and clear reporting to facilitate a broad public peer review.

REFERENCES

Abraham, J. (1995) *Divide and School: gender and class dynamics in compre-hensive education*, Falmer Press, London.

Aitken, M., Bennett, S.N. and Hesketh, J. (1981) 'Teaching Styles and Pupil Progress: A re-analysis', *British Journal of Psychology*, 51, pp. 170–86.

American Sociological Association (1995) 'Symposium on Prediction in the Social Sciences', *American Journal of Sociology*, 100(6), pp. 1520–6.

Andrews, F.M. (1984) 'Construct and Error Components of Survey Measures', *Public Opinion Quarterly*, 48, pp. 409–42.

Atkinson, P. (1984) 'Wards and Deeds: taking knowledge and control ser-iously', in Burgess, R.G. *The Research Process in Educational Settings*, Falmer Press, Lewes, pp. 163–86.

Atkinson, P. (1996) *Sociological Readings and Re-readings*, Avebury, Aldershot.

Averch, H.A. (1974) *How Effective is Schooling? A critical review of research*, Educational Technology Publications, Washington.

Avila, M. (1969) *Tradition and Growth*, University of Chicago Press, Chicago.

Bales, R.F. (1950) *Interaction Process Analysis*, Addison Wesley, New York.

Ball, S. (1981) *Beachside Comprehensive*, Cambridge University Press, London.

Ball, S. (1993) 'Self-doubt and Soft Data: social and technical trajectories in ethnographic fieldwork', in Hammersley, M. *Educational Research: current issues*, Paul Chapman, London.

Banks, M., Bates, I., Breakwell, G., Bynner, J., Emler, J., Jamieson, L. and Rob-erts, K. (1991) *Careers and Identities*, Open University Press, Buckingham.

Barnard, H.C. (1952) *An Introduction to Teaching*, University of London Press, London.

Becher, T. (1989) *Academic Tribes and Territories*, Open University Press, Buckingham.

Becker, H. (1963) *Outsiders*, Free Press, New York.

Beloff, H. (1986) *Getting into Life*, Methuen, London.

Belsen, W.A. (1981) *The Design and Understanding of Survey Questions*, Gower, Aldershot.

Bennett, S.N. (1976) *Teaching Styles and Pupil Progress*, Open Books, London.

Bennett, S.N. (1987) 'Surveyed from a Shaky Base', in Murphy, R. and Torrance, H. (eds) *Evaluating Education*, Harper & Row, London, pp. 81–3.

Berger, P. and Luckmann, T. (1966) *The Social Construction of Reality*, Penguin Books, Harmondsworth.

Bernstein, B. (1958) 'Some Sociological Determinants of Perception', *British Journal of Sociology*, 9, pp. 159–74.

Bernstein, B. (1960) 'Language and Social Class', *The British Journal of Sociology*, 11, pp. 271–6.

Beynon, H. (1973) *Working for Ford*, Penguin Books, Harmondsworth.

Blackburn, R. (1969) 'A Brief Guide to Bourgeois Ideology', in Cockburn, A. and Blackburn, R. *Student Power*, Penguin Books, Harmondsworth.

Blatchford, P. and Mortimore, P. (1994) 'The Issue of Class Size for Young Children in Schools: what can we learn from research?', *Oxford Review of Education*, 20(4), pp. 411–28.

Blatchford, P., Ireson, J. and Joscelyne, T. (1994) 'The Initial Teaching of Reading: what do teachers think?', *Educational Psychology*, 14(3), pp. 333–44.

Bloom, B.S. (1964) *Stability and Change in Human Characteristics*, John Wiley, New York.

Blumer, H. (1939) *An Appraisal of Thomas and Znaniecki's 'The Polish Peasant in Europe and America'*, US Social Science Research Council, New York.

Bowles, S. and Gintis, H. (1976) *Schooling in Capitalist America*, Routledge & Kegan Paul, London.

Bowles, S. and Gintis, H. (1986) *Democracy and Capitalism*, Basic Books, New York.

Bradshaw, J. (1988) *The Family*, Health Communications Inc., Deerfield Beach.

Bramel, D. and Friend, R. (1981) 'Hawthorne: the myth of the docile worker and class bias in psychology', *American Psychologist*, 36, pp. 867–88.

British Psychological Society (1980) 'Supplement', *Bulletin of the British Psychological Society*, 33, November.

British Psychological Society (1992) 'Council Statement of 22 February 1992', *Bulletin of the British Psychological Society*, 5(4).

Broad, W. and Wade, N. (1982) *Betrayers of the Truth*, Oxford University Press, Oxford.

Brown, R. (ed.) (1973) *Knowledge, Control and Cultural Change*, Tavistock, London.

Browne, N. and Ross, C. (1995) 'Girls' Stuff, Boys' Stuff: young children talking and playing', in Holland, J., Blair, M. and Sheldon, S. *Debates and Issues in Feminist Research and Pedagogy*, Multilingual Matters, Clevedon.

Bryant, P.E. and Trabasso, T. (1971) 'Transitive Inferences and Memory in Young Children', *Nature*, 232, pp. 456–8.

Burgess, R.G. (1983) *Experiencing Comprehensive Education*, Allen & Unwin, London.

Burgess, R.G. (1984) 'Autobiographical Accounts and the Research Experience', in Burgess, R.G. *The Research Process in Educational Settings*, Falmer Press, Lewes, pp. 251–70.

Burgess, R.G. (ed.) (1985a) *Field Methods in the Study of Education*, Falmer Press, Lewes.

Burgess, R.G. (1985b) *Strategies of Educational Research: qualitative methods*, Falmer Press, Lewes.

Burstall, C. (1979) 'Time to Mend the Nets', *Trends*, 3, pp. 27–33.

Bynner, J. (1992) *The ESRC 16–19 Initiative: the route to careers and identities*, City University, London.

Cain, L.D. (1969) 'The AMA and the Gerontologists: uses and abuses of "A profile of the aged USA"', in Sjoberg, G. *Ethics, Politics and Social Research*, Routledge & Kegan Paul, London, pp. 78–114.

Calder, A. (1985) 'Mass Observation', in Bulmer, M. *Essays on the History of British Sociological Research*, Cambridge University Press, Cambridge, pp. 121–36.

Cannell, J.J. (1987) *Nationally-Normed Elementary Achievement Testing in America's Public Schools; how all 50 states are above the national average*, Daniels: Friends of Education, West Virginia.

Carey, A. (1967) 'The Hawthorne Studies: a re-analysis', *American Sociological Review*, 32, pp. 403–16.

Charles, E. (1938) 'The Effect of Present Trends in Fertility and Morality upon the Future Population of Great Britain and upon its Age Composition', in Hogben, L. (ed.) *Political Arithmetic*, Allen & Unwin, London, pp. 73–105.

Church, J. (1973) *Understanding Your Child From Birth To Seven*, Wildwood House, London.

Church of Scientology International (1992) *What is Scientology?* Bridge Publications, Los Angeles, pp. 453–92.

Cicourel, A.V. (1967) *The Social Organization of Juvenile Justice*, John Wiley, New York.

Clarke, J. (1978) 'Football and Working-class Fans: tradition and change', in Ingham, R. *Football Hooliganism*, Inter-Action Imprint, London.

Clarke, A.D.B. and Clarke, A.M. (1974) *Mental Deficiency*, Methuen, London.

Cole, M. (1988) *Bowles and Gintis Revisited*, Falmer Press, Lewes.

Coleman, J.S. (1966) *Equality of Educational Opportunity*, US Government Printing Office, Washington.

Comfort, A. (1967) *The Anxiety Makers*, Nelson, London.

Comte, A. (1848) *A General View of Positivism*, Routledge, London.

Cronbach, L.J. (1987) 'Issues in Planning Evaluations', in Murphy, R. and Torrance, H. *Evaluating Education*, Harper & Row, London.

Dahrendorf, R. (1995) *The London School of Economics*, Oxford University Press, Oxford.

Dale, A. and Marsh, C. (1993) *The 1991 Census*, HMSO, London.

Davies, B., Corbishley, P., Evans, J. and Kenrick, C. (1985) 'Integrating Methodologies: if the intellectual relations don't get you then the social will', in Burgess, R.G. (ed.) *Strategies of Educational Research*, Falmer Press, Lewes, pp. 251–70.

Davies, L. (1982) *Life in the Classroom and Playground*, Routledge & Kegan Paul, London.

Davies, S. (1995) 'Leaps of Faith: shifting currents in critical sociology of education', *American Journal of Sociology*, 100(6), pp. 1448–78.

Dawtrey, L., Holland, J. and Hammer, M. with Sheldon, S. (1995) *Equality and Inequality in Education Policy*, Multilingual Matters, Clevedon.

Day, C. (1996) *Class Size and the Quality of Education*, National Association of Headteachers, Haywards Heath.

Dearing, R. (1993) *The National Curriculum and its Assessment: interim report*, School Curriculum and Assessment Authority, London.

Delamont, S. (1992) *Fieldwork in Educational Settings*, Falmer Press, London.

DeMause, L. (1974) *The History of Childhood*, Souvenir Press, London.

Denzin, N. (1970) *The Research Act*, Aldine Press, New York.

DES (1977a) *Education in Schools*, HMSO, London.

DES (1977b) *Ten Good Schools*, HMSO, London.

DES (1978) *Primary Education in England*, HMSO, London.

DES (1979) *Aspects of Secondary Education*, HMSO, London.

DES (1985) *Better Schools: evaluation and appraisal*, HMSO, London, p. 25.

DES (1986) *Science in Schools, Reports 4 and 5*, HMSO, London.

Ditton, J. (1977) *Part-time Crime: an ethnography of fiddling and pilferage*, Macmillan, Basingstoke.

Dollard, J. (1935) *Criteria for the Life History*, Yale University Press, Yale.

Donaldson, M. (1978) *Children's Minds*, Fontana, Glasgow.

Douglas, J.W.B. (1964) *The Home and the School*, McGibbon & Kee, London.

Douglas, J.W.B., Ross, J.M. and Simpson, H.R. (1968) *All our Future*, Panther, London.

Downing, J.A. (1964) *The i.t.a. Reading Experiment*, Evans, London.

Dukes, E. and Hay, M. (1949) *Children of Today and Tomorrow*, Allen & Unwin, London.

Durbin, J. and Stuart, A. (1951) 'Differences in Response Rates of Experienced and Inexperienced Interviewers', *Journal of the Royal Statistical Society*, pp. 163–205.

Durkheim, E. (1952) *Suicide*, Routledge & Kegan Paul, London.

Durkheim, E. (1966) *The Rules of Sociological Method*, Free Press, New York.

Elashoff, J.D. and Snow, R.E. (1971) *Pygmalion Reconsidered*, C.A. Jones, New York.

Eysenck, H.J. (1965) *Fact and Fiction in Psychology*, Penguin Books, Harmondsworth, pp. 127–30.

Eysenck, H.J. (1971) *Race, Intelligence and Education*, Maurice Temple Smith, London.

Festinger, L., Riecken, H.W. and Schachter, S. (1956) *When Prophecy Fails*, Harper & Row, New York.

Fielding, N. (1981) *The National Front*, Routledge & Kegan Paul, London.

Firth, I. (1969) 'N-rays – ghost of a scandal past', *New Scientist*, 25 November, pp. 642–3.

Flavell, J.H. (1963) *The Developmental Psychology of Jean Piaget*, van Nostrand, London.

Fleming, C. (1959) 'Class Size as a Variable in the Teaching Situation', *Educational Research*, February, pp. 35–48.

Floud, J.E., Halsey, A.H. and Martin, F.M. (1957) *Social Class and Educational Opportunity*, Heinemann, London.

Flynn, J.R. (1989) 'Rushton, Evolution and Race: an essay on intelligence and virtue', *The Psychologist*, 9, pp. 363–6.

Foddy, W.C. (1993) *Constructing Questions for Interviews and Questionnaires*, Cambridge University Press, Cambridge.

Fogelman, K. (ed.) (1983) *Growing Up in Great Britain*, Macmillan, Basingstoke.

Fontana, D. (1995) *Psychology for Teachers*, BPS and Macmillan, Basingstoke.

Ford, J. (1969) *Social Class and the Comprehensive School*, Routledge & Kegan Paul, London.

Freeman, D. (1984) *Margaret Mead and Samoa*, Penguin Books, Harmondsworth.

Fuller, M. (1984) 'Dimensions of Gender in a School: reinventing the wheel?' in Burgess, R.G. *The Research Process in Educational Settings*, Falmer Press, Lewes, pp. 139–62.

Galton, F. (1889) *Natural Inheritance*, Macmillan, London.

Galton, M. and Delamont, S. (1985) 'Speaking with Forked Tongues? Two styles of observation in the ORACLE project', in Burgess, R.G. *Field Methods in the Study of Education*, Falmer Press, Lewes, pp. 163–90.

Giddens, A. (1984) *The Constitution of Society*, Polity Press, Cambridge.

Gillie, O. (1976) 'Crucial Data was Faked by Eminent Psychologist', *Sunday Times*, 24 October.

Gilligan, C. (1982) *In a Different Voice*, Harvard University Press, Harvard.

Gitlin, A., Siegel, M. and Boru, K. (1989) 'The Politics of Method', *Qualitative Studies in Education*, 2(3), pp. 237–53.

Glaser B. and Strauss, A. (1967) *The Discovery of Grounded Theory*, Weidenfeld & Nicolson, London.

Goldberg, D.P. (1972) *Detection of Psychiatric Illness by Questionnaire*, Oxford University Press, Oxford.

Goldthorpe, J.H. (1983) 'Women and Class Analysis: in defence of the conventional view', *Sociology*, 17(4), pp. 465–88.

Goldthorpe, J.H. (1994) 'The Uses of History in Sociology – a Reply', *British Journal of Sociology*, 45(1), pp. 55–78.

Goldthorpe, J.H., Llewellyn, C. and Payne, C. (1980) *Social Mobility and Class Structure in Modern Britain*, Oxford University Press, Oxford.

Goldthorpe, J.H., Lockwood, D., Bechofer, F. and Platt, J. (1968) *The Affluent Worker*, Cambridge University Press, Cambridge.

Good, I.J. (1962) *The Scientist Speculates*, Heinemann, London.

Goodchild, M.E. and Duncan-Jones, P. (1985) 'Chronicity and the GHQ', *British Journal of Psychiatry*, 146, pp. 55–62.

Goodson, I. (1982) *School Subjects and Curriculum Change*, Croom Helm, London.

Gottschalk, L., Kluckohn, C. and Angell, R.C. (1945) *The Use of Personal Documents in History, Anthropology and Sociology*, Social Science Research Council, New York.

Gouldner, A.V. (1962) 'Anti-Minotaur: the myth of value-free sociology', *Social Problems*, 9, pp. 199–213.

Government Statisticians Collective (1993) 'How Official Statistics are Produced: views from the inside', in Hammersley, M. (ed.) *Social Research*, Sage, London, pp. 146–65.

Goyder, J. (1987) *The Silent Majority: non-response in sample surveys*, Polity Press, Cambridge.

Gray J. (1982) 'Publish and be Damned? The problem of publishing examination results in two inner-London schools', *Educational Analysis*, 4(3), pp. 47–56.

Gray, J. and Wilcox, B. (1995) '*Good School, Bad School'. Evaluating Performance and Encouraging Improvement*, Open University Press, Buckingham.

Gray, J., Jesson, D. and Sime, N. (1990) 'Estimating Differences in the Examination Performance of Secondary Schools in Six LEAs: a multilevel approach to school effectiveness', *Oxford Review of Education*, 16(2), pp. 137–58.

Gray, J.L. and Moshinsky, P. (1938) 'Ability and Opportunity in English Secondary Education', in Hogben, L. (ed.) *Political Arithmetic*, Allen & Unwin, London.

Grosskuth, P. (1991) *The Secret Ring*, Jonathan Cape, London.

Hall, G.S. (1904) *Adolescence*, Appleton, New York.

Hall, K. (1994) 'Conceptual and Methodological Flaws in the Evaluation of the "First" British Reading Recovery Programme', *British Educational Research Journal*, 20(1), pp. 121–8.

Hall, S. and Jefferson, T. (1975) *Resistance through Rituals*, Hutchinson, London.

Halsey, A.H., Heath, A.F. and Ridge, J.M. (1980) *Origins and Destinations: family, class and education in modern Britain*, Clarendon Press, Oxford.

Hammersley, M. (1981) 'The Outsider's Advantage', *British Educational Research Journal*, 7(2), pp. 167–72.

Hammersley, M. (1984) 'The Researcher Exposed: a natural history', in Burgess, R.G. *The Research Process in Educational Settings*, Falmer Press, Lewes, pp. 39–68.

Hammersley, M. (1992) 'On Feminist Methodology', *Sociology*, 26(2), pp. 187–206.

Hammersley, M. (1993) 'Research and Anti-racism', *British Journal of Sociology*, 44(3), pp. 429–46.

Hammersley, M. (1994) 'On Feminist Methodology: a response', *Sociology*, 28(1), pp. 293–300.

Harding, S. (ed.) (1986) *Feminism and Methodology*, Indiana University Press, Bloomington.

Hardyment, C. (1983) *Dream Babies: child care from Locke to Spock*, Jonathan Cape, London.

Hargreaves, D.H. (1967) *Social Relations in a Secondary School*, Routledge & Kegan Paul, London.

Harré, R. (1993) *Social Being*, Blackwell, Oxford.

Harrold, M.V. and Temple, M.H. (1959–1960) A study of children in the admission classes of four infant schools, making a comparison between those who have attended a nursery school and those admitted direct from home, unpublished thesis, University of London, Child Development Centre.

Hart, N. (1994) 'John Goldthorpe and the Relics of Sociology', *British Journal of Sociology*, 45(1), pp. 21–30.

Hearnshaw, L.S. (1979) *Cyril Burt: psychologist*, Hodder & Stoughton, London.

Henry, S. (1978) *The Hidden Economy*, Robertson, Glasgow.

Hite, S. (1991) *The Hite Report on Love, Passion and Emotional Violence*, MacDonald, London.

Hite, S. (1994) *The Hite Report on the Family*, Bloomsbury, London.

Hobhouse, L., Ginsburg, M. and Wheeler, H. (1915) *The Material, Cultural and Social Institutions of the Simpler Peoples*, Chatto & Windus, London.

Holland, J., Blair, M. and Sheldon, S. (1995a) *Debates and Issues in Feminist Research and Pedagogy*, Multilingual Matters, Clevedon.

Holland, J., Ramazanoglu, C., Sharpe, S. and Thomson, R. (1995b) 'Pleasure, Pressure and Power: some contradictions of gendered sexuality', in Blair, M., Holland, J., with Sheldon, S. *Identity and Diversity*, Multilingual Matters, Clevedon, pp. 260–78.

Holmes, L.D. (1974) *Samoan Village*, Holt, Rinehart & Winston, New York.

Homan, R. (1978) 'Interpersonal Communication in Pentacostal Meetings', *Sociological Review*, 26(3), pp. 499–518,

Homan, R. (1991) *The Ethics of Social Research*, Longman, Harlow.

Howard, J. (1985) *Margaret Mead: a life*, Harvill, New York.

Hoxby, C.M. (1996) 'How Teacher Unions Affect Education Production', *The Economist*, 19 October, pp. 655–66.

Hudson, L. (1971) 'Review of Eysenck's "Race, Intelligence and Education" ', *New Society*, 1 July, pp. 29–30.

Huizenga, J.R. (1993) *Cold Fusion: the scientific fiasco of the century*, Oxford University Press, Oxford.

Humphreys, L. (1974) *The Tearoom Trade*, Aldine, Chicago.

Husen, T. (1967) *International Study of Achievement in Mathematics*, Almquist & Wicksell, Stockholm.

Inner London Education Authority (1969, 1972, 1975, 1977) *Literacy Survey*, Schools Subcommittee, London.

Ironside, M. and Roberts, S. (1965) *Mathematics in the Primary School*, National Froebel Foundation, London.

Isaacs, N. (1955) 'The Wider Significance of Piaget's Work', in Lawrence, E., Theakston, T.R. and Isaacs, N. *Some Aspects of Piaget's Work*, National Froebel Foundation, London.

Isaacs, N. (1960) *New Light on Children's Ideas of Number*, London: ESA.

Isaacs, N. (1964) 'Memo to the Plowden Committee', in Hardemann, M. (ed.) *Children's Ways of Knowing: Nathan Isaacs on education, psychology and Piaget*, Teachers College Press, New York, pp. 159–80.

Isaacs, S. (1933) *Social Development in Young Children*, Routledge, London.

Janowitz, M. (1972) *Social Methods and Social Policy*, General Learning Systems, Morristown.

Jayaratne, J.E. and Stewart, A.J. (1995) 'Qualitative Methods in the Social Sciences', in Holland, J., Blair, M. and Sheldon, S. *Debates and Issues in Feminist Research and Pedagogy*, Multilingual Matters, Clevedon, pp. 217–34.

Jensen, A.R. (1969) 'How Much can we Boost IQ and Scholastic Achievement?', *Harvard Educational Review*, Winter, pp. 1–123.

Jencks, C.S. (1973) *Inequality*, Allen Lane, Harmondsworth.

Jesson, D. and Gray, J. (1991) 'Slants on Slopes', *School Effectiveness and School Improvement*, 2(3), pp. 230–47.

Jowell, R. and Hoinville, G. (1969) 'Opinion Polls Tested'. *New Society*, 7 August, pp. 206–7.

Joynson, R.B. (1989) *The Burt Affair*, Routledge & Kegan Paul, London.

Kamin, L. (1974) *The Science and Politics of IQ*, Lawrence Erlbaum, London.

Kelly, G. (1955) *The Psychology of Personal Constructs*, Norton, New York.

Kerlinger, F. (1977) 'The Influence of Research in Educational Practice', *CEDR Quarterly*, Bloomington, Illinois, September, pp. 5–12.

Kinsey, A.C., Pomeroy, W.B. and Martin, C.E. (1953) *Sexual Behaviour in the Human Female*, W.B. Saunders, New York.

Kohn, A. (1986) *False Prophets*, Blackwell, Oxford.

Kühl, S. (1994) *The Nazi Connection*, Oxford University Press, Oxford.

Lacey, C. (1970) *Hightown Grammar*, Manchester University Press, Manchester.

Lawrence, E. (1960a) 'Piaget and Education', *National Froebel Foundation Bulletin*, 123, p. 12.

Lawrence, E. (1960b) 'Experimental Work on Piagetian Lines', *National Froebel Foundation Bulletin*, 127, pp. 8–12.

Lewis, O. (1951) *Life in a Mexican Village: Tepoztlan revisited*, University of Illinois Press, Illinois.

Lindsay, K. (1926) *Social Progress and Educational Waste*, Routledge, London.

Linz, D., Donnerstein, E., Land, K.C., McCall, P.L., Scott, J., Shafer, J., Klein, L.J. and Lance, L. (1991) 'Estimating Community Standards: the use of social scientific evidence in obscenity prosecutions', *Public Opinion Quarterly*, 55, pp. 80–112.

Lippitt, R. and White, R.K. (1965) 'An Experimental Study of Leadership and Group Life', in Proshansky, H.P. and Seidenberg, R. *Basic Studies in Sociology*, Holt, Rinehart & Winston, New York, pp. 523–37.

Little, A. and Mabey, C. (1973) 'Reading Attainment and Ethnic Mix of London Primary Schools', in Donnison, D. and Eversley, D. (eds) *London: urban patterns, problems and policies*, Heinemann, London.

Lovell, K. (1961) *The Growth of Basic Mathematical and Scientific Concepts in Children*, University of London Press, London.

Lynch, K. and O'Neill, C. (1994) 'The Colonialisation of Social Class in Education', *British Journal of the Sociology of Education*, 15(3), pp. 307–24.

Mac an Ghaill, M. (1994) '(In)Visibility: "race", sexuality and masculinity in the school context', in Blair, M., Holland, J. with Sheldon, S. *Identity and Diversity*, Multilingual Matters, Clevedon, pp. 244–59.

Mac an Ghaill, M. (1996) 'What about the Boys? Schooling, class and crisis masculinity', *Sociological Review*, 44(3), pp. 381–7.

Mackintosh, N.J. (1995) *Cyril Burt: fraud or framed?*, Oxford University Press, Oxford.

McCaghy, C.H. and Skipper, J.K. (1970) 'Striptease: the anatomy and career contingencies of a deviant occupation', *Social Problems*, Winter, pp. 391–405.

McDougall, W. (1908) *An Introduction to Social Psychology*, Methuen, London.

McNamara, D. (1980) 'The Outsider's Arrogance: the failure of participant observers to understand classroom events', *British Educational Research Journal*, 6(2), pp. 113–26.

Mars, G. (1982) *Cheats at Work*, Allen & Unwin, London.

Marsh, P. (1978) *Aggro: the illusion of violence*, Dent, London.

Marsh, P., Rosser, E. and Harré, R. (1978) *The Rules of Disorder*, Routledge & Kegan Paul, London.

Masson, J. (1992) *The Assault on Truth*, Fontana, London.

Mead, M. (1943) *Coming of Age in Samoa*, Penguin Books, Harmondsworth.

Mead, M. (1972) *Blackberry Winter*, Angus & Robertson, Glasgow.

Mead, M. (1977) *Letters from the Field*, Harper & Row, New York.

Medawar, P. (1964) 'Is the Scientific Paper a Fraud?' in Edge, D. *Experiment*, BBC, London, pp. 64–70.

Medawar, P. (1986) *The Limits of Science*, Oxford University Press, Oxford.

Mennell, S. (1974) *Sociological Theory*, Methuen, London.

Milgram, S. (1963) 'Behavioural Study of Obedience', *Journal of Abnormal and Social Psychology*, 67, pp. 371–8.

Mills, C.W. (1959) *The Sociological Imagination*, Oxford University Press, Oxford.

Morgan, M. (1996) 'Qualitative Research: a package deal', *The Psychologist*, January, pp. 31–2.

Mortimore, P. and Goldstein, H. (1996) 'The Mortimore/Goldstein Letter to the *Observer*', *Research Intelligence*, 58, pp. 9–10.

Mortimore, P., Sammons, P., Stoll, L., Lewis, D. and Ecob, R. (1988) *School Matters*, Open Books, Wells.

Mouzelis, N. (1991) *Back to Sociological Theory*, Macmillan, Basingstoke.

Moyle, D. (1968) *The Teaching of Reading*, Ward Lock, London.

Murray, C. and Herrnstein, R. (1994) *The Bell Curve: intelligence and class structure in American life*, Free Press, New York.

Nash, R. (1973) *Classrooms Observed*, Routledge & Kegan Paul, London.

National Froebel Foundation (1961) 'Translation of a Talk by Piaget on 18 October 1960's, *Bulletin*, 130, June, pp. 1–6.

Newby, H. (1977a) *The Deferential Worker*, Allen & Unwin, London.

Newby, H. (1977b) 'Appendix: editorial note', in Bell, C. and Newby, H. *Doing Sociological Research*, Allen & Unwin, London, pp. 63–6.

Newson, J. and Newson. E. (1976) 'Parental Roles and Social Contexts', in Shipman, M. (ed.) *The Organisation and Impact of Social Research*, Routledge, London, pp. 22–48.

Oakley, A. (1991) 'Eugenics, Social Medicine and the Career of Richard Titmuss in Britain, 1935–1950', *British Journal of Sociology*, 42(2), pp. 165–94.

O'Connor, P. (1995) 'Understanding Variations in Marital Sexual Pleasure: an impossible task?', *Sociological Review*, 43(2), pp. 342–62.

Office of Population Censuses and Surveys (1982) *General Household Survey*, HMSO, London.

OFSTED (1994) *The Handbook for the Inspection of Schools*, OFSTED, London.

OFSTED (1995) *Class Size and the Quality of Education*, OFSTED, London.

Oldcom, M.T. (1960) 'The ABC of Groupness', *Journal of Abnormal Psychology*, 5, pp. 6–45.

Olssen, E.P. (1993) 'Science and Individualism in Educational Psychology' and 'Educational Psychology – its Failings and some Additional Failings: a reply to John Joshua Schwiesco', *Educational Psychology*, 13(2), pp. 155–72 and 183–6.

166   References

Papert, S. (1988) 'The Conservation of Piaget', in Forman, G. and Pufall, P.B. *Construction in the Computer Age*, Lawrence Erlbaum, Hillsdale.

Parsons, T. (1951) *The Social System*, Free Press, New York.

Patrick, J. (1973) *A Glasgow Gang Observed*, Eyre, London.

Pearson, G. and Twohig, J. (1975) 'Ethnography through the Looking Glass', in Hall, S. and Jefferson, T. *Resistance through Rituals*, Hutchinson, London, pp. 119–25.

Peel, E.A. (1960) *The Pupil's Thinking*, Oldbourne, London.

Piaget, J. and Inhelder, B. (1941) *Le Développement des Quantités chez l'Enfant*, Delachause & Niestle, Paris.

Piaget, J. and Szeminska, A. (1952) *The Child's Conception of Number*, Routledge & Kegan Paul, London.

Pile, S. (1988) *The Return of Heroic Failures*, Secker & Warburg, London, p. 207.

Plowden Report (1967) *Children and their Primary Schools*, HMSO, London.

Plummer, K. (1983) *Documents of Life*, Allen & Unwin, London.

Pollard, A. (1985) 'Opportunities and Difficulties of a Teacher–Ethnographer: a personal account', in Burgess, R.G. (ed.) *Field Methods in the Study of Education*, Falmer Press, Lewes, pp. 217–34.

Popper, K.R. (1945) *The Open Society and its Enemies*, Routledge & Kegan Paul, London.

Popper, K.R. (1959) *The Logic of Scientific Discovery*, Hutchinson, London.

Popper, K.R. (1989) *Objective Knowledge*, Clarendon Press, Oxford.

Porter, M.A. (1984) 'The Modification of Method in Researching Postgraduate Education', in Burgess, R.G. *The Research Process in Educational Settings*, Falmer Press, Lewes, pp. 139–62.

Powell, P.J. (1978) *Class Size: a summary of research*, Educational Research Inc., Washington.

Power, M.J. (1967) 'Delinquent Schools', *New Society*, October, pp. 542–3.

Prais, S.J. (1996) 'Class Size and Learning: the Tennessee Experiment – what follows?', *Oxford Review of Education*, 22(4), pp. 399–414.

Price, G. (1966) 'Education as a main course', *Education for Teaching*, 70, pp. 4–12.

Punch, K.F. and Tuettemann, E. (1990) 'Correlates of Psychological Distress among Secondary School Teachers', *British Educational Research Journal*, 16(4), pp. 369–82.

Ramazanoglu, C. (1992) 'On Feminist Methodology: male reason versus female empowerment', *Sociology*, 26(2), pp. 207–12.

Redfield, R. (1930) *Tepoztlan, A Mexican Village: a study of folk life*, University of Chicago Press, Chicago.

Redfield, R. (1968) *The Primitive World and its Transformations*, Penguin Books, Harmondsworth.

Reynolds, D. (1976) 'Schools Do Make a Difference', *New Society*, July, pp. 223–5.

Reynolds, D. and Cuttance, P. (eds) (1992) *School Effectiveness: research, policy and practice*, Cassell, London.

Ritchie, J. and Ritchie, J. (1979) *Growing Up in Polynesia*, Allen & Unwin, London.

Roethlisberger, F.J. and Dickson, W.J. (1929) *Management and the Worker*, John Wiley, New York.

Ronai, C.R. (1992) 'The Reflexive Self Through Narrative: a night in the life an erotic dancer/researcher', in Ellis, C. and Flaherty, M.F. (eds) *Investing Subjectivity*, Sage, London, pp. 102–24.

Rosenthal, R. and Fode, K.L. (1963) 'Psychology of the Scientist: V. Three experiments in experimenter bias', *Psychological Reports*, 12, pp. 491–511.

Rosenthal, R. and Jacobson, L. (1968) *Pygmalion in the Classroom*, Holt, Rinehart & Winston, New York.

Rossi, P.J. (1970) 'Evaluating Social Action Programmes', in Denzin, N. *The Values of Social Science*, Trans-action Books, New York, pp. 89–90.

Rushton, J.P. (1987) 'Toward a Theory of Human Multiple Birthing: sociobiology and r/K reproductive strategies', *Acta Geneticae Medicae et Gemellologiae*, 36, pp. 289–98.

Rushton, J.P. (1990) 'Race Differences, r/K Theory and a Reply to Flynn', *The Psychologist*, 5, pp. 195–8.

Rutter, M., Maughan, B., Mortimore, P. and Ouston, J. (1979) *Fifteen Thousand Hours*, Basic Books, London.

Sandelands, L.E. (1990) 'What is so Practical about Theory? Lewin revisited', *Journal of the Theory of Social Behaviour*, 20(3), pp. 235–62.

Scharff, D.E. (1976) *Between Two Worlds*, Careers Consultants, London.

Schwiesco, J.J. (1993) 'Educational Psychology and its Failings: a reply to Ollsson' and 'Are the Failings those of Educational Psychology or Part of Mark Olssen's Theories?', *Educational Psychology*, 13(2), pp. 173–82 and 187–9.

Seeley, J.R. (1966) 'The "Making" and "Taking" of Problems', *Social Problems*, 14, pp. 382–9.

Seeley, J.R. (1964) 'Crestwood Heights: intellectual and libidinal dimensions of research', in Vidich, A., Bensman, J. and Stein, M.R. (eds) *Reflections on Community Studies*, John Wiley, New York, pp. 207–32.

Shaw, C.R. (1931) *The Natural History of a Delinquent Career*, University of Chicago Press, Chicago.

Shelley, D. and Cohen, D. (1986) *Testing Psychological Tests*, Croom Helm, Beckenham.

Shipman, M. (1967) 'Environmental Influences on Responses to Questionnaires', *British Journal of Educational Psychology*, 27, pp. 54–7.

Shipman, M. (1972) *Childhood*, NFER, Slough.

Shipman, M. (ed.) (1976) *The Organisation and Impact of Social Research*, Routledge & Kegan Paul, London.

Shipman, M. (1980) 'The Limits of Positive Discrimination', in Marland, M. (ed.) *Education for the Inner City*, Heinemann, London, pp. 69–92.

Shipman, M. (1988) *The Limitations of Social Research*, 3rd edn, Longman, Harlow.

Shipman, M., Bolam, J. and Jenkins, D. (1974) *Inside a Curriculum Project*, Methuen, London.

Silver, H. (1994) *Good Schools, Effective Schools*, Cassell, London.

Smith F. (1978) *Reading*, Cambridge University Press, Cambridge, p. 4.

Smith, D. and Tomlinson, S. (1989) *The School Effect: a study of multiracial comprehensives*, Policy Studies Institute, London.

Snodgrass, J. (1973) 'The Criminologist and his Criminal. The case of Erwin H. Sutherland and Broadway Jones', *Issues in Criminology*, 8(1), pp. 1–17.

Snodgrass, J. (1978) 'The Jack Roller at Seventy: a fifty-year follow-up of the delinquent boy's own story', paper read at the American Society of Criminology, November 1978.

Spencer, F. (1990) *Piltdown: a scientific forgery*, Oxford University Press, Oxford.

Spock, B. (1963) *Baby and Child Care*, Pocket Books, New York.

Spock, B. (1989) *Parenting*, Michael Joseph, London, pp. 134–9.

Stein, M.R. (1964) 'The Eclipse of Community: some glances at the education of a sociologist', in Vidich, A., Bensman, J. and Stein, M.R. (eds) John Wiley, New York, pp. 207–32.

Stenhouse, L. (1980) 'The Study of Samples and the Study of Cases', *British Educational Research Journal*, 6(1), pp. 1–6.

Stierer, B. (1982) 'Testing Teachers? A critical look at the Schools Council Project "Extending Beginning Reading"', *Primary School Review*, 13.

Stone, M. (1981) *The Education of the Black Child in Britain*, Fontana, London.

Sully, J. (1884) *Outlines of Psychology*, Longman Green, London.

Sully, J. (1893) *Studies in Childhood*, Longman Green, London.

Sutherland, E.H. (1966) *Professional Thief*, University of Chicago Press, Chicago.

Sutherland, G. (1984) *Ability, Merit and Measurement: mental testing and English education 1880–1940*, Clarendon Press, Oxford.

Taylor, I. (1969) 'Hooligans: soccer's resistance movement', *New Society*, 7 August, pp. 204–6.

Thomas, F.C. (1935) *Ability and Knowledge*, Macmillan, London.

Thomas, W.I. and Znaniecki, F. (1918–20) *The Polish Peasant in Europe and America*, University of Chicago Press, Chicago.

Thorndike, R.L. (1968) 'Review of Pygmalion in the Classroom', *American Educational Research Journal*, 5, pp. 708–11.

Thrasher, F.M. (1927) *The Gang*, University of Chicago Press, Chicago.

Tizard, B. and Hughes, M. (1984) *Young Children Learning*, Fontana, London.

Tizard, B., Burgess, T., Francis, H., Goldstein, H., Young, M., Hewison, J. and Plewis, I. (1980) *Fifteem Thousand Hours*, Bedford Way Papers, London.

van der Eyken, W. (1967) *The Pre-School Years*, Penguin Books, Harmondsworth.

Vidich, A., Bensman, J. and Stein, M.R. (eds) (1964) *Reflections on Community Studies*, John Wiley, New York.

Vogt, E.Z. and Hyman, R. (1959) *Water Witching USA*, University of Chicago Press, Chicago.

Walker, R. and Macdonald, B. (1976) 'Curriculum Innovation at School Level', in *Course E203*, Open University, Milton Keynes.

Wallechinsky, D., Wallace, A. and Wallace, I. (1981) *The Book of Predictions*, William Morrow, New York.

Waller, W. (1932) *The Sociology of Teaching*, John Wiley, New York.

Wallis, R. (1976) *The Road to Total Freedom: a sociological account of scientology*, Heinemann, London.

Warburton F.W. and Southgate, V. (1969) *i.t.a.: an independent evaluation*, Murray & Chambers, London.

Ward, J. (1993) 'Sir Cyril Burt: last casualty of the Cold War or the first in the battle for political correctness?', *Educational Psychology*, 13(1), pp. 69–77.

Warnock Report (1978) *Special Educational Needs*, HMSO, London.

Watkins, J.W.N. (1964) 'Confession is Good for Ideas', in Edge, D. (ed.) *Experiment*, BBC, London, pp. 64–70.

Watson, J.B. (1928) *Psychological Care of Infant and Child*, Norton, New York.

Watson, J.D. (1968) *The Double Helix*, Weidenfeld & Nicolson, London.

Wax, R.H. (1979) 'Gender and Age in Fieldwork and Fieldwork Education', *Social Problems*, 26, pp. 508–22.

Weber, G. (1971) *Inner City Children can be Taught to Read: four successful schools'*, Center for Basic Education, Washington.

Webster, R. (1976) 'The Future of Teacher Training' in Raggatt, M. and Clarkson, M. *Education for Teachers*, Falmer Press, Lewes.

Weiner, J.S. (1955) *The Piltdown Forgery*, Oxford University Press, Oxford.

Weiss, C. (1982) 'Policy Research in the Context of Diffuse Decision-making', in Kallen, D., Kosse, G., Wagenaar, H., Klopkogge, J. and Vorbeck, M. (eds) *Social Science Research and Public Policy-Making – a Reappraisal*, NFER-Nelson, Windsor.

Wells, C.G. (1985) *Language, Learning and Education*, NFER, Slough.

Whyte, W.F. (1943) *Street Corner Society*, University of Chicago Press, Chicago.

Wiggins, J.W. and Schoeck, H. (1960) *Scientism and Values*, Van Nostrand, New York.

Wiggins, J.W. and Schoeck, H. (1961) 'A profile of the aged: USA', *Geriatrics*, July, pp. 336–42.

Willis, P. (1978) *Learning to Labour*, Saxon House, London.

Wolff, K.H. (1964) 'Surrender and Community Study: the study of Loma', in Vidich, A., Bensman, J. and Stein, M.R. (eds) *Reflections on Community Studies*, John Wiley, New York, pp. 233–64.

Woods, P. (1985) 'Ethnography and Theory Construction in Educational Research', in Burgess, R.G. *Field Methods in the Study of Education*, Falmer Press, Lewes, pp. 51–78.

Woods, P. (1990) *The Happiest Days? How Pupils Cope with School*, Falmer Press, Lewes.

Wootton, B. (1959) 'Daddy Knows Best', *Twentieth Century*, October, pp. 247–61.

Word, E. (1990) Project STAR: final executive summary. *Contemporary Education*, 62(1), pp. 13–16.

Wright, A. (1992) 'Evaluation of the First British Reading Recovery Programme', *British Educational Research Journal*, 18(4), pp. 351–68.

Wright, A. (1994) 'Evaluation of the Reading Recovery Programme in Surrey: a reply to Kathleen Hall', *British Educational Research Journal*, 20(1), p. 129.

INDEX

Abraham, J., 32
Aitken, M., 31
American Sociological Association,
    16, 120
Andrews, F.M., 82
Angell, R.C., 109
assumptions about the human, 6–8,
    24–6, 39–41
Atkinson, P., 41, 105
Auld Tribunal, 99
authors, 118–28
Averch, H.A., 143
Avila, M., 74

Bales, R.F., 73
Ball, S., 40, 56
Banks, M., 36
Bantock, G.H., 107
Barnard, H.C., 127
Becher, T., 128
Bechofer, F., 81
Becker, H., 44, 47
Bell, C., 49
Beloff, H., 63
Belsen, W.A., 80, 81
Bennett, S.N., 31, 133, 148
Bentham, J., 22
Berger, P., 6
Bernstein, B., 46, 132
Beynon, H., 19
Binet, A., 83
Blackburn, R., 19, 81
Blair, M., 126
Blondlot, R., 6, 73
Blatchford, P., 46, 91
Bloom, B.S., 134
Blumer, H., 109
Bolam, D., 49, 72
Booth, C., 12, 14
Boru, K., 19

Bowles, S., 67
Bradshaw, J., 123
Bramel, D., 99
Briault, E.W.H., 153
British Cohort Study, 13
British Crime Survey, 110
British Psychological Society (BPS),
    22, 48, 142
British Sociological Association
    (BSA), 106
Broad, W., 6, 120, 140
Brown, R., 107
Browne, N., 9, 10
Bryant, P.E., 129
Bulletin of the BPS, 101–2
Burgess, R.G., 40, 43, 61, 75,
    106
Burstall, C., 90
Burt, C., 77–8, 101–4, 142
Bynner, J., 13, 62, 64

Cain, L.D., 124
Calder, A., 13
Cannell, J.J., 152
Carey, A., 99
Cattell, R.B., 83
Census, 13, 56, 64, 81, 87
Central Intelligence Agency, 17
Charles, E., 151
Chicago School of Sociology, 33,
    37, 108–9
Chomsky, N., 30
Church, J., 134
Church of Scientology, 123
Cicourel, A.V., 108
City University Social Statistics
    Research Unit, 13
Clarke, A.D.B., 103
Clarke, A.M., 103
Clarke, J., 34–5